Mr. Beller's Ne

BEFORE & AFTER
STORIES FROM
NEW YORK

Edited by Thomas Beller

Volume I

Mr. Beller's Neighborhood Books
225 Lafayette Street, Suite 1114
New York, NY 10012
www.mrbellersneighborhood.com

Designed by Nick Stone
Cover photographs by Nathan Chaffee
Illustrations and map by Elisha Cooper

Printed in Winnipeg, Canada.

10 9 8 7 6 5 4 3 2
Second printing

Library of Congress Control Number: 2001098768
ISBN 0-393-32353-6
Distributed by W.W. Norton

Almost all of the essays in this book originally appeared on
Mrbellersneighborhood.com. The Web site is designed by Tomas Clark.
Sabin Streeter and Elizabeth Grove are the superb senior editors. This
book's existence owes a great debt to the amazing Joanna Yas, perennial
All-Star. Thanks also to Dorothy Spears, Bryan Charles, Nick Stone, Nick
Mamatas, Kip Kotzen, Vince Passaro, and Parker Posey.

CONTENTS

Thomas Beller   7   Introduction: Before

Leelila Strogov   11   A Pantomime of No

Rick Rofihe   15   The Bowery Scene

Alexander Chancellor   18   Fish Abuse at Vanity Fair

Heather Byer   22   Fifty-eight Inches of Ambiance

Thomas Beller   25   Memo to CBS: Electronic Ed Is Your Man!

Jim Merlis   28   Sal the Barber and the Make-Believe Ballroom

Said Shirazi   33   The Hundred Views

Jeanette Winterson   36   My Secret Socks Life

Maura Kelly   38   Kissing the Cab Driver

Snooder Greenburg   43   The Dynamite Brothers Meet the Slapper

Luc Sante   45   The Tompkins Square Park Riot, 1988

Carolyn Murnick   52   To the Man Who Forgot His New Books . . .

E. Franke   56   Mother's Day

Rebecca Donner   60   In a Swamp of Reusable Souls

Meghan Daum & Thomas Beller   64   Wedding Proposal at Café Loup

Nick Mamatas   70   Old Boilers and Old Men

Ariele Fierman   78   The Coffee Hut Slut

CONTENTS

Denise Campbell	81	Code Blue: A Police Officer Unwinds
Zachary Levin	85	Kenny Colman's Elevator Logic
Vince Passaro	89	Tom's Restaurant
Michael Cunningham	92	Visit With a Drag Queen
Denise Campbell	97	Harlem Love Story
Susan Connell-Mettauer	101	Speed Freaks
Snooder Greenberg	104	One Stroke
Thomas Beller	109	The Turtles in Central Park
Minter Krotzer	112	Trash Like White Elephants
Manny Howard	114	The Jumper
Josh Kramer	117	The Parakeet Book
Sabin Streeter	121	Everybody Poops
Josh Gilbert	127	Bubby's Departure

"I'm one of these guys that says, 'Why can't we all just get along?' But then again, I don't talk to my brother."

—Rick Rofihe

Introduction: Before

New York City
by Thomas Beller

All the essays in this book, both "Before" and "After" were initially published on a Web site called mrbellersneighborhood.com. It was conceived in January 2000, a time when the before/after dynamic would probably be understood in terms of the moment the Internet became a mass medium, and the words "catastrophe" and "attack," were most likely to refer to the Y2K problem, which had threatened to knock out our computer networks at the turn of the millennium.

I had just finished a novel and was walking around town feeling a bit lost; the cold, bright air was making my eyes tear. Like a lot of people who have finished (and therefore in some way lost) their project, I was coming down hard, but the world into which I was returning seemed oddly weightless. We were entering a digital age in which the numbers were all going up. The numbers were everywhere and they were intoxicating. Even the calendar had become a novelty. The numbers moved on a ticker tape, they sped around buildings on zippers, they were announced with an incredible sameness of voice on the sports pages and the business pages and the weather channel. They were sleek, comprehensible, and had as their subject both now and tomorrow.

It seemed like a good time to start something porous, something textured, and, in its essence, about now and also then. The plan was to marry certain old school editorial values with the new-fangled technology of an interactive map of New York. The map would provide a spatial, physical context to a rather abstract, ephemeral medium.

Like many people besotted with technology, I went and bought some gadgets—I replaced my 1993 Powerbook 160 with a G3, and I got a digital camera. The Internet generally, and the map interface in particular, had aroused in me some voyeuristic impulse, and for all my admiration of the personal essay, I was very excited about what it would be like to start zooming into the city from the height of a satellite, and continue zooming, down to a bird's-eye view, a roof-top view, and then right into someone's kitchen.

I romped around the city taking pictures. Eventually I came upon a Hot Dog Lady on Forty-seventh Street and Sixth Avenue who did not want her picture taken. She was adamant about it.

"No picture!" she said when I held up my camera.

Her hot dog stand had the usual blue and yellow umbrella over the cart, and a hand-painted sign with the price of a hot dog, a sausage, a knish, a pretzel, a soda, and so forth, and off to the side a pile of steaming pretzels and chestnuts. It might have been the chestnuts that caught my eye, or my nose, but there was something about the woman that made me want to take her picture. It was a cold day in February and she was all bundled up. All I could see was her angry face. Her expression seemed to say, "It's my body, my hot dog cart, *my life*." She wasn't standing out here in the cold so tourists could take cute pictures. She was running a business.

"How about if I buy a knish?" I said.

She stamped her booted foot on the pavement. "No picture!"

A guy from the next cart came over and joined the conversation. "No picture," he said protectively.

I left empty-handed. She came to mind a few weeks later, when Sabin Streeter, who along with Tomas Clark and Marisa Bowe played such an important part in building the Web site, stressed the importance of having a prominent feature that would allow the site's readers to send in their own stories. It struck me that, regarding the Hot Dog Lady, the most interesting thing on the site wouldn't be a photograph of a proud, heavily bundled woman standing beside her hot dog cart, or even an interview with her; it would be a piece of writing by her.

She has not, to date, written in. I haven't had the nerve to ask. But hundreds of others have written. The site has been an experiment in finding the middle ground between the necessary exclusivity of our best print magazines, with their traditions of excellence and their large pools of staff writers, and a bulletin-board like the one to be found on Amazon.com, where getting published is mostly a matter of not using curse words. The site's ambition is to provide a venue for pieces with no pitch, no angle. This site makes the neighborhood, and the individual, the angle.

In August 2001, over a year after the site began publishing, I sat down with Elizabeth Grove, Joanna Yas, and Sabin Streeter, and began compiling selections for this book. Three weeks later, everything changed; suddenly the numbers were all you wanted to hear; you stayed close to the TV and, if you lived in New York, stuck your head out the window now and then to remind yourself that what you were watching was happening in your backyard. Who cares about Snooder Greenberg and Susan Connell-Mettaur's recollections of the East Village of the sixties, or Luc Sante's memories of that same neighborhood in the eighties? Who cares that Maura Kelly ended up making out with her cab driver on New Year's Eve, that Carolyn Murnick found some guy's brand new books on a subway bench, that Jeanette Winterson is obsessed with the socks at Saks, or that Michael Cunningham paid a visit to Dorian Corey, one of Harlem's legendary drag queens? Jim Merlis found heaven on Mott Street in a barber shop run by an old guy named Sal. So what?

But a few weeks after September 11, I looked at this material again and found it not only relevant, but possessed of an urgency that it hadn't had before. Now more than ever the small moments of life in the city—the funny, pleasant ones and the awful, bitter ones—seemed worth documenting. And then there were the strange ironies and odd resonances strewn throughout these pieces. "New York is the safest big city in the world," writes Merlis, somewhat bitterly, about gentrification on Mott Street. Reading Leelila Strogov's piece in the wake of September 11 one wonders: Is it belittling to talk about loss in terms of love? and concludes, no, it's not.

A Pantomime of No

The L Train, 14ᵗʰ St. and First Ave.
by Leelila Strogov

I had not seen V. in the flesh for about eight years, nor in my dreams for at least three. Once in a while I would see him in a phone booth or at a corner hot dog stand, but whenever I'd get close enough he would inevitably turn into someone else.

He was that someone I think everyone in the world has a story woven around—the one who breaks you in such a way that when you heal, you heal as a different person; a person you don't completely recognize but who you like just a little bit better. I have always thought that this is why people often hate those they once loved too much. They are embarrassed and humiliated by their old selves, the selves that used to do things and feel things for a person they have now convinced themselves wasn't worth all the effort.

I have often considered it one of my greatest accomplishments that I have never hated anyone at all. So I'm boarding the L train at Sixth Avenue heading east, and as soon as I get on, V. is there. Right in front of me. Too close to be a mistake. He's wearing jeans and ratty sneakers and a T-shirt that depicts a faded Mona Lisa in a series of expressions starting from her usual smirk to one where she's hysterical with laughter, tears flying everywhere.

Sitting to his right is a pleasant-looking, brown-haired girl wearing a short skirt and carrying a large artist's portfolio. This must be the Artist-Who-Got-A-Great-Write-Up-in-*Time-Out-New-York* girlfriend, I figured. The one before, I had heard, was the African-American-*New-York-Times*-Journalist. He chose his women by occupation, distinction, education, birthright, sometimes beauty, though this was usually not the main appeal. I never imagined him being caught off-guard with longing for a sassy ER nurse with a charmingly crooked front tooth or a bartender whose hair was on fire and who ate maraschino cherries one after another as if they were sex on a stem.

No, there had to be something more tangibly impressive, either about you or some former version of you. And if he was impressed enough, he wanted you. It was that simple. I knew this from the beginning and didn't particularly mind. I thought it would be fun to turn everything upside down on him and make him love me for reasons he hadn't originally thought of.

And he did.

And it was.

And then it was over because that is what happens when you're twenty-three and the world seems to be full of magnets pulling you in more directions than you can count. He had tried to call about once a year since, but I would never take his calls. He had been unfaithful, and while I didn't necessarily think that was a cardinal offense (he hadn't enjoyed it enough for it to be), I thought it was my duty to at least pretend it was. So I'm holding onto the pole in front of him and I take my backpack from my shoulder and place it on the floor between my legs, and am about to say hello, how are you, where are you living these days, when he gives me a strange panicked look and shakes his head in a movement that if made by a compass would draw only about an eighth of a circle. It is a pantomime of "No" that tells me that the brown-haired artist sitting next to him has issues with my existence and that I am not to speak if I have any respect at all for what we once had.

I hold my tongue.

In the meantime, to his left, a disheveled Ricki Lake look-a-like takes out a nail file and starts grooming herself. Not really knowing what to do, I take my book out of my bag, a copy of Walker Percy's *The Last Gentleman*, and try to read. I am nearly at the end, on page 357: "Dark fell suddenly and the stars came out. They drew in and in half an hour hung as large and low as yellow lamps at a garden party."

That is pretty, I think. But I'm feeling self-conscious. I'm wishing I had put on mascara that morning and that I had worn a different outfit. As it stands, I'm in overalls.

Oh well, I think. He already knows what you look like underneath. And then I can't help it, but I find myself wondering if it's the same for them; if he admires the curve of her hip the way he did mine—like you'd admire a fine-looking tree; if he likes her noises as much as he did mine. He is still just the right amount of handsome, I think, despite the fact that his side-burns are too long.

He's shaking his left leg back and forth and staring at my shoes. I am tempted to leave the train even though it is not my stop, just to make the first exit, to be the one to leave, but I conclude that that would be childish and I stay put. I'm already late as it is. As First Avenue approaches, V. and his artist get up to leave. He tilts his body so that he is standing directly in front of me.

"Excuse me," he says, looking right into my eyes. "Do you happen to have the time?"

I am wondering why. Does he want to hear my voice? Does he want to see my expression when I answer him? I decide I will never know and that that is ok by me. I tell him it is 6:10 according to my watch but that my watch is generally a little fast as I tend to run late and this keeps me in check. I realize too late that this is probably more information than I would have given an ordinary stranger. But I am nervous. He lets his arm very gently touch mine, as if by accident. Then he thanks me and purses his lips in a way I imagine a teacher might do when watching his favorite student graduate.

It's something a little sad, but mostly fond, and it makes me hope that I never see him again just so things can stay this way. When V. leaves the train, I take his empty seat next to disheveled Ricki and put my book away. She keeps sitting up straight and looking over at me as if she has something on her mind, but then rests her back against the chair again.

I am a hundred miles away and not really paying much attention. And then finally, as if she's been holding something in for hours, she looks at me and says in an exasperated, Brooklyn, sandpaper voice: "Do you mind if I ask you something?"

"No," I say, "go right ahead." She raises one of her hands in the air as if she's about to make a presentation on a whiteboard. "That guy who was sitting in your seat . . ." She pauses. "Did you know him?"

"Yes," I say, "I knew him a long time ago."

She nods dramatically and lets out a hum to show me she understands.

The Bowery Scene

Spring St. and the Bowery
by Rick Rofihe

1. Recently, a cousin of mine stopped over on his way from Beirut, a city which now has most of its politics in the street, and almost no sanitation services. Standing outside my door, he looked up and down the Bowery and marveled, "They keep it so clean!"

2. My most persistent fantasy is that one day, when I'm gathering up the garbage that the bums have sifted through and scattered on the sidewalk out front, along comes Dan Rather. I'm dressed for being with garbage and the he's doing a story on the Bowery. He says to me, "How'd you like a square meal and a cup of coffee? You don't mind the cameras, do you?"

3. When the real estate agent sent me to look at the place where I now live, on the Bowery, I almost didn't go. To walk down here is not so much to take your life in your hands, but your change purse. A half-dozen pan-handlers at twenty-five cents, that's . . .

4. A woman I know who moved from the United States to England was showing me around her neighborhood in London when we came upon a

shabby-looking man collapsed on the sidewalk. She ran inside her house and got a blanket for him. After the ambulance she called had departed, she remarked to me, "In New York I used to just step over them."

5. Motorists waiting in traffic on the Bowery are faced with a brigade of bums who are going to wipe their windshields, like it or not, need it or not. Some refuse to pay for the service, while others give change, or bills, or a handy gift. Still others, squirming in disgust, learn that the bums and themselves are participants in the same society and that no matter how much you pay for a car or how shiny you keep it, a drooling man with dirty cloth can revoke these privileges, if just for a little while, on the Bowery.

6. Last spring, I was wakened by the amplified words "Back on the sidewalk!" I heard it a few times but could not give it meaning. The next day things were different on the Bowery. Police on loudspeakers were ordering bums working the stopped cars for change to get "back on the sidewalk." That evening, one who did not get off the street fast enough was cornered by two policemen who poked around until they found his wine bottle which, with a nightstick, one cracked in his pocket.

7. A bum can be a beacon. Once, outside a fashionable shop on Fifty-ninth Street, I saw an old hobo spot a half-eaten candy bar still in its wrapper, on the sidewalk. As he contemplated it, some passersby pointed callously, some laughed nervously, some smiled sympathetically, and some acquired what I took to be thoughtful, almost introspective expressions. Nobody ignored him. He was a beacon.

8. Not all bums drink. Not all smoke. Not all ask for money and some will not take it if it is offered.

9. It's no fun being a bum. There are the campfires, but it's not romantic to be cold, hungry, and homeless unless you have hope of warmth, food, and shelter.

10. It is easy to look out on the Bowery and say, "There are the bums." Encountering one, however, even one who asks to "bum a quarter" or tells you he's "on the bum" the word "bum" slips away in one's mind, perhaps given over to a "man" of "fellow," or, probably, no label at all.

11. Last winter, the city, having a surplus of homeless men, charter-bused them nightly up to a dormitory on Ward's Island, and, in the mornings, gave them subway tokens to get back to the Bowery.

12. Free Thanksgiving diners at a couple of the missions draw hundreds

of homeless men and women who usually frequent other areas of Manhattan. The milling and mixing of these people with needy tenement dwellers and Bowery regulars combine with the classic quiet of Thanksgiving Day to give the area the atmosphere of a religious festival. Some of these pilgrims linger for days, feeling at home on the Bowery.

13. One morning, a platoon of sanitation men descended on the Bowery and cleaned up all the wine bottles. That afternoon a U.N. motorcade took the Bowery route to take the Chinese delegation to Chinatown.

14. Some real-estate developers, some co-op owners, some shops that attract mainly suburban customers may want to clean up the Bowery, sanitize it, make it safe for money. They can try. Meanwhile, men with plenty of time to pass will pass it with Night Train wine. Incoherent babblers will be released from psychiatric institutions into the cool fast world. Amputees will sling their extras clothes over a crutch. And they'll all find their way to the Bowery.

15. Do I feel at home on the Bowery? A few years ago, I forgot to finish addressing a letter to a friend of mine, a college student. It was mailed with only his name and "University of Toronto" on the envelope. He got it. He wrote back to me that someone once wrote to "Albert Einstein, Europe." He got it. Recently, my mother, who lives in another country, wrote to "Rick Rofihe, Bowery, New York." Do I feel at home? I got it.

Fish Abuse at Vanity Fair

The Condé Nast Building
4 Times Square
by Alexander Chancellor

Here in New York I have been put in charge of a small tropical fish. Its owner has gone to Los Angeles to organize *Vanity Fair*'s annual Oscars party and won't be back until the end of the month. Her parting instructions were minimal. I was just asked to sprinkle a little fish food on it from time to time. That was all. I wasn't told how much food to give it or how often (if at all) to change its water.

I have never looked after a fish before, and everyone tells me it is a difficult task. For example, fish do not know how to stop eating: if you give them too much food, they burst. And changing a fish's water is a delicate operation. Not only is the fish easily lost in the process, but the water has to be the right temperature or it may die. It may well die anyway, of course. Fish usually do.

This fish has so far contented itself with occasionally pretending to be dead. At other times it is quite frisky. But it has very little space to be frisky in. Its home is a square glass jar on the top of the desk—so small and square that it cannot even do circles. A visitor to the office the other day said he thought that its owner should be charged with fish abuse. But I don't suppose he knows any more about fish than I do, and the size of the jar is probably just right for a fish of this particular kind.

It is not a colorful fish. In fact, it is completely black. But it is curious to look at, having several seemingly superfluous fins almost as big as its little body. It's a bit like several fishes stuck together. This appearance suggests rarity—and therefore considerable expense if it should die and have to be replaced before its owner returns from Hollywood. Maybe it is a million-dollar fish and we will have to sell the house in London.

When I aired this anxiety to Chris Garrett, the managing editor of *Vanity Fair*, she told me a cautionary tale about a dog that was flown recently from Europe to New York to be re-united with its lady owner. It traveled in a crate in the hold, but turned out on arrival to be dead. The airline staff could not face the idea of presenting the owner with a corpse, so they rang her to say that her dog was now arriving on a later flight and spent the time thus gained searching the pet shops of New York for one that looked the same.

Returning triumphant from their mission, they replaced the dead dog in the crate with a living one and told the owner that her dog was now ready for collection from the airport. When she arrived and saw it she shrieked and then fainted. Her dog had died in Europe, and she had been bringing it home for burial. There is little relevance in this story to my dilemma, but I was much amused to hear it.

I suspect that fish anxiety is widespread. In the 1980s, when President Reagan was about to hold his first ever meeting with Mikhail Gorbachev in Switzerland, he rented a villa from the Aga Khan on the shore of Lake Geneva. One of the Aga Khan's children had left a note in the house asking him to keep an eye on the goldfish. At the appointed time, the President's Chief of Staff, Donald Regan, came by to pick him up and take him to the historic summit.

He found Mr. Reagan standing gravely in front of the fish tank. "Don, we've got a problem," he said. One of the goldfish was lying dead on the bottom. So, as the peace of the world hung in the balance, members of the President's staff were urgently dispatched to find a replacement. If only the fish in my care were a humble goldfish, instead of this strange, multi-finned specimen, I would have rather less to worry about.

In case you are wondering how I find myself in this situation, the answer is that I am spending a month in New York working at *Vanity Fair*, thanks to the kindness of its editor, Graydon Carter, who, along with all of his senior staff have gone to Hollywood for the great Oscars extravaganza. It is the most popular party of the year, and Mr. Carter is besieged by people angling for invitations.

I haven't been one of them, though. I am perfectly happy where I am; and anyway, I have an onerous duty to perform here in New York feeding the fish.

The worst possible thing has happened. The fish has died. A week after I wrote about the stress involved in looking after somebody else's fish, the little creature snuffed it. This was not my fault, I promise. An assistant to Sara Marks, the fish's owner, took it to the coffee alcove to change the water in its glass jar, and I followed him there to get myself a cup of coffee. I saw him pour the fish into a cardboard coffee cup, change its water in the sink, and then pour it back into the jar.

I don't know whether the water was too cold or too hot, or whether he decanted the fish too roughly, but it dived headfirst into the gravel at the bottom of the jar and expired. I have yet to speak to Ms. Marks, the Director of Special Projects at *Vanity Fair* whose office I am temporarily occupying, but I gather she is not well pleased. She is said to be particularly distressed that nobody had the courage to tell her what had happened for a couple of days. She had had the fish for a year, which is quite a long time, so she has every reason to feel a little upset. However, I have decided against looking for a replacement, since I have grown convinced that people oughtn't to keep fishes in their offices, especially when they are not there.

For some reason, the dead fish was returned to my desk in its jar, where it remained for a day upside down with its nose in the gravel, slowly changing color. A day later, when I was beginning to wonder whether I shouldn't give it a formal burial somewhere, perhaps in Central Park, I returned from lunch to find it gone. To my surprise I slightly miss it. The good thing about a dead fish is that it is the antithesis of the Buzz. There is nothing "hot" about a dead fish. And since New York is ruled by the Buzz and "hotness,"there is something rather comforting in that. I even kept its death secret for a while, like countries with dictators do when their leaders have died, just to enjoy the peace of being with something dead.

Fifty-eight Inches of Ambiance

3rd Ave. between 19th and 20th St.
by Heather Byer

I choose what I'm wearing carefully on Tuesdays. I like to show a little midriff, some shoulder. In a bar, before I play, I look around and notice other people's midriffs and shoulders. I look at the curve of bodies bending across tables and feel my own. I want to laugh the throaty laugh of a James Bond ingenue.

I favor the side pockets and can cut a ball nicely, but my break is weak and I invariably clutch on the eight, a maddening condition that once caused me to throw and splinter a cue, McEnroe-style.

I own my own cue, a fifty-eight-inch McDermott. I carry it in a soft red canvas case, which I throw over my shoulder every Tuesday. People stare at it—and me—on the subway. Their stares, for once, are not crude or hostile or blank, but curious, aroused.

I took up pool a year-and-a-half ago, after years of fantasizing about it. I loved watching people play the game, in bars or on TV. They seemed so confident. They didn't have to talk: they thought, decided, moved. I liked that the balls came in so many colors, that you had to keep track of them—their numbers meant something. I liked listening to the elegant click click of a game, liked the way players faced each shot like they were behind the plate, anticipating the next pitch. I liked cigarettes hanging out of mouths, long-necks tapping thighs, ambiance. I liked Paul Newman.

It took me five years to walk into a Manhattan pool hall and ask if someone could teach me; it took me another nine months to play in front of people without shaking. When I first learned to shoot, that's all I wanted to do. I would stroke the same shot over and over, allowing the instructors to set up situations for me, but backing off when asked to play against the other students. I just liked the math, the thinking, the green felt, the silence—so quiet compared to my jabbering media friends.

Then I joined a league, learned to face an opponent, and started playing pool. And everything changed. There is something sexual and powerful (or is it powerful and sexual?) about a woman who plays pool. And no, it has nothing to do with sliding a stick through your hands or putting balls in pockets or any of the other obvious visual double entendres. Sometimes I think about my former teammate, Patty, who wore a lot of red. She had a big, curvy body and she hated to lose. When she won her face lit up and she laughed that throaty laugh and was extra nice to her boyfriend.

In pool you use your brain but communicate through your body, slowly, sometimes languorously. If you sit at a computer all day and type words, or use your large vocabulary in long, boring meetings, then playing pool—communicating this way—is like taking off a nun's habit and being given a pair of spiked boots and a whip.

About a year into it, I joined one of the Monday night leagues and learned how to stalk a table. I learned how to get people to take me seriously—or playfully—without uttering a word. Pool players pretend to ignore each other but are, in fact, reading every twitch, cigarette puff, beer swig, grin flashed at a teammate for a sign of their opponent's game. You have to be close, intimate, alive to notice these things. You think, aim, shoot, smile dangerously, taking as long as you want. And in eight-ball, the kind that's played in the New York bar leagues, you'll often hear someone explain that "slop counts." It's an indelicate expression for an important rule: if you try to sink a ball but miss and sink one of your others instead, it counts. Your accident, your excess, is sweet.

Last summer, in my first league match, I went up against a much better player, a cocky guy named Simon who was from somewhere in Northern England. He wore an ugly gold chain and had big teeth. Our face-off took place in a garishly lit Irish-style pub on the east side of Third Avenue, between Nineteenth and Twentieth. I set up the balls in their triangle but worried that I might not have done it quite right. Simon shrugged and said, "It's all right, it looks nice."

"Gee, no one's ever told me I had a nice rack before," I said.

He grinned, and proceeded to kick my ass. At one point, the trouncing was so bad that he actually ordered a pizza, which was delivered during the third game of our match, and he turned his back to me while he ate it. So I went for the billiard equivalent of a Hail Mary and smacked the cue ball across the length of the table, where it hit the rail and sliced back, knocking the three-ball into the far corner pocket. The bar erupted. Simon didn't move. He continued to chomp coolly on his slice, so I said, "Turn around, asshole," or something equally Clint Eastwood. And he did turn. And gave me a nod. He also beat me, but it didn't matter.

I look at the women in my bar in the East Village, and they look at me, and we seem to have this silent bond, like we're all addicted to the same thing. The same body thing. The same sex thing. And yes, I guess it was bound to happen: I had an affair with a pool player (no, we never did it on a pool table), a tall, gangly guy, a bit dopey, not someone you would think could be graceful, or steely, but he was both at the table. He had beautiful hands; something seemed to fall off of him when he played, his outer coat. His essence came through, like I think mine does. We had nothing else in common, and the sexual charge lasted only as long as a night of pool, which is why our affair endured barely three months. I switched to the Tuesday night league, but I have no regrets. Slop counts.

Memo to CBS:
Electronic Ed Is Your Man!

11th St. just off Waverly Pl.
by Thomas Beller

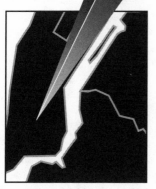

Electronic Ed called out to me and I pulled my bicycle over and heard his news: CBS is interested in his story.

He was lounging on a stoop on West Eleventh Street, in the dappled shade.

"This girl, this *woman*," he corrected himself, "from CBS, she stopped me. She saw something on your inner-net thing. She wants to pitch it to these producers at one of those news shows. She works there. She did all this research."

Now, Ed is a homeless person, more or less, and it may seem somehow wrong, condescending, to throw around a word like dappled in this context, but Ed is also a very stylish guy, in demeanor, in looks, and in the way he conducts his interactions. He's humane, and his face has the dignity of an El Greco. He can handle a little dappling.

"She went back and did all this research and she knows that I got a medal in Vietnam for saving my platoon, and the metal plate in my head, and she found these photos of me in the ring," he waved his craggy (filthy) biblical hand, a gesture encompassing himself, stretched out on the stoop, and also about the last twenty or thirty years, a pantomimed ellipsis, as though to say, "one things leads to another."

"And now I'm out here!" he said. "And there's this court case going on with my wife, there's sixty five thousand dollars that's supposed to be mine that she got locked up.

"And there's a house I'm supposed to be living in. She had her fifteen years. Now it's my turn. This was all agreed on fifteen years ago! The kids have grown, it's my turn. Time for them to get out!"

I listened to this and thought: My God, the city has another acrimonious divorce on its hands.

In some way the Mayoral divorce situation was having some bearing on this friendly chat with Ed. When someone like Raul Felder, who is smart, well-heeled, rich, active in the life of the moment, behaves with such ugly, gruesome, barbarity—"squealing like a stuck pig"—is that what he said about Donna Hanover? I mean, those crazy rednecks in *Deliverance* and Raul Felder are operating on about the same level here. Ed looks very good in comparison, a bastion of civility, even if his hands are dirty and he's missing a front tooth.

It's hard not to think of Ed as a guy doing really well, sometimes, seeing him roam around, his spirit hanging in there. He once told me he is dying of cancer. "It's not long for me," is how he put it. He didn't blurt it out. He mentioned it after we'd been talking on and off for a while, in the depths of a cold winter. He said it, "Cancer," and I had to stand there and watch the horrific reflex of my own doubt. Who am I to doubt Ed?

By his side was the big black bag of his that he always carries around. From this bag emerges, from time to time, objects of really impressive aesthetic value: Once I saw him with a small whicker rhinoceros, which, placed in the right modern furniture store on Lafayette Street could have sold for a few hundred dollars. Often these objects were electronic. He had an eye for vintage objects. Apparently people throw them out, and Ed finds them. He's got a good eye.

The "inner-net thing" is a series of pictures Josh Gilbert took of Ed this past winter that appeared in a series, Eleventh Street Characters. It had its little run in New Stuff and who know who sees these thing? Suddenly Ed has opportunities with CBS.

He says internet with a Western Cadence. "Inner-net."

He took something out of his bag. It was a small lock box, spray-painted gold.

"It still has keys," he said, and he opened the box and there in a small envelope were a pair of keys.

Ed spent some time demonstrating that the keys worked.

"Do you want me to write something for your inner-net thing?" he said. "Because now that all this stuff is happening, I think I might like to write some things down."

Last winter I had advanced him a twenty for some bit of reminiscences. I told him if he would just keep some sort of diary of what he's been up to, but it's never that simple, you ask someone to take a nibble of their life and soon they are staring with numb horror at the enormity of it, the whole history, a mountain towards which one can't take a single step, or, on the other hand, maybe he didn't have a pencil. Either way, the famed manuscript drop at the M&M grocer never occurred. It was going to be some weird kind of drug deal: I give this vagrant a twenty and he delivers the goods. But the good, they never came. ("Success, it never comes."—Pavement)

I told him if he wrote something down I would love to publish it. Then I put my foot on the pedal.

"What's her name, from CBS, her last name?" I said in parting.

"I don't know. Her name was Cindy, Cynthia?"

On one hand, the whole thing sounded dubious. But then again, he had told Josh Gilbert all about his days in the boxing ring. Maybe he told this woman at CBS, and she has been looking into it. She verified he has the medal—for saving his entire platoon. Is Ed for real?

Oh hell: It sounds real! Someone out there has taken the time and energy, put the CBS research department to work, Rather and Morley Safer and Mike Wallace are not yet alerted to these developments, I realize, but hey! Get on the ball! Electronic Ed is an interesting guy and he should be on your network.

Sal the Barber and the Make-Believe Ballroom

‖ 209 Mott St.
‖ by Jim Merlis

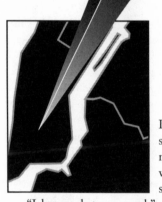

I needed a barber, not a stylist, in a barber-shop, not a salon, owned and operated by one man, not a local franchise of a national chain, who would cut my hair, not tag my head like some graffiti artist. I wanted a barber.

"I know what you need," my friend Nick said as he interrupted the litany of haircutting demands I was making. He was smiling, sitting across from me at our regular restaurant. He's been going there for years, the food is good, but most importantly they let him smoke. Before telling me what I needed he slowly put his cigarette to his lips, puffed out a cloud of smoke and watched it rise before it gently broke apart into the air.

"You need to see Sal the Barber." My mind immediately leapt to Sal "The Barber" Maglie, former New York Giant and Brooklyn Dodger pitcher nicknamed "The Barber" because he often threw at batters' heads, giving them close shaves.

"His shop is on Mott between Prince and Spring," Nick continued. "They got two chairs there, but he does all the cutting. He doesn't have a phone, so just show up, and if you have to wait he's got these photo albums of pictures he took in Naples. Get a shave too, it's the closest thing to heaven. The whole thing will run ya twenty. That's without the tip." Then he leaned in and turned his head slowly to the left and then to the right, as if he were telling me a secret. His eyes were bright, his eyebrows raised as he said the words he knew would send me directly to Sal, the one thing I wanted from a barber, "Pal, he's even got one of them old fashion barber poles outside his joint." He moved back and took another drag on his cigarette, but instead of looking at the smoke or me he folded his arms and looked away giving me a moment to contemplate what he had just said. He knew what I wanted, I wanted the old school barber, the old school haircut, one that was classic and timeless and nothing symbolized that more than the barber pole.

The next morning on my way to Sal's I was struck by how much Mott Street had changed. It used to be a neighborhood where men wearing untucked shirtsleeves would sit outside their homes and social clubs on folded chairs on nice days; talking, yelling, reading papers while other men passed and shook their hands and joked. Where gangs of boys would walk aimlessly with purposeful strides up and down the street all day, stopping only to gawk at pretty neighborhood girls. It was a neighborhood of juxtapositions: a hub of organized crime with no street crime, an ancient village in the most modern of cities replete with customs and shibboleths that separated its locals from outsiders.

These days the barriers have been broken down and the outsiders have opened up boutiques where you can be guaranteed that you're paying the highest price possible; young and beautiful men and women walk up and down the street with a certain these-are-the-good-old-days swagger, and a fearlessness that these good old days will last an eternity. These are halcyon times in the city, it's the safest big city in the country, the only crime, one could say, are the prices at the Mott Street boutiques, but these new Mott Street pedestrians don't seem to mind.

Sal's barber pole seemed to be out of place in this space where it once fit so comfortably. Walking in I knew immediately that the shop was the last vestige of the old neighborhood and old village ways. I later learned that Sal's business hours were indicative of this. Like a mom and pop shop he keeps flexible hours. "Sometime I open at nine," I would hear him tell a customer in his thick Neapolitan accent on a subsequent visit. "Sometime I open later."

On the walls were three brilliant celebrity photos unlike any I had ever seen. There was the picture of Martin Scorcese with his parents (Scorsese grew up a few blocks away on Elizabeth Street. His autobiographical film *Mean Streets* takes place in Sal's neighborhood). Next to Scorsese was a picture of an actor, whose name I didn't recognize but underneath his name read the line, "The Robert DeNiro look-alike." The third picture was of the Robert DeNiro look-alike smiling that side of the mouth squinty-eyed Robert DeNiro smile standing next to an uncomfortable and serious looking Robert DeNiro.

I asked for a haircut and shave.

"No shave, buddy," he said sharply, and then turning on his clippers asked, "you want it short?"

Two things I have learned about Sal: he calls everyone Buddy and he always wants to cut your hair short.

"Not too short," I said nervously. Sal chuckled and said under his breath, "Not too short," and put down the clippers and grabbed his scissors. "Buddy, I won't make it too short," he laughed as he began snipping furiously.

As the haircut proceeded, I tried to angle for the shave. I asked him if he knew my friend Nick, but he said he wasn't sure.

He asked me if I lived nearby, and I told him that I lived in Brooklyn. He stopped cutting and said, "I live in Brooklyn too, Borough Park, I started cutting fifty-five years ago, right after the war." Before we could bond over Brooklyn, he turned on the clippers to shave the nape of my neck. When that was done I started to talk about Brooklyn, but he didn't seem interested.

I had given up. He was putting the finishing touches on my hair when he asked, "You like this music?" The music was coming from a radio in the corner of the shop. It helped supply much of the old time ambiance, playing nostalgic big band music on an AM frequency. The DJ announced in an easy and dulcet tone that the station was from a small town I'd never heard of in New Jersey. He thanked us for being in *The Make-Believe Ballroom*. It was a great station, playing not only big band music, but also some of the more obscure songs by well known artists. It was as if *The Make-Believe Ballroom* was created and broadcast solely for Sal's Barbershop.

"Yes," I said.

"Really?" he chuckled skeptically.

"Oh sure, I like Louis Prima, Frank Sinatra, Benny Goodman."

"You really like Frank Sinatra?" He was still skeptical.

"I love Frank Sinatra," and I told him which albums I owned and how I went to see Frank the last time he ever played Madison Square Garden.

"Okay, I give you a shave." I had passed the ultimate test of the old school barber, the appreciation of Frank Sinatra.

It was incredible. The many sides of Sal.

First there were the hot towels, and the warm shaving soap and the gentle brushing of the straight razor across my face. My eyelids grew heavy and I closed them. Occasionally, I opened them to see Sal's eyes behind his black framed glasses studying the small motions he was making as though he were sculpting my features. Then came the details. With his fingers he pulled my nostrils apart and cut my nose hair, he put his hand in my mouth so that it was smooth and he shaved around its edges. When he was done my face was smoother than it had been since I hit puberty.

"So, you like your first Mott Street haircut and shave?"

I did, although I am a little miffed that he asks me that every time I see him. But then, we're all just Buddy to him.

That was how the story was going to end, but then I called my brother. On my recommendation, he'd started getting the short haircut I had turned down from Sal. After his first cut, he called me. "He's like an artist," he said.

"He's great," I said.

"He's better than great, he's an artist," he said.

"Like van Gogh," I said.

"That's a bad choice of artist for a barber," he said.

"Sure, with the ear and all," I said.

"Michelangelo works better, because he sculpted too and he's Italian and all."

"Michelangelo," I said.

But just yesterday, my brother actually got a bad cut from Sal, one that he had to cut further when he got home, because Sal had missed a spot. And there were other things wrong too. There's no Make-Believe Ballroom, anymore. The music is from a soft rock station, an FM station, no Sinatra, only contemporary classics. My brother learned that someone broke into his shop and stole his radio, and the new radio can't get AM that well. Maybe that's why Sal didn't seem quite himself.

"Poor Sal, did they take anything else?" I said.

"I don't know, I didn't ask," he said.

Who breaks into a barbershop? I wondered. Is there a big black market for scissors, clippers and AM radios? What kind of people would have done this? Was it vandalism or theft? Did Sal keep a secret stash of money in the shop, and how much could that have been? And, besides, I thought the city had rid itself of crime. Maybe the radio could be replaced, but where can one find a good AM radio these days?

The Hundred Views

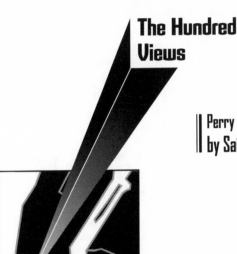

Perry St. and West 4th St.
by Said Shirazi

We had been fantasizing about what it would be like to live in a brownstone when we saw a man in a motorized wheelchair scooting slowly back and forth in the middle of the intersection. Like us, he was crossing at a diagonal, the one opposite to ours, and as we passed each other he asked if I could carry him up the stairs to his apartment. I looked to my girlfriend. There was no sign on her face of a world in which people who need help are annoying.

We followed him to his building and he began to give us our instructions. She was to take his bags and his keys, unlock the entry doors and prop them open with the wedges of wood she'd see there, go up the stairs to his apartment and twist the knob just inside the door to turn on all the lights. Meanwhile I moved each of his feet out from its resting place so his body turned to the side, plugged his chair into the middle socket of a thick orange extension cord, wrapped a chain around the axle and locked it, and lifted him in my arms.

He spoke slowly, so you naturally tried to finish for him by guessing, but this only flustered him more; you had to learn to wait. All things considered he was surprisingly undesperate.

I had taken his request partly as a challenge to my strength. He was a fairly small man, and I had calculated that whatever disease was wasting him away would have taken at least twenty more pounds off his frame. There was an element of drama in that I understood I was not supposed to set him down until we reached his apartment; it wasn't grocery rules. Putting his limp left arm around my neck, I carried him like a bride through the gate, up the wide stone steps and through the two entryway doors, up the long flight to the second floor and over the waiting threshold.

"Here we come," he called out, "we're going very fast."

The apartment had been entirely redone for the sake of his condition. There were wooden railings on every wall for him to pull himself along and the kitchen and bathroom were specially equipped to put things within his reach. You could see the whole place at a glance because all the doors had to be left open. The walls were covered from top to bottom with framed black-and-white photographs, and on his shelves were dirty, brittle paperback editions of old classics, the kind that would crumble at another reading.

The photos made me think of the hundred eyes of the guardsman Argus, which after his death came to decorate the peacock's tail. The apartment vanished into the world of the photos, like a prisoner's body vanishing under a web of tattoo ink. It was a room with a hundred views.

Settling into his upstairs wheelchair, he told us he had gone to hear a lecture about poetry, and asked if we liked poetry, which got my girlfriend very excited. It was Randall Jarrell, he said, and we understood he meant Jarrell was the subject, not the lecturer. At this point it was on the verge of him having us over. Who do you like, he asked me.

Well, I said, I see you have a picture of Yeats on your wall, I like him.

Do you like Wallace Stevens? he asked us eagerly. My girlfriend said that she did but knew I didn't, for I had recently been complaining about his vagueness. He liked to memorize poems, he said, and began to declaim some Dylan Thomas for us, one which my girlfriend also knew; they took turns reciting the lines and correcting each other's lapses while I looked around the room.

> *In my craft or sullen art*
> *Exercised in the still night*
> *When only the moon rages . . .*

I think between the two of you, you've almost got it, I said, and laughed. That was about the only trace of what an asshole I usually am.

My first thought was that he was a brilliant photographer who'd had a tragic accident. There were a few pictures of a man with a motorcycle, and the obvious thought occurred to both of us that the man might be him. But he couldn't have taken the picture of Yeats as a young man; in fact he said he hadn't known who the photo was when he got it. Looking around, I began to recognize some of the other photos, including what might be the most famous photo ever, two French people kissing. Our new friend was not a brilliant anything, just another lonely fan. Besides, he had told me downstairs it was multiple sclerosis.

So poets, keep on scribbling; poetry saves lives, though I suppose in the end it does so by saving us from life, from having to look at it. It gives us a way to figure out strangers and a reason to get out of the house even when we're not sure we'll make it back in. And I wouldn't be surprised if much of what I've gathered so far of how to be humane and kind—or how to seem it, which is close enough—I got from poetry too; the rest I got from watching my girlfriend.

My Secret Socks Life

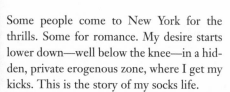

Saks Fifth Avenue, at 49ᵗʰ St.
by Jeanette Winterson

Some people come to New York for the thrills. Some for romance. My desire starts lower down—well below the knee—in a hidden, private erogenous zone, where I get my kicks. This is the story of my socks life.

I was traveling along Broadway in one of those reassuring black Town Cars. My agent was with me. She wore black. I wore black, all frivolity buried, this was working-woman funeral chic. Then she noticed my socks, which were made of silk, and patterned in the thinnest possible black and dulled-silver stripe. When I wear trousers, socks are to me what ties are to guys—the only way of discreetly breaching the uniform, a way of adding difference without drawing attention it.

"I love those socks." She said.

"Saks." I said.

"In small sizes?"

"The smallest."

This matters. While your average Ugly Sister can paddle about in size six and going up, we Cinderella princesses take a three. A sock has to fit. I don't want the toe folded over like a hotel bedspread, or the heel puffed out like a snake bite above my ankle. Worse, I don't want socks without heel or toe, you know the sort of thing—a badly made tube that could be used to warm winter pipes or store tennis balls. It's not a sock, it's a leg bandage.

What I want has to be beautiful, natural, perfect. A tall order in life and love, but worth the hunt if it's socks or art. Anyway, I'm a Virgo with Leo rising, so beautiful, natural, perfect, is where I stand—at least when I can get something to put on my feet.

I live in Cool Britannia, or Cruel Britannia, or Kooky Britannia, or Cotton Socks? Forget it Britannia, where the Land of Compromise is most at home in retail. We are a nation of shopkeepers, and as such, know that the easiest way to turn a profit is to sell shoddy goods. Shoddy goods are always expensive even when they're cheap. They're not worth buying at all, that's why. So, if you find yourself unsocked in England, too bad. Look on the labels and you'll find Cotton-Mix. Silk and Lycra. Woolrich. Woolrich? What the hell is Woolrich? A sheep? No. A sock made of forty percent wool. The rest will be nylon. This marvelous euphemism leaves the language as threadbare as the goods. If I am rich, I have an abundance, not forty percent. On the footsie, my sock-stocks are junk bonds.

So I am prepared to travel six thousand miles to New York, Saks Fifth Avenue, looking for toe-to-toe contact. I am severe. I am practiced. No one pulls the lycra over my eyes. I take a magnifying glass to read the labels, a calculator to convert the price, and scutter off with my booty in bags the size of cabin trunks.

If you want to know where I am, that's where you'll find me, on the ground floor, in the corner, with my feet up, head over heels, in a new romance, with that elusive, must-have, slinky little number that glides over the foot like a geisha.

Home is where the heart is, but lower pleasures must be accommodated too. I'm thinking of buying that New York pied-à-terre.

Kissing the Cab Driver

Spring and Hudson St.
by Maura Kelly

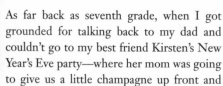

As far back as seventh grade, when I got grounded for talking back to my dad and couldn't go to my best friend Kirsten's New Year's Eve party—where her mom was going to give us a little champagne up front and her older brother was going to hide a bottle of vodka for us in the basement bathroom—New Year's Eve has sucked.

There was the New Year's Eve bash at my best friend Erin's house during my junior year of high school. I'd recently gone out on a few dates with this blond-haired, blue-eyed quarterback named Matt Jezior and he was supposed to show at Erin's. Her parents were away and her basement was full of liquor. They'd never notice a few missing bottles. It was a night full of possibility. By then, I'd given a few back-seat blow jobs, sure, but I'd never kissed anyone at midnight at the turn of the year or had a boyfriend. I figured Matt was my sure thing on both accounts.

As I waited and waited for him to show up, I drank and drank. When he finally arrived, around eleven, I was wasted on the two beverages that, since

my missed date with destiny four years before, had become synonymous with
New Year's celebration in my mind: vodka and champagne. And I was marching around the house soldier-style, sporting Erin's dad's old army jacket.

After spotting Matt, I ran over and hugged him, clocking him on the
forehead with the green wicker Christmas basket I was wearing as a helmet.
Then I tried to remove it, but the handle that I'd somehow pulled under my
chin like a strap made it too tight; why are things always easier to get on
than to get off? When I finally freed myself, Matt and I sat on the couch and
talked for about five minutes until I passed out.

Matt was shaking me when I woke up. "Listen," he said, "I'm going to
go home to ring in the year with my mom."

Matt and I said a polite good-bye. I watched him cross the porch and
head to his black Volvo. Before he reached it, I started screaming, "You
mama's boy! Fuckin' mama's boy! Yeah, that's right, go home to your mama.
Wuss!"

Despite all this, every time the holiday approached I thought with hope:
this year will be better. Different. Special. Finally.

But for the first time, as New Year's 2000 approached, I had no such
belief. I was in the midst of a pretty intense period of depression. Mourning,
I guess, is the more accurate word. As the psychological torture ran its
course, I'd been forcing myself not to drink, even though boozing is something I usually like to do when I feel down, because I finally realized getting
drunk actually *does* make things worse in the long run. So I was feeling pain
as clearly and sharply as a patient without anesthetic would feel a wisdom
tooth being pulled.

This year, an old college friend of mine was throwing a NYE 2000 party
at her father's penthouse apartment in SoHo. I had no excuse not to go. I
hadn't seen any of my college friends in about three months, and one of the
lines I'd been using to put people off was: "Well, I'll definitely see you at A.'s
New Year's party." The idea of making polite party conversation made me
feel sick to my stomach, but I was equally horrified by the idea of staying
home alone.

At 10:30 I was in my red party shoes and fuchsia party dress and at the
door of A.'s dad's apartment: full of old friends, demi-starlets, rich kids,
original paintings by big-deal real artists like Picasso and Matisse, four
makeshift bars, a full staff of wait people passing hors d'oeuvres and pour-

ing drinks, silver holiday decorations, and a giant tree in the corner with silver lights.

I had a hard time talking to anyone—I was too busy conducting an interior dialogue. I ordered a Wild Turkey and Diet Coke to try and shut myself up. It was too easy: the drinks were free, I could have anything I wanted, and no one was without a glass in hand as far as my eye could see.

By the time my friend J. and I decided to leave the party shortly after midnight to do some serious drinking, I'd had four more Diet Turkeys. We met up with another friend and headed to the Emerald Bar on Spring to start drowning our souls in earnest.

I was still drinking my Turkeys at 5 A.M., across the street from the Emerald at a club called Sway—dark lights, cigarette smoke, and women with backless shirts being groped by men wearing designer clothes. By that time I had lost both my friends and my wallet, accidentally scraped half the leather off my red heels, spilled a drink down the front of my dress, and picked up a sexy Portuguese guy with a black leather jacket and a dark goatee who was happy to buy me drinks. We tried to talk at first, but his English was bad and my Portuguese was non-existent. So we gave up and made-out instead.

At 6 A.M. I peeked behind one of the club's black curtains and saw the morning light had started to rise. It sobered me up a bit, made me realize I didn't want a one-morning stand. I told Portugal I was heading home alone.

A cab pulled up to the corner at the same time I walked out the door.

"Where you want go?" said the cab driver.

I told him my address. "But you gotta take me home for free because it's not that far and I have no cash," I said. "I lost my wallet tonight."

He turned to look at me. Maybe he saw the drunkenness in my eyes, the brown stain on my dress, the ripped white fishnets, the washed-out mascara shadows under my eyes.

"Please," I said.

"Okay," he said in a foreign accent.

Considering he was doing me a favor, treating me like a friend, getting in the back seat seemed the wrong thing to do. I hopped into the front, kneeled up on the seat, and gave him a hug. He laughed and started accelerating slowly.

"Are you Iranian?" I said.

"No."

"Iraqi?"

"Saudi," he said.

"You miss your home?"

"Sometimes, some things. But there is more here. It is better."

"Did you have a nice New Year's Eve?"

He shrugged.

"I am in my cab. But I make lot of money. It is okay."

"Will this new year be good for you?"

"Be good?"

"Yes. Will good things happen?"

"Oh yes, very good things. It will be good."

"It will?" I said.

He glanced over at me. "Oh yes," he said, eyes back on the road.

I started crying.

"Why you are crying?" he said.

Then I just said it: "One of my favorite people in the world shot himself in the head last month." I wasn't sure he understood. "My friend is dead and I loved him," I said.

My cabbie put an arm around me and pulled me to him. I let his sweater absorb my tears.

"It will be good," he said. "You are beautiful."

"But why didn't I hold him like you are holding me? Why didn't I know?" I stared at him, waiting, even though I knew by then that nobody had an answer to that question. Then I realized he had pulled to the side of the road. We had reached my corner.

He turned to me, pulled me tight, kissing me firmly on the lips and then working his tongue through them. Partly because my mouth was so used to being open after Portugal, partly because I thought he might not have had a New Year's kiss, because I thought he might be sad like me, and partly just because, I opened my mouth and we frenched for a few seconds.

I pulled back hard against the strong arms enfolding me, like I'd stuck my tongue in an electric socket: I suddenly got scared. But he was too strong and held me tight. I almost couldn't separate my mouth from his but somehow managed to do it.

"No, no," I mumbled against his lips. "Please, no!"

I pushed away from him again and this time he let me go.

"I'm sorry," I said. "I can't any more."

I patted his hand.

He smiled at me. "It is okay. It will be good."

I nodded. "Okay," I said. "Thanks for the ride."

"Happy New Year," he said. We both smiled.

I opened the door and got out.

The Dynamite Brothers Meet the Slapper

188 East 3rd St.
by Snooder Greenberg

I was sitting in my fourth-floor fire escape window on a hot summer afternoon, watching the sparse street life on Third Street, a few people sitting around on our buildings stoop, a couple of guys had lawn chairs, a few guys standing outside the bodega . . . like that.

Mine was a junky/hippie building, yeasty like the rest of the neighborhood, shit happening regularly. At about 2 P.M. a Latin kid said something to a guy standing outside the building across the street from me, the guy slapped him, he left after a few more words and all was quiet again. I was back in the window at 4 P.M. Then, in an instant, out of nowhere, appeared the Dynamite Brothers, kids in leather jackets with their colors; they filled the intersection of Third and B, packed tight they overflowed past the Third Rail Bar on the corner. Maybe two hundred to three hundred of them. Just as quickly the people on the block disappeared into buildings, and they started up the block. They had chains and garbage can lids to shield against the crap that people soon began throwing at them from windows. They systematically smashed all the car windows and threw garbage cans in the street. About this time I broke off to call 911. There is no way the cops didn't get another hundred such calls. (The cops showed up after fifty minutes and a good ten minutes after the Dynamite Brothers disappeared with the same military dispatch with which they had shown up.)

After a couple minutes they closed ranks in front of this building across the street and one of them started yelling in Spanish, I assume demanding that the Slapper come out. After several minutes the Slapper did come out. A brief and, all things considered, surprisingly civil conversation ensued, and then the Slapper was shot in the face with a pistol, and the Dynamite Brothers quickly melted away down Avenue B.

This happening was not newsworthy, nothing in any of the papers, nothing in the media, but so help me God this happened just as I say.

The Tomkins Square Park Riot, 1988

St. Mark's Pl. Between First Ave. and Avenue A
by Luc Sante

On Saturday, August 6, I was possibly even more abstracted than usual, because it was well nigh midnight before I realized that I had neglected to eat dinner, and that the refrigerator contained nothing but half a jar of horseradish[1]. So I set out for a greasy spoon on Second Avenue, in the heart of the sidewalk market district (mismatched shoes, secondhand

---

[1] This piece was submitted to the New Yorker, and a version was published in the issue of August 22, 1988. It appeared in the "Talk of the Town" section and, as was then the custom, was unsigned. The anonymity was especially appropriate in this case, because the version printed differed so wildly from my original (which appears here) as to make it in effect the work of its editor. Still, the piece you are reading is in many ways disfigured by my pathetic attempts at New Yorker style. You see me trying to sound like that magazine's man of the world, who just naturally employs constructions like "well nigh," who "decides to investigate" as if he were Philo Vance. Even the framing is phony. Although it was and is my custom when alone to eat dinner very late, in fact that night I saw the eight cop cars when I was out walking my dog, but I guess that didn't sound sufficiently interesting. And my stylistic contortions got worse: In the typescript I submitted I actually changed the first-person singular to first-person plural. (The published version reverted to the singular, as "A friend writes . . .")

45

pornography). After refreshing myself with rubbery kielbasa slices embedded in an egglike mass, I was proceeding back up the avenue when I saw
eight police vehicles come screeching around the corner of St. Mark's
Place, bearing down on Tompkins Square Park.

I decided to investigate. The park had been much on my mind lately,
and I had been expecting trouble there for at least a year. A decade ago,
when I first moved into the neighborhood, the park had been the undis-
puted province of junkies and muggers, and few others, including me[2], ventured into it after dark. More recently, however, it had regained its position
as a public gathering site. On weekend nights it emanated music and
hijinks as the traffic among the dozens of bars and restaurants nearby just
naturally came to include the park. At the same time it had become an
encampment of the homeless. On bitter January nights, as I headed up
Avenue A from my office to my apartment, I would see groups of people
huddled around trashcan bonfires or packed together sleeping under a
tarp. Late in the winter, though, policemen had been coming around and
dousing the flames, and otherwise harrassing the occupants of this latter-
day Hooverville[3]. When summer came the ongoing party and the homeless
settlement had in some fashion fused; it was a mild commotion, a bit bois-
terous but no threat to anyone. Nevertheless, in view of the cops, it was a
ticking bomb. The park's history for a century had been marked by clash-
es between the police and area residents, from the gun detachments that
were moved in after the 1887 execution of the Haymarket anarchists in
Chicago for fear of local anarchist flareups (none occurred), to the violent
turf wars of the late Sixties and early Seventies, a three-way tangle among
police, hippies, and Hispanic youths. Some of the tension of those post-
Summer of Love days had returned, although now largely devoid of racial

[2] In twenty-eight years of living in New York City the only time I was actually mugged was in the
spring of 1983, when I was visiting a girlfriend who lived on Tenth Street, on the north side of
the park. She fell asleep, the apartment was hot, and I decided to go smoke a joint on a park bench
I could see from her window. Within minutes I was face down on the bench with a knife blade to
the side of my neck as unseen hands went through my pockets and relieved me of my twenty
bucks. I felt like a fool, since I knew better. If you went to the park at night you incurred a tax,
and that was that.

[3] This designation drew letters from readers asking whether the encampment shouldn't rightly
have been called a "Reaganville." Point taken.

[4] A pretty hasty assertion, this, given how many of the homeless were black or Hispanic.

content[4] and set starkly between locals and the authorities. There had been talk, too, that city officials were unhappy with the park's design, disturbed by the darkness provided by the dense, ancient trees and the twisting, European-style paths, and were considering revising the landscape to a more open and policeable plan. It did not come as much of a surprise, then, to hear that the cops were intending the close the park at night, nor that the first such effort, on the last weekend in July, was met with vocal if confused resistance. On that occasion some taunting went on and there were a scattering of arrests, but around two in the morning the thirty or forty cops went home and jubliant locals moved back into the park, convinced that they had won.

On this night, though, things looked different before I had even reached First Avenue. Groups of people massed on the four corners of First and St. Mark's were yelling slogans like "The Park Belongs to the People!" Halfway down the next block a cordon of cops in riot gear was blocking further access in the direction of the park, not even letting through residents of buildings located beyond their post, nor were they deigning to answer questions. Even if one knew that there had been some recent disputes over use of the park—and such knowledge was by no means general in the neighborhood—the obviously hostile police presence appeared inexplicable. Overhead, a police helicopter hovered, coming so low that the roar of its blades seemed to be rising from behind the houses on both sides of the street, and then coming lower still, so that the backwash of its rotors kicked up the debris from the gutters and the trash from the trashcans and drew it upward in spirals.

On Avenue A[5] the helicopter aimed its spotlights at the tops of buildings. Was it looking for snipers? The avenue was full of people, some protesting but many more pulled, dazed, from bars and apartments, some from bed; one guy was wearing a bathrobe and slippers. A group crowded around a man who said he had heard the chief of the Ninth Precinct assert that he was calling for reinforcements due to "Communist agitators" among the protestors. This drew a laugh. Police were everywhere (by the end of the night their numbers would be estimated at 450): beat cops with their caps turned around and badge numbers obscured, plainclothesmen

[5] The cops made a great show of cordoning off St. Mark's Place, but characteristically they didn't bother with any of the other side streets leading to the park.

trying with little success to look like locals, riot cops bearing Plexiglas shields, vehicles marked with designations ranging from "Hazardous Materials Squad" to "DWI Task Force," and, just below the park's main entrance opposite St. Mark's Place, an Emergency Services truck the size of a bus, with lamps like Klieg lights aimed up and down the avenue. Suddenly a detachment of mounted cops went tearing down St. Mark's at full gallop.

On First Avenue, where the horses were headed, all was chaos. Trash cans lay on their sides in the middle of the street, small groups of civilians were being chased this way and that by mounted cops and foot cops wielding nightsticks. The police appeared to be acting in purely random fashion, suddenly deciding to empty a particular corner or stretch of sidewalk of its occupants, or, hearing an insult launched at them from the crowd, undertaking a flanking maneuver, sticks braced, advancing to their own rhythmic chant: "Kill, kill, kill!" More vehicles, patrol cars and paddy wagons, came roaring down St. Mark's Place the wrong way. Then they parked and the cops just milled around, eventually beginning their own game of patternless rousting and containment actions.

Back on Avenue A, the block between Sixth and Seventh streets just below the park was now an empty zone between police lines at either end. A handful of cops were stalking the block demanding that shopkeepers and the owners of bars and restaurants shut their gates. A middle-aged cop who looked a bit like the actor Brian Keith was shouting himself hoarse ordering the owners of the large mid-block Korean grocery to lock their doors. "With a key!" he screamed again and again. Earlier I had heard someone in a crowd say, "You know who's really hurting tonight? S.Y.P." I tried to decipher the acronym: Socialist Youth Party[6]? Now I realized they had been referring to this popular albeit grossly overpriced convenience store, locally known as Save Your Pennies, which under ordinary circumstances would have been doing its heaviest business at just that hour. I watched the activity for about fifteen minutes, virtually the only civilian on the block,

[6] Pretty unlikely that the Trots would have been out in force, but as a veteran of the mid-Seventies at Columbia, when I witnessed a fair amount of violence and near-violence between left and crypto-left factions—often involving Trot splinter groups and thugs from Lyndon LaRouche's National Caucus of Labor Committees—I was still at that late date expecting that a riot would bring the ideologues out of the woodwork. Nobody was selling Workers' Vanguard in Tompkins Square, though.

until finally a small cop came up to me and yelled, half-pleading, "What are you doing? Go home!" as if I were an errant toddler and he a nervous young father.

Below Sixth Street the heaviest concentration of police stood cordoning off the block from a crowd of several hundred locals. Every sort of attitude was present on both sides. There were cops who wanted to talk, for example, trying to reason it out with their opponents, although they were a distinct minority among the blue ranks. The civilians comprised a wide range of ages, dispositions, and sartorial adornments. One long-haired peacock in an incongruous black duster paced around in confusion, preening as if reflexively. A shirtless man paced in front of the crowd with the air of a prophet, lifting his cane in the air as he instigated chants. Most people simply looked dazed. Others kept appearing, homeward bound from work or bars and entirely unprepared for the situation; most ended up staying with the crowd. A knot of people on a corner clustered around two priests, who seemed to have been among the complainants responsible for the police presence. That is, they had asked the precinct to try to reduce the volume of noise emanating from the park, and now they were alternately embarrassed and defensive in the face of the semi-military occupation. A couple of reasonable-sounding passers-by had seen the beginnings of the fray, around eleven o'clock, when the cops had evacuated the park, a group of youths had turned around and rushed the fence, sticks had been wielded and bottles thrown. From there matters had escalated. The passers-by, avoiding ideological argument, were making the point that bad policing had been and was manifest. The priests kept insisting that a large police presence was necessary to protect their parishioners from the crack trade. They didn't seem to register the fact, even when it was pointed out to them, that such trade does not take place in the park but in derelict buildings on side streets that are raided every now and then but reopen almost immediately. Finally, one of the priests lost his cool. "You think this is bad?" he said, having by his own admission perceived that a number of his interlocuters looked Jewish. "You should go to Israel, see what the Israelis are doing on the West Bank. They're really cracking heads[7] there!"

---

[7] This anecdote, or whatever shard of it was preserved in the published version, raised a certain amount of controversy. The pastor of St. Brigid's, on Avenue B and Seventh Street, wrote in to protest that far from the anti-Semitic police-defender he was depicted as, he was actually out

Over the next few hours events became increasingly repetitive as cops and crowd were locked in a face-off, which would momentarily be broken when somebody (always someone invisibly in the rear of the crowd) would lob a bottle and the cops would charge and club heads. A young woman who had done nothing but stand in the wrong place was clubbed so badly her shirt was soaked through with blood. After she had been taken away in an ambulance, others raised her shirt on a stick like a flag. Onlookers wept, screamed in frustration, exhorted their fellows to take up sticks and do battle; the crowd had no leaders and no logic. Neither did the cops, apparently; they spent a great deal of time dispatching units to investigate rooftops from which nothing was being thrown. Periodically cops would go around dumping garbage cans and smashing the empty bottles with their clubs and feet, invariably drawing applause from the crowd. They seemed to be particularly vehement in going after bicycles, deliberately damaging them with their truncheons. Every now and then a fire truck would pull up and, after a few minutes, depart. This remained inexplicable until a radio report the following day quoted police officials as saying that the crowd started fires along the avenue, but no fires were seen, at least by me. A negotiating session between locals and cops, mediated by a third priest, became a circular bout of reiterated arguments.

Finally, about five o'clock or so, I was getting so sleepy, having been up since seven the previous morning, that the tableau before my eyes began to look imaginary. I decided to go. Just then the huge Emergency Services truck began broadcasting news of a Community Board[8] meeting to be held the following Wednesday. Then somebody threw a bottle and the cops charged yet again. All night I had been pretty deft at staying out of their path, but this time I did not move quickly enough down Sixth Street, and I was slammed against a building, and then dragged along the

that night trying to negotiate with the cops on behalf of the protesters. In fact I knew him by sight, and acknowledged his negotiation in the following paragraph, although that part of the piece didn't survive the edit (Father Moloney, if I remember his name correctly, went to prison a few years later for his alleged involvement in a scheme to run guns to the IRA)—there had been two other priests whom I couldn't identify. There are at least five Catholic or Eastern Rite churches within a block or two of the park.

[8] Not as incongruous as that sounds, since the Community Board, a body despised by many local residents (and the feeling was mutual), was always calling for preemptive police actions, allegedly on behalf of "the community."

sidewalk. I limped home, fingering the gashes in my shirt and pants, wishing I hadn't been wearing new clothes that night[9].

---

[9] The next day I took the Hampton Jitney to Sagaponack, where I wrote the piece, and the edits were dispatched on the bus and picked up by me at the Candy Kitchen! Yes, those kinds of strange paradoxes were a feature of the Eighties. I made probably $15,000 a year then, paid less than $200 a month for my apartment on Twelfth Street and an equally trifling sum for my office on Sixth, but I had more successful artist friends with whom I was renting a house near the beach—the Hamptons had not yet been so grotesquely disfigured by money then either, and the rent was not astronomical. My friends had all lived in the East Village when they were poorer a few years earlier, and the major topic of discussion then was the infuriating death of Jean-Michel Basquiat, killed by success. I had known him in the neighborhood—I remembered sitting with him on the fire-escape stairs of the old Center Bar on St. Mark's as, flushed with excitement, he told me he had that day sold Henry Geldzahler one of his color-Xerox postcards. That was the beginning of his rise, and of his fall. The death of Jean-Michel and the debacle in the park are now entwined in my mind, both representative of how beginning in the early Eighties money moved through Manhattan, sucking up and then discarding everything in its path.

To the Man Who Forgot His New Books on the Subway Platform at Lincoln Center

The Uptown 1/9 subway platform at Lincoln Center; the subway; Barnes & Noble

by Carolyn Murnick

Your books were a little bit strange, and that ended up working in your favor since none of us wanted them at first glance. Stuff about yoga and spiritual exercise, something about linguistics, and a medieval text. There were five of them in the bag, complete with your credit card receipt from the Barnes & Noble, with a couple of bookmarks thrown in for good measure.

I was just in the Barnes & Noble, (perhaps I had seen you?), and to my dismay, the book I had wanted was not in stock. They had called other stores for me so I was on my way uptown to another branch where I was told my book would be waiting for me at the information desk.

When I got down to the subway platform, my thoughts flitted between the winter chill and the insidious, yet accommodating energy of the superstore and I sat on the bench right next to your bag of books without even noticing them. There was no one else around and I stared across the tracks with a heavy-lidded focus at the groups of people toeing the edge. It was the sound of that young couple slipping through the turnstile that finally caused me to turn my head.

She was loud and demanding with long painted fingernails curled around the cell phone attached to her ear. Her free hand extended behind her to where her boyfriend grasped it, a step out of sync, giving him the appearance of an animal on a leash being led aimlessly. He carried her Victoria's Secret shopping bags and flinched when she tossed her hair over her shoulder and it hit him in the face. She would leave him first, I surmised.

She snapped her cell phone closed as she approached the bench where I was sitting, and called out, loudly, "Look, someone forgot their new books." She began to pick up the bag.

"Well let's see what we have here," I said.

And then we looked, and again, none of us said anything right off the bat because I think we were a little confused by the subjects you were interested in.

I took one of the books in my hand, one that had a picture of people in leotards on the cover, and noticed that your credit card receipt was tucked into the front page.

"Here's the credit card receipt," I said to the couple, "this guy just bought these a few minutes ago."

They said nothing and the girl continued to leaf through one of your other purchases, periodically pointing something out to her boyfriend.

The train was taking a while and I couldn't help thinking of you. Did you realize you had left your books as soon as you walked on to the train, only to turn around and have the doors close in front of you? Or had you not even realized they were gone yet? Suddenly, I remembered I was on my way to the uptown Barnes & Noble and thought again of the web of interconnected stores in the city. Then, in a burst of inspiration, I said to the couple, "Hey, I just had them put a book on hold for me at the Eighty-second Street Barnes & Noble and I'm going there now and maybe I can take these books to them and they can contact the guy from his credit card receipt and he'll get his books back. Do you think that would work?"

I said it kind of all in one breath, sounding rather dorky and excited.

They said nothing, continuing to page through your purchases.

"Yeah," I said to no one in particular, "I'm going to do that."

This decision left me feeling slightly giddy. I had come into contact with a textbook situation in which to test my moral fiber. That realization combined with the knowledge that I was doing the right thing, was delightful.

Finally, the guy turned to me, "You're going to return them?" he asked.

"Yeah," I said, "I'm going to take them to the uptown store now."

He turned to his girlfriend and continued talking, and finally we hear the train pulling in. We're getting up to walk over to the track and the girl is putting your books back into the bag and I'm standing there waiting to get them from her, when she holds the spiritual exercise book outside of the bag. "I'm just going to keep this one," she says timidly, "Do you think that's OK?"

I stare at her for a moment, feeling a sudden anger toward her and feeling at a loss for words. My simple textbook situation of only minutes before had now mutated. Other people had become involved now, other people who may or may not obstruct my swift carriage of justice. I'm thinking to myself that there must be one perfect thing to say at this moment, and if I don't hit upon those words I've somehow failed. Since there was only a short window of time before the doors of the train closed, I knew that I must act quickly, and this made me even more anxious.

"No," I finally say with a dramatic pause, "I'm not going to return them if they're not all there."

We stare at each other for one more moment. She's not moving and I don't know what else to say so I turn and walk onto the train. The couple follows me and takes a seat on the opposite side of the car, holding your bag and engaging in a heated discussion. The girl is sitting and the guy is standing over her, and she's holding that one book in her her lap and scowling up at him. I'm looking over at them but trying not to let them catch me and I'm really rather angry now. I contemplate whether I should walk over there and give them an abridged monologue on ethics in everyday life, and then I laugh to myself imagining what I would say. But a second later I'm frustrated again, your lost books and these people are really making me mad and now I'm emotionally involved with this situation and I just want to do the right thing and make up for your loss but now it seems out of my hands.

We're nearing my stop and I'm realizing now that I'm going to have to just let it go because I need to get off the train and re-engage with what I was planning on doing anyway, when I see out of the corner of my eye that the young man is walking toward me.

He approaches my side of the car and looks at me with a serious, almost pleading look.

"Here," he says handing me the bag, "they're all here."

"Thank you," I say, and I sincerely mean it, as a triumph for you and for me and also for him, maybe, by winning a small argument with his princess girlfriend.

But what transpires in that moment makes me little anxious at the same time; one stranger is trusting another merely on a leap of faith. When I walk into the uptown store and explain what had happened (minus the supporting characters) and hand over the bag, the man at the counter looks at me with such incredulous gratitude that I almost think they're going to reward me for my good deed by giving me the book I want for free.

But of course that didn't happen.

And instead of them contacting you from your credit-card receipt to come pick up your stuff, which I realize now was rather complicated and illogical, they just credited your account the missing amount and restocked the books themselves. After it was over, I was a little bit exhausted, and a little bit giddy again, but I was glad for you, and I wondered what you would think when you noticed that Barnes & Noble had credited you for the amount you paid for the books you had lost.

You'd never know how it had happened.

Mother's Day

Greenwich Village
by E. Franke

My brother is a twenty-eight-year-old millionaire living in Greenwich Village. He drives a Boxster, owns a beach house in East Hampton, and recently bought an original one-sheet of *Breakfast at Tiffany's* for the bargain price of twenty thousand dollars. Sometimes he asks me, his older sister, what I could "use": cable TV, a new set of bike wheels, a Palm, perhaps? But I always say the same thing: I'm a writer, I'm writing, and someday my writing will pay off.

He respects me, of course. Believes in my talent, though it has yet to be discovered. Thinks I have integrity, even if I did let him "pay off" that $13,000 debt last spring. His profound generosity is matched only by his lifelong shame: for having a dead-beat dad, for having red hair, for having mispronounced "crudités" at his Bar Mitzvah, and for all the rest of the having and not-having that continues to put him at odds with the other haves and have-nots on the planet, myself among them.

As it is, I've been sick for a few months. It's nothing serious, by definition: what began as a virus turned into a sinus infection that turned into a bronchial infection that, in conjunction with seasonal allergies and writer's block and my ex-boyfriend's new wife and the *New York Times Magazine* crossword puzzle I can't finish and the water bug that crawled under my bed last night, has blossomed into plain-old, garden-variety depression. Which is to say that yes, I am clinically depressed; but on most days—with the right recipe of anti's, exercise, friends, and cigarettes—I am perfectly fine and functional, despite the fact that I'm (a) self-involved, (b) self-pitying, (c) annoying, and (d) downwardly mobile. Which brings me back to my brother.

Drew, as he is named, thinks that I am too nice, and that I'll go nowhere in life if I don't ask for the things I need. Like tissues, or an editorial critique from one of our widely-published cousins, or a raise from my boss. "Let people help you once in a while," he said to me last night as I opened and closed cabinet doors in my barren kitchen, trying to find something, anything, for him eat. "And stop trying to please everybody!"

"I don't do that anymore!" I said. "You know, I have become very, very selfish."

"You have?" he asked.

"I even screen my phone calls."

"WOW!" he yelled back. "Call *Candid Camera* headquarters!"

I poured oil into a frying pan, dumped in some popcorn kernels.

"Do you think I suffer from Jewish Mother syndrome?" I asked.

"Not by the looks of your refrigerator," he said.

We were waiting for my groceries to be delivered. It was a Sunday night, and I hadn't been out of my apartment all weekend. I spent hours cleaning the dust beneath the bed, the dirt on the window-bars, the grout on the bathroom floor. Martha Stewart, who is my real-life boss, once told me that "housekeeping is an art, not a chore." I was quick to agree, adding that, for me, housekeeping is essential to my mental health; it's the only thing I can do to "clean up my dirty mind." I had meant to use the word "messy," to note the head-clearing aspect of cleaning. Needless to say, Martha hasn't chatted me up much since then.

"So," said Drew, once we finally sat down for our chips-and-salsa dinner.

"So," I said back.

"When is all this supposed to end?" he asked.

Translation: When is your supposed literary agent going to sell your supposed novel for this supposed large sum of cash? When are you going to stop obsessing over your ex-boyfriend, and the ex-boyfriend before him, and get on with your life? When are you going to stop smoking and start running and get into shape and look better and feel better about yourself? (Do you want me to buy you a treadmill for your thirtieth birthday?) When are you going to accept the fact that life truly does suck. That even though I am rich, I too am looking for love in all the same, rotten places. That driving out to the Island in my convertible, alone, is the closest thing to true happiness I can foresee for myself. That my last girlfriend dumped me because I asked her to chip in for ski tickets in Utah. That I still carry a picture of (our childhood cat) Dottie in my wallet. That you can't go on living in this studio on this crummy block. That you can't be so giving to so many of the wrong people. That you can't address your old boss' envelopes for free just because you have good penmanship. That you can't make mix-tapes of your favorite Sleater-Kinney songs to this kid who blew you off for drinks last week. That you can't date someone who you call "dumb boy," even if he does live in Dumbo. That I can't keep on coming over here and picking up the pieces of your life, gluing them back together, and serving them to you on a cracked plate.

I took a swig of Robitussin and washed it down with a Dos Equis.

"Remember when we took Dottie to the vet and got pulled over for speeding?" I asked him.

"Yeah," Drew said.

"And the police officer saw sick little Dottie in the front seat? And then apologized? And ripped up the ticket?"

"Yeah," he smiled. "I remember."

"I think about that a lot," I confessed.

"Poor Dottie," Drew said.

"*Nebach*," he added, in Yiddish.

"Hey," I said. "Can we please go for a ride in your car tonight? just you and me?"

He started counting on his fingers. "First of all," he pointed out, "my car only seats two, so it can only be you and me. And second, could you please not say please all the time? You're starting to sound like a British talk-show host."

"Sorry," I said.

"And stop saying you're sorry!"

I waved at him with my middle finger, the way he used to do to me at the dinner table when our babysitter wasn't looking.

"Uh-oh," he said. "That's gonna cost you."

But both of us know I'll never have to pay.

In a Swamp of Reusable Souls The Collaborative Poem Writte by the People Staying Up All Night for Seagull Tickets

Delacorte Theater, 81st St. and Central Park West retrieved by Rebecca Donner

1. This is the poem that the people in line wrote

2. the day has been beautiful and clear and lots of fun

3. I've enjoyed my time in the dark and the sun

4. The sun always rises. I remember that through convoluted thoughts.

5. It shines, the rays melt the butter, making it soft.

6. which I put on my toast in the early morning.

7. Morning? Sweet potato, sausages, and pot.

8. with *arepas con queso*

9. or maybe just a glass of wine.

10. a robust port and some Camembert cheese

11. followed by mint leaves and dill

12. will be a great recipe

13. for all the children living beyond the trees.

14. Then they all got butt nekkit, and

15. Jumped into a lake in the clearing

16. the monkeys walked along the edge
17. eating burgers with only one hand
18. alone in a city with myself
19. nothing but smoke and filthy sheets to keep me going.
20. Conductor and chorus! it's easy to attach meaning to meaningless things
21. silly swank, but not so easy with meaningful things
22. And he passes forward toward the blue gray . . .
23. uttering words of disjuncture slipping from his tongue
24. then writing them down quickly with careful penmanship
25. and erasing them with slickly subtle lips
26. as the lines of sand smoothed by the sea crested white
27. their faces, contorted by the pain of their recent ordeal,
28. strained, smiling, laughing, singing, all in solidarity.
29. Long, long, line, I like Natalie
30. I woke up this morning with a sore neck
31. I have no idea what to say
32. [Blank]
33. [Ditto]
34. boogie down, Otto, boogie down
35. come, come home, to a passage of India, and stay forever
36. fill us up with love and sky and breathe
37. The bounty of mother earth fills me.
38. The heart of life is in my sweet soul
39. For love is lost in words intention
40. I lost my pocket change in San Francisco
41. And then my dog barfed up my jelly donut that I fed him the night before
42. And then he slept with my whore
43. She was named Benjamin of Edge wave
44. but the horse had a cold so he went to see the dog
45. In reality the horse was depressed so . . .
46. Or maybe she was obsessed so . . .
47. Think, as you were in it and in part
48. I am here and I am tired
49. These trees aren't the usual tombstones.
50. The life of those beneath them spread upwards and over.
51. Moving through the forest like a cool swift breeze

52. I stop to listen to a lark sing—so sweet.
53. My heart swells with the joy as I reach out to greet
54. Eternally filled forever swimming
55. Through pools of mist cool on my face
56. I will move a mountain
57. and fill it up with morning rains
58. Until the hourglass drains
59. my corpuscles the grains of sand
60. often shocked with sinking hands (a llama man)
61. the opus neared its end
62. take it to the end of the line
63. and then start all over again
64. What a long strange road it has been
65. Over the top
66. *plus haut que le soleil* [higher than the sun]
67. Lower than a bug
68. I think I need a hug
69. I'd tell you the word but I can't pronounce it.
70. P is for Potter, Harry Potter
71. I can't say flower if it's a sunflower?
72. But dummy is the noun form of dumb.
73. Y . . . 74. i shoot the blues like trashy heroin.
75. the gash spews salve-like moist toppings.
76. The life seems too easy to comprehend
77. Depends who tries
78. To make the biggest impact
79. In a swamp of reusable souls
80. *cést une fleur* "lotus" . . . a New York [it is a lotus flower in New York]
81. Forever in bloom...the petals never falling away
82. Requesting a chance . . . A chance if I may
83. To be who I am and be who I say
84. White Junk floats around in the air
85. looks like a horse and mare
86. The cows are hunting their pray
87. Lushus Lushus Green Grass Alive, fresh.
88. What the hell is lushus?—Too good to be true?

89. But truth is not what it appears to be.
90. No, I see only lies.
91. And everything is a beautifully elaborate and intricate lie.
92. Except for the way you smile at me.
93. That sax is blowing right through your hair
94. And Butrous-Butrous Gahli smiled at it all, "Ha-Ha!"
95. But nothing could erase the memory of that day
96. Those purple elephants had been incredible
97. And pink imperiled pansies
98. Bloom in the August miasma
99. You pregnant starburst of song
100. I wake up and hum along
101. The leaves, The sky, The . . .
102. Eat Your Mistakes.
103. With just a touch of blue-cheese dressing
104. i knew she was not with me
105. So where could she be
106. Anywhere but here with me
107. I have a dream
108. that there is PORN for all
109. Blame Canada
110. Life is beautiful
111. Beauty is not to hold
112. For once it is attained it will be gone forever
113. And forever and forever until it's gone again.
114. The feeling rises in my chest.
115. And I listen to the sounds around me
116. Wondering where she is now
117. and where He is now
118. swimming in the pool of blood
119. trying to get out from their
120. Something's coming over me

Wedding Proposal at Café Loup

13th St. between 6th and 7th Aves.
by Meghan Daum
and Thomas Beller

Proposals of marriage are becoming the most public moment of people's private lives.

I ran into a cast member of Cabaret, *the other day, and he told me about a marriage proposal that took place at the end of a recent performance. The fiancé paid the producers of the show, who then asked Matt McGrath, who plays the emcee (who ends the play dressed in a concentration camp uniform; very romantic), to ask the departing audience to "hold up for a moment." Matt McGrath brought the pair onstage and the man got down on a knee in front his perplexed girlfriend (who was apparently cringing), and popped the question. The woman did not say no. But she did not say yes. On her way out she was heard to remark, "My mother raised me right."*

All of which is a round about way of introducing the following two pieces that describe a public proposal of marriage that took place recently in Café Loup. — TB

By Meghan Daum

Every Sunday the local newspaper in the midwestern town where I live prints engagement and wedding announcements that look like the pages of a high school yearbook. The faces are fair skinned and robust, some still marked with acne. Their pictures are taken at portrait studios by photographers who appear to have directed them to gaze into each others eyes and said, "Think about the moment he proposed to you, imagine the scene, try to recreate the look on your face . . . okay, there!"

Sometimes couples simply send in their senior prom pictures. I often suspect that the guy popped the question on the dance floor while the Titanic theme played over the loudspeaker and some tattooed girl in a spaghetti strap dress smoked a joint hundreds of yards away in a bathroom stall covered with phrases like "If you love something set it free. If it doesn't come back to you, hunt it down and kill it."

Recently, my friend Tom and I were in Café Loup recently drinking non-alcoholic beverages around 6 in the evening. Café Loup is located in Manhattan on 13th Street between

By Thomas Beller

The other day, through no fault of my own, I was a witness to a very public proposal of marriage that took place at Café Loup.

It was a humid early evening and my friend Meghan and I were at the bar drinking non-alcoholic beverages. Club soda for her. Tea with lemon for me (I was hung over; I don't know what her excuse was). Meghan lives in Nebraska now, and we began catching up. Then, in the vestibule area at the front of the restaurant, a man started singing. Right away there was something about his tone of voice that made me cringe a little. His voice wasn't awful, but it had this weird emotional charge that made us stop talking. He was singing something about a Valentine. We craned our necks; our view of the bar was obscured by a pillar.

I could see this guy singing, and the look of unbridled happiness and emotion sweeping over him, as though he were serenading a newborn baby. He had a cell phone in one hand. A tape recorder was on the table beside him. And he was looking at . . .

Sixth and Seventh Avenues and the newspaper I just mentioned is published in a town that is located in the south eastern corner of a state that's sandwiched between Kansas and South Dakota. I bring this up because at some point during that six o'clock hour an event occurred that probably occurs all the time, except that neither Tom nor I had ever seen it occur in quite that way and for about ten minutes we got the feeling that we were witnessing something bizarre and extraordinary, even though no one else in the restaurant seemed to notice it. A man in the front of the restaurant, about ten feet from where we were sitting, started singing a song I'd heard many times on the radio. It was by an artist like Celine Dion or Leanne Rimes and went "you're my love, my valentine." It sounded a bit odd coming from a male singer with a Broadway belt. He was singing to a young couple who was with him. The woman's face suggested she was nonplussed but trying to be polite. The man had his back to me, but suddenly he was on his knees, evidently proposing marriage. The woman started weeping. They hugged. The man pulled out a cell phone and made a call. When they walked towards the bar Tom and I could see their faces. I don't know what he made of them but I recognized them right away. They

something, someone, I couldn't see. Then I saw that there was a couple standing in front of him, and I understood.

"I think someone is getting married," I said.

"No!" Meghan gasped. She craned her neck. I craned my neck.

The bartender sat at the far end of the bar, reading the paper.

I leaned back in my seat to get a better view. There was a guy down on one knee in a black T-shirt, blond hair, wispy mustache. Before him stood a woman: long brown hair, flowery dress through which you could see her nice shape. Big honest face. Beaming, blushing more and more as the guy on his knee spoke to her. The guy who had been singing was beaming as he looked on, the maître 'd, standing near by, was beaming, we were craning our necks. The bartender kept reading.

A ring was produced. He slid it on. Hugs. The cell phone was handed around. Who was on the other line? For some reason I imagined it was her father. "Sir, I have just proposed to Caroline, and she said yes. Is that OK with you? It is? Great! I love your daughter!" That is what I imagined being said.

"We have to ask them what is going on," said Meghan.

were the faces from my town newspaper, dressed up like New Yorkers, or at least like midwesterners who, after a few years in New York where they were probably temping while trying to make it as actors or playwrights or clog dancers, had acquired some errant New York trappings. The woman wore an imitation Betsy Johnson dress. The man wore a black tee shirt and shoes that I cannot remember as anything other than Capezio jazz shoes, which I'm certain they were not. They lived in Jersey City.

I figured their first date had been at Café Loup or that they had met on Valentine's Day (hence the song) or at least that Café Loup was a favorite spot or they shared an affinity for Celine Dion or whomever had recorded that song. But when Tom and I began questioning them, like reporters interrogating flustered Oscar winners backstage, they told us they had never been to Café Loup. It had no particular significance in their relationship. Until now, of course. The man, whose name was Walt, was from Oklahoma. I think the woman's name was Caroline, but I didn1t catch where she was from, only that it was far away. I admired her engagement ring, which seemed like the sisterly thing to do, even though engagement rings all look the same to me. Tom

"But it might spoil the moment," I said.

This was dishonest. I was put off by the moment, so I shouldn't have been defending it. But maybe I wanted to protect them from disgust. What was my problem anyway? I had long ago trained myself to smile with beneficent life-affirming goodwill at the site of couples kissing in the park. Love blooms, it's great for all of us, how wonderful, et cetera. I mean these smiles, really! I'm happy for kissing couples! But now I was hung over and all this earnest "There is no one in the world I would rather be with than you" emoting was making me a little sick.

"I don't think they would have done this in public if they didn't want people to watch," she said.

"Watching and asking questions are not the same thing," I said. The woman was crying a little. She was on the phone now. Was it her father? This was a big surprise for her, obviously. The happiest day of her life.

And then they were near us. The singer, who had performed the role of surrogate religious figure in the choreography of the whole scene, was now standing out on the sidewalk on the phone, and the happy couple were beside us.

and I shook their hands and congrat-
ulated them. They went off to have
dinner. I ordered another club soda.
Tom and I had a conversation that
skirted around our tacit belief that
this couple was, in a certain sense, not
as sophisticated as we were or liked to
think we were. His term was "goofy,"
which was not a groundless observation, and without coming right out
and saying it we both seemed to agree
that the only people who can fall in
love and get engaged over a Celine
Dion type of song and weep about it
are people whose imaginative stan-
dards are such that a café in which to
propose marriage can be chosen not
based on its nostalgic value or even
champagne selection but solely on
the fact that it is located on
Thirteenth Street between Sixth and
Seventh Avenues in New York. The
moment seemed to have made Tom
somewhat melancholy. I didn't feel
much emotion, but I felt the emotional conflict. I've experienced it so
many times by now that it no longer
elicits feelings, merely a replay of the
thoughts I've had a thousand times.
It's what happens when happiness is
held in front of your face like a painting you don't want to own, but whose
placard, nonetheless says "This Is
Happiness." I asked Tom if there was
anyone he respected who could feel
romantically satisfied for longer than

So we launched in. Straight-
forward questions, honest questions, yet it was peculiar, as though
they had just won an award or
been on a game show and were
now at the post-show news conference.

His name is Walt. I forget hers.
They live in Jersey City. They had
never been here before. He was
from Oklahoma originally. His
friend, the singer, was friends with
the manager of this place . . . and
his best friend couldn't be here:
"He was going to start the whole
thing off by reading a poem,"
explained Walt, but since he couldn't
be here they called him so he could
hear it, and yes, it was a total surprise for her . . .

"Did you guys meet on
Valentine's day?" asked Meghan.
There had been this Valentine
theme to the song.

"No," she said.

"Yes," he said.

They looked at each other.

Oh shit, I thought. We've done
it. A pang of excitement and guilt
welled up within me. We've gone
and contaminated the thing with
our questions. For a brief moment
the bloom was off the rose. Their
first matrimonial spat. But they figured it out. Their first date was on
Valentine's Day. The bloom was

one day. He kind of laughed and looked away and later he would recall me as saying "Do you know anyone who is smart who is romantically happy for more than one day at a time."

That's not how I phrased it. I know I didn't use the word "smart," although "respect" isn't much better. It doesn't really matter though, because the more I think about that couple the more certain I am that in fifteen years, when some version of Tom and me are still sitting at that bar, Walt and Caroline will have a house in Oklahoma or Nebraska or even Jersey City and it will have a basement family room where they keep their photo albums and when they show their wedding pictures to their children Caroline will say, "your father proposed to me in a café in Greenwich Village in New York. A man sang. We drank champagne. That was a beautiful day."

back on, big hug, wet eyes, time to go back and finish the meal, best regards, bon voyage, we all shook hands as though we were on line to enter a special zone, a circle of light. What is it about proposals of marriage that lends itself to these public performances?

"They were goofy," I said, pouring more hot water into my tea.

"Of course they were goofy," said Meghan. "Do you know anyone who is smart who is romantically happy for longer than a day at a time?"

Old Boilers and Old Men

|| Jersey City
|| by Nick Mamatas

My boiler broke this winter, after the pedestal sink on the second floor of my home gave way and tipped over, thanks to an aging six-penny nail. The upstairs bathroom quickly filled with water and began seeping through the gaps in the floor's tile grout. The ceiling of my first floor kitchen started leaking in spots where spackled-over drywall gave way. Once in the kitchen, the water swirled across the room and down into the basement, thanks to the holes in the floor where the water pipes stand. We quickly turned off the house feed, righted the sink and mopped up. When I turned the main valve back on, cold water hit my fifty-year-old cast iron standing pilot steam boiler which, thanks to it being February, had been running at 100+ degrees. The cheap, silvery paint-job the previous owner had applied was flaking off, and the iron chambers inside cracked when room temperature water hit red-hot iron. Isaac Newton was right when he said, after the apple landed on his head, "Physics is a bitch!"

So is getting a new boiler. Cast-iron boilers, the kind one needs when one's home is heated with those big, accordion-style radiators, are different in two crucial respects from the boilers of homes with baseboards. They cost twice as much, and are three times as heavy. I'm a child of the Internet Age I make my living writing term papers for stupid college kids and business obituaries for magazines nobody reads. I can't fix a boiler, and I couldn't afford new one. So I did what anybody in my situation would do, I called on old men for help the next morning.

The first old man I called was Azad. He was the previous owner of the house, and my former landlord in Jersey City. Azad owns about nine buildings and has perfected the black art of slumlordery. When I lived in one of his other apartments, I saw garden hose in the place of piping in bathrooms, pennies jammed into fuse boxes, entire closet walls made of caulking and spackle tape, electric lights powered by inserting loose wires into outlets, and, in the backyard, a small mountain of Army surplus typewriters, stacked up against the window of my living room, and exposed to the elements. He tried to sell me one when I asked about them. "Just like new, except for the leaves," he said.

I wasn't stupid enough to buy a used typewriter from this man—I own a computer, after all—but I was stupid enough to buy a house. Anyway, in the cosmic algebra of Jersey City real estate, Azad owed me.

He brought me to another old man, a man named Moe. Moe was very old, about 117, if wrinkles can be believed, and he worked in a hardware store on Duncan Avenue. Moe knows. He was on a ladder in the plumbing aisle when we approached him, and glared at us with basset hound eyes. Azad called him "Mister Moe." Mister Moe didn't acknowledge my existence, since I was obviously too young to have any worthwhile information or questions. Mister Moe must have known he was coming, since he was on a ladder doing nothing but waiting by the sealant can I needed to buy. I imagined that when my boiler went SPUNG at 2 A.M. the previous morning, Mister Moe sat up in bed across town and screamed, "A boiler! In danger!"

Moe wasn't confident the sealant would work. In fact, he said "He'll need a new boiler" to Azad. Azad shrugged. Moe was right. We poured in the sealant and turned on the water, and I had a metal box full of rain. "It's leaking too much," Azad said, about twenty times. When the water drowned our ankles, he turned off the water, but too hard, breaking the switch. We went to Home Depot. There, we were approached by a plumber named Sam. Sam instantly diagnosed our problem: we needed a new boiler, there was nothing the orange-smocked man-ape we were drawing diagrams for could do for us. He'd give us a new boiler and install it, in one day, for $1,800. He'd even, Sam the Plumber said, find us the same exact boiler, so that we wouldn't need to buy any new fittings. Finally, Sam the Plumber shook both our hands and announced, "I am Arabic!" perhaps hoping to capitalize on some secret industrial stereotype I wasn't familiar with. Italians are all in the mob, Greeks make the best greaseburgers, Jews are great with money, when you want a bitch of a boiler installed, call upon an Arab.

Azad is an Arab too, a Pakistani. As Sam walked off, he leaned in and explained, "That man isn't a real Arab. He's an Egyptian. Always watch out for an Egyptian." Another set of stereotypes only old men know. Never buy a baby from a gypsy, it'll be defective; don't stare at a Finn's shoes, you'll make him imperceptibly more self-conscious; never buy a boiler from an Egyptian, they don't really know what they're doing.

It doesn't even get cold in Egypt.

We never found the switch at Home Depot. I spent the rest of the afternoon mopping up a slow drip flood. I needed a better quality of old man. I needed to let the genie out of his bottle, no matter what the consequences. I needed to call my father.

My father is a child of the industrial age, and is entirely perplexed by my lifestyle, as his own father was by his. My father was raised on the cliffs of Ikaria in Greece, and was expected to do nothing more than strangle goats, go to church and press olives. But my father was always mechanically inclined, and mechanically inclined is an unfortunate thing to be on the poorest island in the poorest country in post-war Europe. No phones, no toilets, no internal combustion engines, no electricity, no precision instruments, no watches, no factories, no paved roads, nothing but boats, and old men didn't let strange kids near their boats. My grandfather, the blacksmith, was the most technologically advanced person in the area. His son wanted more. And eventually he got it.

Drafted into the Navy by the military junta, trained to fix diesel engines, weld steel plates while at sea and repair factory systems, my father is living in his own little space age. Physics became his bitch. TV commercials like to amaze us by explaining that the Internet can send images and information to our door at the speed of light. That isn't hard. Hard would be getting those bundles of electrons to move much slower than the speed of light. We're just along for the bitch's ride. Hard would be, hard is, getting natural gas, water, waste water, steam and exhaust to mix and trade places on demand without leaving behind a wayward drop of water, a telltale sooty smell, or without blowing up the goddamn house. Installing a boiler is hard. Installing a boiler is a bitch, said my father, paraphrasing Isaac Newton. But he could do it. There's almost nothing that can be done with two hands that he can't do.

Installing a boiler is a bitch for one simple reason. Boilers are standardized. Houses are not. Boilers are designed to be moved once. Doorways are designed for people, not boilers. More often than not, the upper floors of a house don't even go up these days until the boiler is already there, in the basement.

So, my old man had to remove the old boiler, piece by piece, and I had to help. I bought a wrench and unscrewed what I could, usually having to rescrew something else back in first, or to knock off a nut with a hammer. My father noticed my wrench. Did I buy it just for this? he wanted to know. Yeah, I did. It's a piece of shit, he told me. Go get the wrench from the car. The wrench covered in grease. The wrench that smells like an oil spill. The wrench that has actually been used before.

Father: 1, Nick: 0.

I can't help but keep score when working with my father. He knows how to do everything that requires physical labor and heavy tools. He's the gawky computer nerd of the nineteenth century. He built his own home and still likes to drive by banks and point and laugh at them, because he didn't need to take a mortgage, unlike those twentieth century suckers and their credit economies. When a contractor built a home behind his backyard, my father quickly bought the lot between the two houses and poured two and a half tons of compost on the property, just to teach the guy a lesson about trying to develop in his small town. He knows everything, and he lets you know that you know nothing.

We peeled the tin off the sides of the boiler, and found cardboard and brown powder covering the works. "Don't put any in your mouth," he told me, "it's asbestos." Like I had a tablespoon standing by. While cutting away at the fittings, I banged my head against a wayward pipe hanging from the ceiling twice. My fault for not watching. My father, who is all of five foot two, banged his head against the same pipe seven times (I counted, of course). That was the pipe's fault.

Father: 1, Nick: 1.

We pulled apart the cast iron chambers of the boiler and discovered something interesting. Part of the job, the removal of the pilot light, is actually easy. Turns out that my fifty-year-old cast iron steam boiler with the standing pilot was actually a conversion job. It was a 110 year-old manual coal fed steam boiler, retrofitted to work with all this fancy natural gas and running water. All the old men lose a point for not recognizing this! I wanted to call Sam the Plumber, and demand he mount an expedition to raise the Titanic so he could install the exact boiler, an American Radiator Company model CL–003, right now.

Father: 0, Nick: 1.

My father speaks the language of old men, so he was incredibly useful. I ordered a new boiler and got a price quote for $2,000. He calls the same place a moment later and got a quote of $1,650. The difference was a single syllable. In response to "So, you wanna standing pilot Mclean?" I answered, "Uhm . . . yes." My father just answered "Yes."

At the store, Sanitary Plumbing Supplies, a large warehouse with every possible permutation of pipe, but without a working cash register, the old men rule. While we were there, a middle-aged man showed up, looking for a part for his toilet. What was the model of toilet? He didn't know. Did he want a rubber or plastic flapper? Dunno.

"Is your toilet," asked the suddenly very bored old man behind the counter, "one piece or two?" He didn't know. Even I know that my toilet is a two piece job. Sheesh. The middle-aged man rubbed his bald head and announced he was just going to go to Home Depot.

That man was a fool. I had already tried Home Depot, with Azad, and then, again, with my father. Some eleven-year-old employee tried to sell us galvanized pipe settings, the sort very useful for putting up a fence, but only useful for boilers if you want to kill yourself and your neighbors, all at once, in a terrible explosion. There are no old men there. Home Depot is the exclusive province of the young, stupid man. No wonder it's so popular.

A young man's skills do come in handy though. My father had to map out a Rube Goldbergesque pathway of black steel and copper pipe fittings.

Twenty-five elbow joints, four and a half feet of two inch pipe. Seven two to one-and-a-half-inch reducers. Seven six-inch copper nipples. My father wasn't sure how to spell the word nipple. I was there, ready with my immense bank of knowledge, gleaned from writing 5,000 crooked term papers, enough papers to buy this bitch of a house. En eye double pee el ee.

Father: 0, Nick: 2.

At the end of the day, after pulling out three quarters of a ton of cast iron and dumping it in my driveway, my father went home. I stayed home, shivering with my dog. My girlfriend and roommate spent the night elsewhere.

Father: 1, Nick: 2.

He was back the next night, Monday, after work. My father works in Brooklyn, on the docks, and reports to work at 7 A.M. That means getting up at five, squeezing into an ancient Volkswagen Jetta, and driving from lovely Port Jefferson to shithole Red Hook. He spends most of the day on the crane, four hundred feet in the air, whipped by freezing wind coming off the bay, fixing the crane. He works on those huge cranes most people only see in silhouette when crossing the Brooklyn or Manhattan bridges. Few people know that they are designed to lift sixty-ton containers from tanker ships, but that they spend most of their time lifting eighty-ton containers. Most people don't know, even those people who depend on these cranes, which includes everyone who likes . . . things, that these cranes break down a number of times a day. Most people don't know that workers have been crushed by these cranes as they roll across the piers. And only my father knows what it is like to hose the corpse meat off the huge steel wheels of one of these cranes after it runs over one of his friends. That day, everyone else was given the afternoon off, but my father, who had the most seniority—who was the oldest of the old men there—had to stay behind for two hours, with a hose and a shovel, helping the police put his pal into a garbage bag.

So after work on Monday, my Father showed up again to work on the boiler. He left at 1 A.M. and went back to the docks to sleep on a bench. He didn't want to embarrass my roommate or my girlfriend with his overnight presence. And on Tuesday, he did the same. Wednesday as well. Also Thursday. It takes a long time for one man to fit a standard boiler into a 110-year-old house.

I'm not quite sure how to score that. I get free labor, but I regret it. I want to be able to do something for my father, but there is nothing I can do that he can't, that he wants. I can make money with a computer, and this amazes him. Back when I lived at home, I'd write term papers in the living room, typing a hundred words per minute with only two fingers, and my father and his cousins and his uncles, old men even more capable than he, would just stare. I didn't have to leave the house. I didn't have to bend my back and work twice as fast because some fat foreman with mob connections wants to get home while mama's tomato sauce is still warm. I didn't have to comb my hair. Of course, neither does my father, but he feels bad about it. The only job worth having, he'd tell me as a kid, is one where you walk in with combed hair and a pressed shirt, and walk out at the end of the day the same way. Even though I've never had to hose the corpse meat off a crane, I feel bad that I'm not able to get a job like that, for him.

Father: 2, Nick: 2.

Finally it is Friday again, and my boiler works, sort of. I have to go downstairs to the basement, connect two wires, get a little shock from the twenty-four-volt switching mechanism, and then go back upstairs to enjoy the heat. My roommate lives down there, and whenever I go into the boiler room, he asks me, "Gonna turn the boiler on?" The old man's answer would be, "Of course not. I'm just going to give her—boilers are female, like ships and other bitches—a massage. What are you, stupid?" Forty minutes later, when I go back to the basement to turn off the boiler, my roommate asks me, "Gonna turn the boiler on?" The old man answer to that stupid question would consist of a six-inch copper nipple to the head. This I know from experience. Luckily for my roommate, I'm still a young man, and we have a new boiler, one guaranteed for ten, rather than 110 years.

It's next Tuesday when my thermostat is installed. I haven't spent even five minutes with my lovely new boiler since then. I also haven't spent even five minutes with my father either, who lives in lovely Port Jefferson. He built a greenhouse last week, after work. I wrote a term paper on NAFTA, for work. He fixed a fifty year-old tractor he bought at auction from an old bankrupt man and used it to move four tons of compost around the lot between him and his young man enemy. I wrote a little something on the thrilling topic, "self-published books tends to suck" for the *Village Voice*. His own boiler broke, during what the news mistakenly called "the Storm of the Century." He fixed it himself, for free, in one day.

Father: 3, Nick: 2.

Then I realized something. Lots of immigrants' sons have these imaginary competitions with their highly skilled nineteenth-century fathers. We can never measure up, never fully be on our own, never navigate the planet without the help of an old man. Our own fathers were much smarter when they were young men. They didn't have these ridiculous hang-ups. They knew how to win. They left the continent their fathers were on behind them, and dove into a crazy new world without money, family or even the ability to spell the word nipple, and grew old here on their own terms. Meanwhile, I can't even consider moving further from my parents than Jersey City. After all, what if my boiler breaks again?

Final score: Father: 4, Nick: 2.

The Coffee Hut Slut

41st St. and Third Ave.
by Ariele Fierman

I have been flirting with the coffee man for about three weeks now. Every morning, as I am about to round the corner into the construction site I work near, I ask him for a large coffee, skim, no sugar, three Equals. The first time I went to him, he asked me how many sugars I wanted.

"No sugar," I politely stated, "Equal."

Then I smiled and the coffee man smiled back at me. Maybe he saw something in me, I don't know.

"Ohhhh," he said way too knowingly. "Equal and coffee, okay!" And then he emptied the content of three pale blue packages into my coffee. He handed me my coffee cup, I slid him my money, and as he wished me a pleasant day, I turned around to say thanks.

This has been our routine for about three weeks now, it's never different. And yet, every day there is something new I notice about the coffee man. Yesterday I noticed that his gold watch sparkled when the light hit it the right way, today I noticed his tanned forearms. The other day I swore I saw reddish auburn-esque highlights in a full head of hair. It is hard for me, however, to get the full picture of the coffee man because the coffee man operates from within a coffee hut.

Nonetheless, I will never forget the time coffee man offered me assurance things will get better when everything to me was left in the city dump.

That morning of misery I stumbled to his coffee hut and could barely look up into his eyes. "Large coffee, skim, no sugar, three Equals." I barely managed the words. As he was sliding my loose change back to me, he cupped it in his hands for a moment, and uttered those most memorable words: "Cheer up," he said to me, "Things will improve!"

I looked into his square, eyes. "Thank you, thank you so much." We held eyes for a second or two, I then clutched onto my coffee bagged in brown paper, rounded the corner and headed into my construction site, with an improved attitude, thanks to coffee man.

That day in my cube, I thought about coffee man. Does he have a family? How did he get into the coffee business? Does he brew his own coffee, grind his own beans, handpicking only the best of them? So many questions I had for coffee man. He was such a sweet man working in such a tough city, a city in which one is forbidden to talk prior to coffee.

This got me thinking, coffee man is a middleman. He hands over the coffee, allowing his loyal customers to enter the stage of normalcy and acceptance, leaving behind the one of despond and revulsion. Coffee man acts as the medium between the world of the non-normal and the world of the normal. I need my coffee; I need my coffee man.

The next day I sauntered to the coffee hut, checked my watch, looked at his usual breakfast items for sale, and ordered, surprise, my usual. But this time I tried to jazz it up. Why not, I was in better spirits. I had already had some caffeine via my roommate's flat Diet Fanta left out all night. "Let's try one sugar, two equal," I said coyly.

Coffee man stopped dead in his tracks. He looked up at me under his floppy head of black bangs which too often dangled in his face. "You have good morning?" He uttered, stunned at my decision.

"Yes!" I said, too enthusiastically for my pre-coffee stage.

Nonetheless, he tore open my blue packets, poured them into my cup, put the cup in a brown paper bag, looked up at me and then smiled. "You have great morning!"

I slid him my usual, but since today I was feeling good, I gave him a little extra something. An extra quarter to improve his wonderful coffee grinding technology.

Coffee man did not like this. No sooner than leaving his hut, I heard his faint footsteps behind me, "Ma'am!" He screamed. He sounded like a little boy, which was surprising since he was a coffee man. "You forgot your change!"

On this I whipped my head around. I looked for coffee man but couldn't find him in the herd of people. Where was he coming from? Where was my Colombian coffee grinder, my Spanish lover, my inspiration for goodwill towards others?

And then, I found him. I felt as if the wind was knocked out of me. My feet were glued to the hot cement of the New York city pavement but my mind was spinning out of control. In front of me stood the coffee man. Coffee man stood no taller than my waist with a hand like that of a boy's extended outwards. "Here ya go! Your change!" He had to yell over the loud roar of passersby.

My life, up until now, flashed before me like a car zooming through an orange light. Before me stood a man that was a midget, a Colombian midget.

Poor coffee man, he hid his height by standing on a platform behind the coffee hut! I took the change and walked down the block, where I spilled out my coffee out, as though it were something shameful and contagious.

Code Blue: A Police Officer Unwinds

‖ 125th St. and Amsterdam Ave.
‖ by Denise Campbell

Most evenings will find Michael Johnson, a New York City Police Officer, sitting at home alone in front of his TV with a bottle of Hennessy near by. Hennessy is top shelf, he says. It doesn't leave you with a hangover. Michael doesn't drink every night to get drunk, according to Michael. He doesn't even drink to unwind from a stressful day because most of his days are not that stressful, according to Michael. According to Michael, he's just chillin.'

Michael recently broke up with a girlfriend, a fellow police officer. His co-workers had warned him: never date a cop. He sees now what they meant. He's contemplating whether or not he should go to Internal Affairs because of the latest spree of incidents with this lady cop. She's having a hard time letting go of him. She follows him in her car. He's able to lose her because according to him she's not a good driver. She has cut his tires. In the cold early hours of winter mornings he has had to change flats. Once she even ticketed his car. It was a big laugh for his fellow officers when he went in to the precinct to complain about the ticket. He didn't know at that time that she had issued it. In several phone conversations with her, he tried resolving their issues. He really did not want to take his personal business to the department. One day he left his apartment and found her sitting in his car. She refused to get out so he left her there and did not drive to work that day.

Like many New York City police officers, Michael moonlights as a security guard. He is presently working at The Wiz on Fulton Street in Brooklyn. On several occasions he sees her cruise by the store. He makes up his mind. He's going to report her to his superiors first chance he gets. He knows that the way the Department works, he will come under just as much scrutiny as she will. That was part of the reason for his hesitancy. But it was evident at this point that this woman was not of sound mind. And he felt she might be pretty close to slipping over the edge.

Michael has been on the force for six going on seven years now. No, he did not as a child dream of growing up and becoming a cop. His mother drives a school bus, and his father is a dentist. They are divorced. The way he tells it, the opportunity arose for him to take the Civil Service Exam. He did pretty good on it and was called to begin training at the Police Academy. "It was a city job, that offered a decent salary and early retirement," he summed it up blandly. Michael had gone to SUNY New Paltz on a football scholarship. He dropped out after one year. Since dropping out, he had held several menial jobs. He didn't think of police work as particularly dangerous. He was not going to try and be anybody's super cop. He would go to work like any other city employee and not place himself unnecessarily in harm's way.

An accidental pepper spraying landed him in the hospital. After having his heart monitored for several days, the department decided that he should be removed from the street beat. He was moved to the Youth Officers Unit. At the time of his transfer, he couldn't say that he particularly liked kids. But it was certainly a relatively safer assignment than running down criminals. As a youth officer, he and his female partner patrolled around schools and responded to incidents inside school buildings. His sensitivity towards kids whose parents and home lives he came to know increased. He says after having met some of the parents, he understood better why the kids were the way they are. Michael has lots of stories to tell about promiscuous thirteen-year-olds and their boyfriends who are grown men, fourteen-year-old daily pot smokers, kids who can't put together an articulate sentence. Kids who are physically, verbally and sexually abused. Kids raising kids.

Despite all of the social ills Michael sees on a daily basis, he remains pretty much apolitical. He doesn't bother to vote because he doesn't believe it will change anything. "The world is going to be the same as I found it when I leave it," he says pessimistically. Somehow he hasn't connected the kids' deviant and anti-social behavior with social, political and economic realities. Some of his other values run along the same line of a devil-may-care attitude. When asked about going to church and God, he jokes that the only God he worships is the dollar bill. He supports capital punishment as opposed to life in prison. About convicted rapists and murders, he says, "Fry their asses. Why should taxpayers' dollars feed, clothe and shelter these people for the rest of their lives?"

When asked about racism within the police force, Michael readily admits its existence. He says he deals with it on an individual basis, though, not institutionally. He told of once threatening a fellow officer with taking him "out back and kicking his f-ing ass" because of a racist comment he made. He said he never had a problem with that officer again.

While Michael was willing to talk about racism within the police department, the blue wall of silence came up immediately when asked his view around the latest spate of police killings. "We are experiencing a bad moment between police and civilians," he explained. "But every job has its good and bad workers. I can't speak for the cops who were involved in these incidents. I don't know them." When asked about both the acquittals and convictions in the recent police trials, Michael's response was "The jury spoke, and the people spoke." When pressed to expressed his personal feelings about the incidents involving Abner Louima, Amadou Diallo and Patrick Dorismond, Michael insisted he had no comments.

"I can't afford to pick up a paper and see me quoted somewhere," he said very seriously. "I have a daughter to take care of." He offered to talk about his unit, the Juvenile Unit. "I work in the schools. Now, I can tell you anything you want to know about Bloods, Crips, juveniles, whatever. I don't deal with other units in the Department. I get dressed, join my partner and go do my job. That's it."

What is Giuliani's role in the tension between police and the black community? According to Michael, Giuliani has nothing to do with anything. "The department is going to always be the same." As for his future as a policeman, Michael responded solemnly, "I'll be in and out in twenty years, retired."

When that time comes, he will be forty-three.

Kenny Colman's Elevator Logic

80 Centre St.
by Zachary Levin

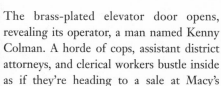

The brass-plated elevator door opens, revealing its operator, a man named Kenny Colman. A horde of cops, assistant district attorneys, and clerical workers bustle inside as if they're heading to a sale at Macy's rather than for work at the state court building at 80 Centre Street.

In his mid-forties, thin-faced and short, and wearing a fedora, a Western string tie and a jean jacket, Kenny perches on the end of his stool next to a panel of buttons. He pulls a lever.

The door closes. It's a strange sight to see on this thermometer-busting day at the height of summer: all those people cramming into one particular elevator car while five other cars stand empty, their operators waiting anxiously in front of them.

"Okay, folks, welcome to Camp D.A.!" Kenny calls as the elevator rises. "Today's activity: water sports!"

Not one rider raises an eyebrow. They've gotten used to this over the three years he's been running the elevator. Kenny's worked for the D.A. for a quarter of a century, formerly as a messenger and clerical worker.

But it's in his present position that he's flourished. "Are we ready for today's trivia question?" Kenny asks, in his best game-show host voice.

"I was born ready, Kenny. You know that," says a burly cop, rolling his neck as if steeling himself for a confrontation.

"Okay, sir. Would you like TV or movies, history or science, art or sports?"

"TV," the cop shoots back. "I been boning up."

A small fan on the ceiling struggles against the steamy air. Kenny takes his time. A tall man working on a half-moon armpit stain is standing in the middle of the six-by-eight-foot space. Behind him, a fat man is breathing so hard you'd think he was taking the stairs. Mounted on the wall, at eye-level, is a corkboard displaying photographs of several attractive women whom Kenny considers friends. Next to them are pictures of his loved ones: a Siberian Husky named Lobo and a good-looking man in a black leather jacket—his older brother Dave, who died of colon cancer a few years ago. This is not like being transported in an institutional elevator; it's like riding in a gypsy cab dressed up to feel like someone's home.

"On the TV show *All in the Family*," Kenny says, "what was Michael's last name?"

The cop bunches up his features, says, "I love that show," but offers no answer.

Other passengers murmur to themselves, but volunteer nothing. Meanwhile, the elevator man whistles the *Jeopardy!* theme song. The elevator arrives at the fourth floor—Parole, the cop's destination.

"Okay, what is it?" the cop demands.

"Stivic," answers Kenny, "Michael Stivic. Better luck next time."

"Quick, gimme one more," the cop begs as he squeezes out of the elevator.

"What was Edith's maiden name?" Kenny asks.

The cop stands silent, slackjawed, as the door closes on him and the elevator moves on.

Now, heading toward Special Narcotics on the sixth floor, the tall man with the armpit stains blurts out, "Baines! She was Edith Baines before she became Edith Bunker."

"This is correct, sir," says Kenny, searching his pockets for a lollipop.

Lollipops are his gift to those who answer correctly, but he's out of them. He promises to restock at lunch.

"Make sure it's the kind with the gum in the center," the tall man says.

"You bet!" Kenny says.

Before getting off, the tall man receives a high five from a fellow passenger—to the chagrin of most of the people on board, whose heads are level with his wet underarms.

"I don't quiz the people to make them feel bad, or to see them get it wrong," Kenny confides. "It's not about 'Look how much I know and you don't.' My goal is to put a smile on somebody's face, make the day pass a little easier for us all."

In turn, Kenny's supervisors allow him to make his own weather. He has become the building's mascot, its intermission zany, its half-time show between tedious dockets. Kenny admits that his strength is TV and movie trivia, especially Hollywood films from the thirties through the seventies. But he's strong in world history, too, and dabbles in art, science and sports. His love of movies was in part inspired by his bother Dave who, while attending NYU, had to write a paper on *Red River*, the Howard Hawks classic starring John Wayne. Kenny researched the paper for his brother. Dave received an A. Soon thereafter, Kenny began to devour the classics. To this day, John Wayne is one of Kenny's favorite actors—Kenny can quote from *El Dorado*, *The Quiet Man*, and *The Alamo* verbatim.

He can even tell you the running time of every Wayne picture, and probably who catered lunch. It makes sense that the diminutive elevator man, made smaller sitting on his stool, spending his days in a claustrophobic box, daydreams of the imposing Wayne, high in the saddle out on the prairie as he surveys the land.

Having finished his one-hour lunch break, the elevator man reenters his small office and sits on his stool. He crosses his legs, affecting a nonchalant air he didn't exhibit earlier in the day and hums the theme song from *The Magnificent Seven*. Moments later, two plainclothes cops walk into the elevator, one short with a beard, the other tall and clean-shaven. A rare draft kicks up the short one's unbuttoned overshirt, revealing his holster and the butt of his gun.

"Six, Kenny," says the tall cop. Kenny's finger is already on the button.

"What's the good word?" the short cop asks.

"How do you fellas feel about John Wayne today?" Kenny responds.

"Naw," says the tall cop.

"*Die Hard*?" asks Kenny.

"I'm no good at *Die Hard*," the short cop says, giving a wink to his snickering partner. "What else you got?"

"How about Clint Eastwood?" Kenny asks.

"Go," says the short cop.

"Name the actress who played Eastwood's partner in *The Enforcer*?"

The two cops stare quizzically into each other's eyes as the elevator creaks to a stop. Then, simultaneously—nearly screaming like schoolgirls at a Ricky Martin concert—they exclaim, "Tyne Daly!"

"This is correct!" says Kenny, adding, "it was made in 1976 and has a running time of ninety-six minutes. But for my money I'd recommend *The Enforcer*, 1951, Humphrey Bogart and Zero Mostel. Mostel made a great crook."

As they get off the elevator, lollipops in hand, the partners chant, "Who's the boss? Who's the boss?"

The elevator man, now heading down to the ground floor, looks pleased with himself. He shakes his head and smiles. "That was a lob directly over the plate—my gift to the NYPD. They'll feel smart all week."

Tom's Restaurant

112th St. and Broadway
by Vince Passaro

I took two of my kids to see the new Adam Sandler picture, *Little Nicky*, and there it was again, behind Sandler as he sniffed some flowers: Tom's Restaurant at 112th and Broadway.

When I was at Columbia College, in the gray and bankrupt and crumbling 1970s, my friends and I had a joke that someday, older and successful, we'd make a date to gather for lunch, and Tom's would be so famous we'd be able to jump in a cab and say, "Driver, take me to Tom's." It would be the Sardi's of the Bromo-Seltzer set.

This turned out, bizarrely, to be nearly true. Tom's is a Columbia haunt and home to senior citizens on fixed incomes looking for an inexpensive full-sized Sunday meal available all week long. Its arrival as a second-tier New York icon, getting up there with the Margaret Bourke-White art deco bird jutting from the Chrysler Building or the arches at Washington Square, came first with the house-mix version of Suzanne Vega's "Tom's Diner," and was cemented by a decade as the exterior of the diner where Jerry Seinfeld confabbed with Elaine, Kramer, George, and, when worse came to worst, Newman.

Now visitors come from out of town and around the world just to see the place. One pauses on the sidewalk in order not to walk in front of them as they take their snapshots. The management sells postcards at the register.

Its fame always strikes me as a piece of bittersweet personal comedy. I spent hundreds of hours there, through every stage of our romance, with the woman I dated through my college years, now my wife and the luckily-absent-from-*Little Nicky* mother of our three sons.

Not long after we'd met, I ran into her on a sunny afternoon in front of Tom's and watched her eyes blazing green in the bright light, during some minutes of long-forgotten talk, before calling up the nerve to invite her for a coffee.

Later we would go on Saturday evenings, spending our last money on the early editions of the Sunday papers and coffee and a shared sugar-soaked glazed donut, which was roughly the size of a hubcap and best eaten with forks. Invariably, as I remember it, we'd argue about literature. "You don't like any women writers," she said. I offered Flannery O'Connor and Joan Didion. "They're not really women," she said. "Henry James is more of a woman writer than they are." I also liked George Eliot and the two most prominent Brontë sisters and Austen, but nineteenth-century British writers didn't qualify. It wasn't until she introduced me to Grace Paley, who could do more in two pages than most writers can do in two hundred, that I liked a woman writer who did make it.

After fights, after rapprochements, after movies (dozens and dozens and dozens of movies, at the Thalia, the New Yorker, the Embassy, and later the Metro, which had an Ozu and Mizoguchi festival we went to every Wednesday afternoon); we'd retreat to the window seat in the corner, do the crossword, watch for friends, and work out the boundaries of a shared world view. When we were flush, we had cheeseburger specials, with the great fries and the always near-flat cokes from the fountain. One of us might even go for the roast turkey supper, which on weekends came with stuffing, soup to start, salad, two vegetables, and coffee, an extravagance at $3.75.

One day in the summer of 1977, before the blackout and during the Son of Sam spree, I went in, had an iced coffee at the counter, and read my *Daily News*, which had three great columnists covering New York: Michael Daly,

Pete Hamill, and, the writer we thought the best newspaperman of our era, Jimmy Breslin.

Then I walked out into the brutal heat and saw on the median that runs down the spine of Broadway two old men. They were faced off and arguing very loudly. One took out a cheap-looking gun and shot the other in the leg, pop, just like that. In those days, cops thought it a good idea to ride "undercover" together in cabs, so much so that in a neighborhood such as ours, you'd see more off-duty cabs with two white guys in the front than you'd see real ones that could actually take you somewhere. About six of the undercovers showed up in the next forty-five seconds, or so it seemed, cops leaping out the doors with pistols drawn, until the middle of Broadway was like a gun show. I meandered on home. The two old men were still yelling.

We had times apart, of course, Beth and I, and if I were to meet any other woman at a local hole, it would be at the College Inn up the block. Tom's was for her and me. They all knew us there, not by name but by the matching narratives of maturing faces and growing intimacy: Betty, the sixty-ish waitress with her flaming red hair: "How are ya ba-bay . . ."; and the other waitress, of similar years, so shy we never learned her name, knowing her only by her tiny, little-girl voice and her fabulous jet black wig. The guys behind the counter, Tommy and the rest of them, were dark and muscular young men forever wiping things down with white cloths and hot water from the coffee urns.

"Yes, my friend, whatever you like my friend." When we were broke, "No problem, pay me next time, sure sure."

This is still our neighborhood, vastly more expensive now but in some way still incurably grubby. We like it that way. Beth took one of our boys in for an ice cream recently, and Tommy, with hair and mustache gone gray, like the aging Giancarlo Giannini, asked her,"You still married to that guy?" Yes, she said, in a tone that, I'm certain, very much depended on the day.

"How many kids, two?"

Three, she said.

"Good, good, I stay married to my wife all these years, too," he said. "Too expensive to get divorced, and what for? Another one is better?" He makes that face, and waves his hand: *bah!* to the modern world.

Visit With a Drag Queen

Times Square; Harlem
by Michael Cunningham

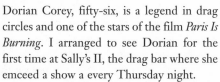

Dorian Corey, fifty-six, is a legend in drag circles and one of the stars of the film *Paris Is Burning*. I arranged to see Dorian for the first time at Sally's II, the drag bar where she emceed a show a every Thursday night.

Sally's II, just off Times Square, was a hustler bar for men who prefer their men in dresses. It's a gaudy, threadbare joint where drag queens, not generally of a recent vintage and some downright geriatric, aggressively peddle themselves to skeevy-looking guys who look as if they have unhappy wives and a few fucked-up kids and a little patch of dying lawn somewhere in the suburbs. It's a destination, the last stop on the train, and you'd have to be a deeply dedicated romantic to find any appreciable element of glamour there.

Corey's show took place in a largish room behind the bar proper, a left-over from some other incarnation, its walls covered with faded murals of Edwardian men and women cavorting heterosexually. The room was furnished with scarred garden furniture, wobbly white plastic tables, and molded plastic chairs.

Corey's show started forty-five minutes late, at almost 1 A.M. Although the bar up front was crowded, only four or five of us sat scattered among the lawn chairs, and everyone but me seemed more interested in his drink or his cigarette or some vaguely upsetting dialogue going on in his own head. Sally himself, a raging canary-yellow blond missing his front teeth, introduced Dorian, and she appeared from behind the Masonite partition that served as a dressing room.

Though you'd have to have been legally blind to think of Dorian as a beauty, she was undeniably spectacular. Six feet tall, she had on another foot and a half of silver hair. She wore more makeup than some women apply cumulatively over their entire lives. Her low-cut black bugle-beaded gown showed a few stray curly hairs nestled in her silicone décolletage.

She lip-synched a rendition of "Georgia," walking the edges of the dance floor with the bulky, unswerving grace of a steamship. She was a focused if not an inspired performer, and she made glacial, unrelenting eye contact. She dared you to dislike her act.

After her opening number she picked up the microphone and shouted toward the bar, "It's showtime back here, you girls don't know what you're missing." But the girls were doing business. Dorian gamely introduced a couple of other queens, whose style was more in the classic drag mode: torchily animated, sexualized, exaggerated. Then Dorian performed her stately closing number, "Stormy Weather," and that was that.

I followed her back behind the Masonsite partition and introduced myself. Pop music was cranked up right after Dorian's show ended, and her rickety dressing room stood next to the deejay's booth. The music was so loud I could feel it humming in the Masonite when I touched the doorjamb.

"Ah, the writer," she shouted. "Hello, baby."

She grandly extended a red-nailed hand. She was already tucking into a rum and Coke.

"Thanks for agreeing to do this," I shouted back.

"You want to talk about Angie?" she said.

"What?"

"You want to talk about Angie?"

"Yes. You knew her, didn't you?"

"What was that?"

"You knew Angie. Didn't you?"

"Sure I did."

The music was rattling the makeup bottles on the plywood counter. I suggested we go someplace else.

"It's awfully late," Dorian hollered. "Why don't you come up to my place next Thursday? You can interview me while I get dressed for the show."

I told her I'd be happy to do that. When she asked me to repeat myself I simply nodded, and she wrote down an address on West 140th Street, in Harlem.

On a Wednesday night in 1993, I got home and found Dorian Corey's voice on my answering machine.

"Mr. Cunningham," she said imperiously. "I naturally assumed you would call before you came. I'm not feeling well. Please call at your earliest opportunity."

I called her the following morning—drag queen morning, which to most other people is three in the afternoon.

"Mm-hm?"

"Dorian? It's Michael Cunningham."

"Oh, Mr. Cunningham."

"I'm sorry you're not feeling well."

"I'm afraid I won't be up to an interview."

"All right. Maybe next Thursday."

"Yes. Maybe next Thursday."

"I'll call first."

"Please do."

"I hope you're feeling better."

"Thanks, baby."

It was three weeks before Dorian Corey was feeling well enough to see me. She lived on the top floor of a snug, four-story, red-brick row house across the street from the City College of New York campus. It was a nice block, well maintained, not at all the residential equivalent of Sally's II. I was relieved, for Dorian's sake.

I rang the bell, and Dorian's voice, which registered somewhere between the sound of an oboe and a pair of pinking shears, wafted down from the top floor.

"Stand out in the street, honey, and I'll throw you the keys."

I stepped out into the street, and a plastic change purse landed at my feet. I took the keys from the purse, let myself in to a clean, crumbling lobby that had been elegant eighty or ninety years earlier. A matronly brown and mocha-colored wainscoting gave way, at shoulder level, to yellow-green paint and sputtering fluorescent light. I walked up the four flights. I'd brought a dozen pale pink roses.

Dorian met me at the door. If you'd have had to be legally blind to consider her beautiful in full makeup, you'd have had to be legally dead to consider her so without it, in a knee length T-shirt, with her hair wrapped up in an old nylon scarf.

But her dowager manner held. She formally invited me in, accepted the roses without comment, as if my bringing them had been assumed. Grocery boys brought groceries; reporters brought roses. She led me into the living room, introduced me to her lover Leo, and disappeared, saying she'd be back soon.

Leo was a sparse, wiry man in his thirties who bore more than a passing resemblance to Charles Manson. He wore jeans and a baggy shirt. He was watching a Knicks game on television. Dorian's and Leo's living room was a grotto dedicated to the goddess of junk. In the spaces between the television, the sofa, several chairs, and a double bed, only a narrow footpath remained negotiable among displays of old crockery, embroidered pillows, assorted lamps, artificial flowers, and gilded trophies won by Dorian at various balls. It was a yard-sale version of Aladdin's cave.

Leo watched the game with an acolyte's rapture. When a commercial for Kool-Aid came on, he told me brightly that he'd bought some just the other day. He jumped up, trotted out of the room, and came back with a large can of something called Pink Swimmingo. It depicted a flamingo in sunglasses, snorkel, and jams.

"See?" he said. "Pink Swimmingo. Not fla-mingo. Swimmingo."

"Uh-huh," I said. "Well."

Soon after, Dorian returned and said to me, "Are you ready to be rescued?" I told her I was, and she beckoned me into her sewing room.

Dorian's sewing room was a treasure cave of a different order, more like the real thing. Or, rather, it was a more faithful fake version of the real thing. Strands of faux pearls and rhinestones looped out of shoe boxes. Leopard prints and gold-threaded gauzes and sequined chiffon were piled everywhere, and in the middle rose a dressmaker's dummy wearing a half-finished contraption of rhinestones and flesh-colored ultra suede, a hybrid of early Bob Mackie and late *Road Warrior*.

We spent slightly more than three minutes on the subject of Angie. Dorian said Angie had been fabulous, a great mother and a promising star. Dorian, unlike some other drag legends, was generous toward her sisters. But still, it quickly became apparent that you didn't go to one major star for detailed information about another. So we talked about Dorian.

She was one of the "terrible five," the five reigning house mothers of the ball world. Angie had been another, along with Pepper LaBeija, Avis Pendavis, and Paris Dupree, whose annual ball "Paris is Burning" gave Livingston the title for her film.

"I used to have a lot of children, but time passes on. Those children who used to come by and talk, they're now the mothers of their own houses. I'm an over-the-hill legend, you know? Leo in there is really the only child I've got left. He was my lover for the first four or five years, then he was my friend the next twenty minutes, and now he's my son."

From the other room, I could hear Leo happily cheering on the Knicks.

I asked her whether she had a favorite outfit and she paused with a look of mingled pride and regret, like a mother being asked if she doesn't really have a favorite among her children.

"Well, this was quite a while ago," she said. "I made a rhinestone gown, then I had a headpiece with rhinestones all over it. I had a back piece maybe about nine feet, covered with white feathers. Then I made two smaller ones about seven feet high, diamonds, and covered them with feathers and had little hand grips. So now I'm getting to be about twenty feet wide and fifteen feet high.

"I'd rented a fog machine. They turned it on and the whole stage filled with fog, and I folded those two side pieces in front of me and I came out and as I got to center stage I opened them and it made the fog part. And everybody gasped. I wanted to run down and see me too. It was the only time I'd ever walked a ball that I had no doubt I'd won."

Harlem Love Story

124th St. and Malcom X Boulevard
by Denise Campbell

"If I should die tonight, oh baby, though it be far before my time. I won't die, no. Sugar, yeah, cause I've known you. How many eyes have seen their dream? Oh, how many arms have felt their dream? How many hearts, baby, have felt their world stand still? Millions never, they never, never, and millions never will, they never will."

—Marvin Gaye

I came out of the print shop carrying two boxes of flyers promoting a march and demonstration in Harlem that coming Saturday. Michael Stewart, a graffiti artist, had been the latest victim in a string of police killings. Caught defacing the walls at a Fourteenth Street subway station, Stewart was severely beaten, hog-tied and brought to Bellevue Hospital d.o.a. The cops responsible for his death had been indicted and were currently on trial. But no cop in the history of New York had ever been convicted for killing a black person. It was certain that they would go free. The rally was a call for an end to police brutality and justice for Michael Stewart. Two weeks prior, I had taken part in an overnight sit-in in Governor Cuomo's Manhattan office. We had demanded a special prosecutor for this case. We did not get one. And when the cops were acquitted, I put the pain I felt in that place where I stored all my other hurts.

Malik had been waiting for me double parked on Remsen Street off of Court Street, in downtown Brooklyn. Prince was playing on the radio when

I scooted into the front seat, and Malik was singing along. "I will die for you," he crooned with Prince. Then he turned to me and matter-of-factly repeated the words, "I will die for you." We were comrades; of course he would die for me and I for him, which is what I at first took the words to mean. Then it occurred to me that wasn't what he meant at all. I felt flushed. He was saying was that he loved me so much, he would give his life for me. Right then and there my soul opened up to him.

Malik was twenty-four when we first met. I was thirty-one. He was living in Harlem, but he was not a New Yorker. He was from Texas and a recent graduate from the University of Texas. I was impressed when he told me he had majored in economics. He had not been in New York long, but already held a position of leadership in the New Afrikan Peoples Organization (NAPO), an organization I had just become a member of. He was mature for his twenty-four years and very intelligent. He did not have a commanding physical appearance. A vegetarian, he was tall, thin and wiry and rather frail looking, which might explain why older women in particular were attracted to him. He had this "I need to be taken care of" look. He was Gandhi-like in demeanor, which bespoke a kind and gentle spirit. But there was that side to him that believed in Malcolm X's motto that if anyone put their hands on you, you send them to the cemetery.

As I said, my soul opened up to Malik the way a flower opens up to the sun. But I was not alone in loving him. Women were captivated by him. All sorts of propositions came his way, some of which he entertained to my grief and consternation. He told me about a Filipino woman in Texas, fifteen years his senior, who had implored him to have a child with her. She had an eleven-year-old son, was approaching forty and wanted another child. She told him she had never known anyone like him before. For this reason, she sought a union to procreate with him, and said there would be no strings attached. I only half believed this story until he went to Texas to see the child soon after it was born. He named their son Mandela. When I got to know Malik, I could see how a woman would want to have him forever be a part of her life through a child they would bear together.

While I felt pretty secure in Malik's "die-for-me" love, I nevertheless found myself fending off ladies the whole duration of our relationship. And it was not just the ladies, mostly everyone with whom he came into contact was drawn to him. I was in constant competition for his attention, particularly with leaders and other members of NAPO who were jealous of our relationship. I really had no choice but to share him. There was work to be done and Malik was key to getting it done. We were both committed to the "Movement," which meant our relationship was secondary. Everything was secondary. The sacrifice for me was that we could not spend a lot of time together. But in our hearts, we were never without the other.

NAPO's New York headquarters was a four-room railroad flat on 124th Street between Malcolm X Boulevard (formerly Lenox Avenue) and Adam Clayton Powell Boulevard (formerly Seventh Avenue). Malik and several others actually lived there. I was living in Brooklyn, but had grown up in Harlem. And although I had moved from Harlem some years prior, I still felt a strong bond with it. I remember reading Piri Thomas's *Down These Mean Streets* and Claude Brown's *Manchild in the Promised Land* as a teenager and being really moved by the depiction of the lives of people who lived in Harlem. Thomas and Brown had succeeded in capturing the harsh realities of life in Harlem. Sunless, airless, roach and mice infested, paint chipped apartments. Scarcity of food. Bedraggled clothes. More tears than laughter. Heart-pumping fear. Misplaced hate and too little love. Incessant fighting to survive.

As a member of NAPO, I came to Harlem three to four times a week. Each time I emerged from the subway at 125th my heart fluttered with excitement. Partly because I was only a few minutes away from seeing Malik. It was also the thrill of being in Harlem. I noticed how little things had changed since I was a girl growing up there. The landscape was still that of crumbling tenements, decay, impoverishment. In some ways, I found comfort in this sameness. I enjoyed the feeling of coming back home again and again. The bond between Malik and I was deepened by the compassion and love we had for the people, who in our eyes were the wretched of the earth that Frantz Fanon wrote about. Our lives were dedicated to changing the conditions that oppressed us. We would give our lives for the people.

Much of what Malik and I felt for one another went unexpressed because we were almost always engaged in "the work." To ward off envy, I took great care to conceal my affections for him. He on the other hand wore his love for me on his sleeve. It was in his eyes when he looked at me, in his voice when he spoke to me or about me. It showed in how he spoke up for me and looked out for me. And when we were alone, it was a time of validation and communion conveyed through his touch, his embrace, his kiss. Malik gave good love.

But deeper than his love for me was Malik's love for the cause. I was not the least surprised when he told me one night as we sat across from one another in a dimly lit diner on 125th Street and Broadway that he was going to Nicaragua.

"I'm going there to work in the coffee fields. It will be good discipline in hard work," he told me. Immediately images of him working side by side with peasants in a field under a beaming sun came to mind. The Nicaraguans will take to his gentle manner and unassuming bearing, I thought.The women, especially, will grow fond of him and take care of him.

When Malik left, Harlem still called out to me. There among its ruins lay the seeds of discontent that would drive me to fight for social change. I thought of Malik and the discipline of hard work whenever we were posting flyers in the middle of the night, or marching or demonstrating. Over the many miles separating Nicaragua and Harlem, our love for the the people bridged our love each other.

Speed Freaks

314 East 6th St.
by Susan Connell-Mettauer

In the summer of 1968 I had an apartment on East Sixth Street between First and Second Avenues. The rent was cheap, and it was on the top floor of a tenement which meant there was a sooty patch of skylight in my bathroom and a tub with feet where I could sit and contemplate the black starless sky.

Decorating was minimal. I painted the floor and radiator and all visible pipes a flat plum; the walls were white; and my mattress lay on crude pallets from large wooden packing crates. There were a few gaudy flourishes—a large antique mirror with an ornate gilt frame, a black and white poster of Mick Jagger kissing a microphone.

My needs were few since I did not eat or sleep, which is to say I was typical of most people in New York at that time. A sort of corrupt Taoist, I lived on air and the weird buzzing that seemed to fuel the city. I shoplifted clothes from Saks and Bloomingdales and Bonwit Teller. People gave me drugs. In this regard I had benefactors who, like me, wanted to be dangerous. Two lived in my building: a drug dealer from Texas and an acting student at NYU who was also a member of a motorcycle gang called the Dustbusters (not to be confused with the rival gang on Fifth Street, the Dirtdevils.)

These two gangs did things like tie each other up in abandoned buildings and set each other on fire. When not engaged in homicidal acts, the Dustbusters lined their many Harleys in front of the tenement on Sixth Street, and the gang—a pack of hirsute sociopaths hung with oily chains, leather vests, and inscribed with tattoos—clanked and banged and tinkered.

At dawn, the hostile spit and manly vroom of ten engines would have woken me up if I had ever slept. It is a safe bet that the Busters didn't sleep any more than I did. And while they were busy torturing rivals, I tie-dyed my plundered satin shirts from midnight to 4 A.M. Joined by invisible threads of amphetamine, we ground our teeth and chewed our respective cuds into the early morning, courtesy of John the acting student and the white piles of crystal meth he doled out so generously.

John didn't expect sex as payment for his drugs. He was anomalously genteel, and he got his thrills from having each foot in a different world. He was handsome too—pale, blond, hollow-cheeked with fish-belly blue eyes. His greatest fear was turning into a goody-goody. I knew this by instinct. I also knew he was a romantic. And in the same way the Dustbusters fascinated him, so did I. But he didn't really want the Dustbusters or me. He wanted the spark we set off in his imagination. Under these circumstances sex was irrelevant.

The drug dealer down the hall was a slightly different story. He expected something in return for his tokens. But that was his bad judgment. He specialized in psychedelics, LSD, mescaline—at least that was what he gave away freely. He was short, not much taller than me, and he wore a leather hat with a wide brim. Straw-like hair wisped down to his shoulders. He would have been good looking if he were taller or broader or healthy. But there was something of the underfed sharecropper about him. Where he shone was in his own environment, which was a large dun-colored apartment with no furniture and black metal gratings on the windows. Here he was the big man or at least the center of attention, while people made furtive entrances and exits with the guilty expression of smiling dogs.

The Texan licked his fingers in between counting leaves of cash, and then he rolled his currency into a thick wad—sometimes he did this many times in a row. And one time, maybe after the fifth counting, someone howled, "Look out they're coming in the window." And they were. They looked Puerto Rican in that they were not black or white but a dark coppery color. They had managed to wrench the corner of a grating off and they were making headway on the next and rattling the windows with implements. They were waving some kind of weapons—knives or guns or something. I don't know because it was dark out there. The drug dealer from Texas did what you would have expected (being from the Lonestar State where the men are men, and the sheep take cover). He told me I had to help him.

I said okay, and we ran down the hall and bolted ourselves in my apartment with the police lock. I also had a metal door you would have needed a hand grenade to bust through, and my windows fronted Sixth Street except for the skylight that for some reason the thieves didn't bother to find. After that the Texan backed off with amorous expectations. But the motorcycle gang did not go away. And one morning after a zippy night of drawing increasingly intricate little pictures with a fine-liner and tie-dying and retie-dying my clothes to hideous shades of green and brown, I experienced what is known to speed freaks as crashing.

In fact, I crashed all the time, but I didn't know what it was, so I hadn't isolated it as particular to the act of taking amphetamine. I thought it was part of life. Crashing is a lot like it sounds: a sudden and utter pitch from happy puttering around to the gloomiest edge of rage. Only the rage doesn't ignite. It sits sodden and immobile and huge. I looked at my fingernails dyed purple with red around the sides. The stove was sloshed with horrible colors. The heap of clothes was as if stained by dung and bile. My drawings were stupid and the fucking motorcycles—vroom vroom vroom—were blasting holes in my teeth. I strode to the window, hoisted it up, shrieking, Shut up you fucking morons.

Well, that didn't really happen because before shrieking, I looked down and thought, "They tie people up and burn them." So instead I suffered into the overly hot afternoon, each noise like a stone bouncing off my tin pate. Shut up. Shut up. Shut up.

One Stroke

3rd St. and Avenue A
by Snooder Greenberg

One February night in 1969 a man knocked on my door and introduced himself; he had heard about me from somebody, he said. He didn't say what he heard. He had just moved into #2 with his wife Jamie and his little girl Hannah. They had just arrived from Alfred University; there was something about the SDS and an ROTC armory that had been set on fire.

I knew in five minutes that he was crazy and that he would be my brother. He loved me too, instantly. We talked for hours in my filthy kitchen with its single bare light bulb and "EYE CONTACT" scrawled in big block letters in red paint on my wall. All the visions, all the plans, they're lost now.

Two days later Jamie showed up with a fifty-page typed manifesto that he asked me to stash in my bedroom bureau because he was expecting the cops to bust him. It stayed in the bottom drawer of that bureau for seven months till narcs took it along with much else that they later denied any knowledge of. I let these sleeping dogs lie.

I guess you would call them florid personalities. Rick introduced himself to several others in the building that night and his brilliance in the phase he was in made many of us an instant community. A friend from the street-life outside told me Jamie had already fucked one of the local tough-but-nice junkies, so from that among other things there came to be a feeling of an even larger community extending into the third world jungle of which our building was the core.

I believe it. Jamie was called *puta* by some on the street, but she was so much more, free and wild and beautiful, but sometimes showing fear of the ride her husband was taking her on. The name of Rick Deohlie's magical community was "Symbiosis Associates." Symbiosis associates was real. Those 188 tenants under his spell changed overnight from being a collection of isolated counter-culture poseurs with various pathologies to being close friends. Many later went on to fuck up each others' lives. Shortly after the events described here, Rick took the front door of #2 off its hinges and declared his home an open peoples' apartment in the name of symbiosis associates—"la familia."

At this point Jamie left with Hannah, went uptown to speak again with his doctors, and saw the legal aid lawyer on Avenue B about divorce papers. She also fucked the peoples' lawyer, and I think they eventually got married and moved to Nyack. Within forty-eight hours Rick had been beaten to a pulp and the apartment stripped clean. But even this was only one of many revolutionary moments, and the sequence of events doesn't matter. It's the light of his life that matters, it's the beauty within the insanity of this child of the Long Island suburbs. You've got to wonder just how many revolutions there were back in those days. Rick's was the best I ever saw.

He was in some kind of outpatient program; that was always vague. The program had gotten him a job as a telephone installer. A few days after we met he came home in the late afternoon wearing a brown monk's habit. All of it, head to toe. They had sent him to St Patrick's Cathedral that day to work in the basement on the phones. There he found the habit and 1,500 autographed color 5x7 photographs of Cardinal Spellman, who Rick thought was a faggot judging by his dress. He had walked home all the way from the cathedral distributing over half the photographs and speaking out about the Cardinal's falseness and hypocrisy. Nothing came of that phase of the revolution. I still have a framed picture of the cardinal on my wall, other than that it's as if it never happened.

Shortly before his hospitalization he began fucking Judy, an ex-girlfriend of mine, who had left her family in Westchester to come to 188 East Third Street and join the revolution. Everybody in the building pretty much fucked in their back bedrooms, on the common airshaft. These were railroad apartments; everybody pretty much heard everybody else fucking. Judy was in the fifth-floor left rear, #2 was first-floor left rear, I was fourth-floor left front.

The night I heard Rick upstairs in the process of fucking Judy, Jamie was downstairs hearing it too. In minutes she knocked on my door. She was crying tears of desolation and begging for something with her eyes. I don't remember any words being said. She hugged me, then took me by my hand and led me the five feet from my apartment door through the chintzy bead curtain to my tiny bedroom. All I really remember of it is the moment I slid into her, the silky sleek tightness of her pussy, those few seconds unlike any I've ever known. One stroke. One. Then the door opened and Rick was standing in my kitchen looking through the curtain at me inside his wife. She pushed me off and told him it didn't mean anything. I don't remember that we had made any noise, but now the mature ex-asshole that I am knows that she did make purposeful noise and that is how he knew to stop his own party and come downstairs.

Rick seemed very nonchalant. In fact neither of them ever discussed that moment with me. I loved her after that. Two days later she gave me a hippie necklace of tiny clear blue beads which has hung on a hook in my bedroom for the last thirty years. But within two weeks she had made it very clear that I was unconditionally dumped despite Rick's collapse. God I hated her then.

This night of my one stroke love fuck was not over. I don't remember how it came to pass, but the four of us got in my van and drove to an empty summer house on a lake in Putnam County, to sort things out I guess. We each dropped 1,000 mikes of Osley Orange Sunshine on the way there. I was hoping to get to finish fucking Jamie and for Rick to finish Judy. When we got there the acid took hold, before long Rick had butchered my ego with the elegance of genius and reclaimed his wife. Now I see that he was magnificent that night, it might have been the finest moment of his life, maybe one of the great moments in the life of our species.

We sat around a simple country living room, and as the acid took control he took off his clothes with a quick fluid sureness. A hunting knife appeared in his hand, he climbed onto an end table and jumped from table to chair to couch to table around the knotty pine walls of this little room. He made a low animal noise, his body lit by the light from the fireplace, murder in his eyes, it was the stone age, I was frozen with terror. Now I blame it on the acid and excuse myself. I couldn't move or speak. I remember him taking Jamie by the hand and the joy and triumph of her as he marched her to a bedroom . . . and his colossal boner, the only time I ever saw his cock. Twice as big as mine.

Judy, who seemed oblivious to what had just happened before her eyes, suggested that I fuck her for old times sake. What I am proud of is that even in abject humiliation my ego knew what I needed to do to survive. I bundled up and walked into the freezing night, walked a mile across the still frozen lake through the dead still cold beauty of that night, and climbed up a pristine snow-covered hillside, sat down in the snow and looked a long time at how the snow sat on one low branch of a pine tree right next to me, bathed in the moonlight. I guess the acid washed it all clean and I felt flooded with the beauty of life and my ego somehow popped up whole again. I had been a coward, but the next morning, still tripping, I took Rick "hunting" in the deep woods behind this house, I gave him a twenty-two rifle to hunt with, I talked very straight about everything and gave him a clean chance to kill me. Instead he said he loved me. It seemed to me that we had completed some sort of circle and were whole again. We went back home to Third Street.

My next recollection is that the following weekend Rick and I, without Jamie, were back at that country house, this time with my brother and a bunch of his friends, maybe eight or nine people. We all did that orange sunshine, and then Rick had a major psychotic breakdown. This time eight or nine tripping people were very scared for themselves and about what might happen when the straight world showed up, all getting progressively into their own acid paranoia as Rick retreated into gibberish, making singsong chants over and over with crazy eyes and slobber on his face . . . "symbiosis associates, symbiosis, la familia, symbiosis associates, la familia" . . . all the way to New York down the Taconic Parkway with its fascist state cops while I held him in my arms in the back seat.

We called his parents from the city. They had been through this before, they came and took him to Creedmore Hospital on Long Island. Jamie told me later that week that his diagnosis had been refined, now his label was mixed-state schizophrenia/bi-polar disorder, not compliant with lithium or anything else. She said they said he was likely to spend the rest of his life in and out, getting progressively worse. As of my last knowledge before we broke off all contact, Jamie was pursuing the divorce and taking up with a better class of revolutionaries from around the corner on Avenue B, her poverty lawyer friends. Rick disappeared. Six months later he showed up again on a late summer afternoon, walking down Third Street looking crisp in new chinos, a haircut, and a golf shirt. He had a cool, detached edge.

We were never close again. He'd been out west, completed a degree in St. Louis at McDonalds' "Hamburger University," and spoke at length about his bright future with the company. He'd also developed what he implied were deep ties with the American Continental Army, some sort of secret armed militia that was going to move the revolution to the far right. Later, in front of our common street friends, he started in on me for being half a jewboy, which I am. I said something about that being my best half, and a comment about character disintegration as a marker in psychosis, and that is the way we ended.

I wrote the author of this piece about his byline. "Snooder Greenberg doesn't sound real. If you want a pseudonym how about something like Randall Snood?" The author, who now lives in North Carolina, wrote back:

"Randall Snood would be acceptable but it does not have inner meaning for me like Snooder Greenburg does. It strikes me that you, or (root of most evil), some fucking lawyer unduly darkening your world, may fear I have chosen someone else's name to write under and you might thus have legal difficulties with Snooder Greenburg. I assure you that is not so. Snooder is the name of my dog who lived with me on Third Street. Greenburg is the name of my present dog. I'd be delighted to send you documentary proof of this, veterinarian records, affidavits from my family, et cetera. T.B., I know you are a man of reason and good will, and so am I. See that I respect your work and would not harm it in any way, and that I appreciate your mission. My God, man, it's going to be eight years of George W. Bush! Cut me a break here. Let's stand together. The ice caps are melting, these are the last days. In fifteen million years it all recollapses to another single point of energy.

The Turtles in Central Park

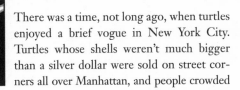

Central Park
by Thomas Beller

There was a time, not long ago, when turtles enjoyed a brief vogue in New York City. Turtles whose shells weren't much bigger than a silver dollar were sold on street corners all over Manhattan, and people crowded around to buy them.

In the midst of this turtle trend, my friend Kip moved back to New York, after two years in Los Angeles, and it was only a few days before he was swept up in the turtle craze. "I got them on the street, in Chinatown, five dollars each," he told me excitedly. "That's the great thing about New York. One minute you're walking down the street and then all of a sudden you're a turtle owner."

When Kip went to buy a habitat for his new pets, he found the store jammed with people looking at aquariums and inquiring about turtle food. "It's turtle mania. I don't understand it," the store manager said. Kip bought an aquarium, some props for inside the aquarium, including a fake plant and a brick ("to give the environment some architecture," he explained), and a supply of minnows, which functioned as scenery until the turtles ate them. Kip named the two turtles Kirby and Rod.

At first Kip acted like a new parent: he doted over the pair with a certain loving anxiety. He stared at them with wonder. He reported on their movement and behavior in detail, as if every little thing they did was of universal interest.

"It was so great," he would say into the phone. "Kirby was asleep, you know, all balled up in his little shell, just sleeping on top of the brick, and then he fell off the brick. He just fell off and floated down to the bottom, and when he landed he stuck his little head out and looked really confused." There was a great deal of speculation about Rod and Kirby's relationship. Did they get along? Who was more powerful? And most importantly, were they happy?

It was around this time that the turtle phenomena began to make the news. They had been smuggled into the city from turtle farms in such far off places as Louisiana and Florida. The ASPCA—who were being inundated with calls from new turtle owners wondering how to care for them—raided a distribution center and confiscated over three thousand tiny turtles, whose scientific name has a pleasing sound: Trachemys Scripta Elegans. City and Federal officials—who were acting on a law which bans interstate turtle trafficking—cracked down on the street venders, and the turtle trade was eradicated. (The United States, it turns out, has elaborate turtle regulations.) Rod and Kirby were contraband.

Kip, however, was having his own, more private drama with Rod and Kirby. He had moved into a new, very small apartment, and was unemployed. His return to New York was not going well. I didn't hear much about the pair until one day he said, "Rod and Kirby are starting to depress me. They paw at the glass. It's kind of disturbing. They swim right up to the glass and kind of paw at it with their little turtle hands like they want to get out. I sit here all day in my little apartment watching them in their little aquarium. I feel like I'm their jailer." Kip began to fasten to the idea that he was somehow holding the pair captive against their will.

Then one day he decided to set them free. He found a place that struck him as a good turtle habitat, the pond in Central Park, and I met him there for the big event. He brought them in a portable aquarium, a plastic case about the size of half a gallon of milk, with some water on the bottom. It was a brilliant autumn afternoon, and Central Park was brimming with strollers. A group of ducks quacked and paddled festively in the center of the pond. The world seemed huge and full of possibilities.

Rod and Kirby, on the other hand, seemed extremely small. Kip set the aquarium down on the grass and we took a close look. Their shells were bright green and they moved around excitedly, sensing a big change. One of them came up to the plastic wall and started pawing at it. Kip was right. It was disturbing. After a few minutes he tipped the box on its side. There was a moment of confusion, and then the pair began to make their way forward, toward the water. Rod jumped right in and started paddling out to the ducks in the center of the pond. Kirby was more reluctant, hesitating at the water's edge for a minute before plopping in. He moved around in the shallows while Rod swam further and further away, a tiny speck of animated green just beneath the water's surface.

"I wonder if they'll stay friends," said Kip.

The events described above took place in the mid-nineties. A few years after Rod and Kirby took their dive into what was then called Belvedere Lake, I was startled to see that there had been a name change. It's now called Turtle Pond. Henry J. Stern, the parks commisioner at the time, explained that the reason for the name change was that Turtle Pond was a kind of mecca for dissafected turtle owners, who would arrive from the East and West sides with their pet turtles and set them free.

Trash Like White Elephants

India St., Greenpoint, Brooklyn
by Minter Krotzer

There is a man who looks just like Hemingway who lives on India Street in Brooklyn in a building called the Astral, a dismal place with huge arching windows to remind you of its past glamour as an apart-ment building for international sailors (Mae West is said to have been born there). He lives right above a woman named Maria who cuts people's hair in her apartment. This man, who I always call "Hemingway," spends every day, all day long, looking through the trash cans on India Street for objects that he is interested in. Whenever he finds something that he likes, he puts it into a basket that is tied to a string leading up to his apartment. He then calls up to his son, Aristotle, who sticks his head out from the window, screams back in acknowledgment, and pulls up the basket. Both are equally excited by the finds.

One day I went up to Hemingway, as he was carefully sorting out pieces of a broken mirror from a bent-up tin of macaroni and cheese, and I told him how much I liked his beard. I don't know why I had the urge to do this.

Perhaps I felt the need to interrupt his persistent activity, to see if he was capable of being distracted and responding to something other than a piece of trash. He slowly turned towards me and made a sound that was a definite expression of disgust and told me that he didn't care for his beard. He said the only reason he keeps it is because a woman down the street pays him eight dollars a week not to shave it off. This left me feeling even more curious than I had been before. So now when I look out the window at Hemingway I think about the woman instead of the trash.

The Jumper

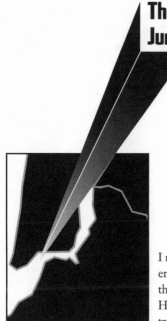

‖ Brooklyn Bridge
‖ by Manny Howard

I recently spent an afternoon watching a guy entertaining three of New York's finest on the eastern parapet of the Brooklyn Bridge. He was wearing what looked like a green track suit.

"Jumper!" the call went up in the office.

The view here is extraordinary: the Brooklyn Bridge, the World Trade Towers, the financial district, the Statue of Liberty, and the harbor beyond. We had seats in the sky box for this one and watched as the police department cleared the roadway of traffic (both to and from Manhattan), set up command posts, moved two pods of Emergency Service Unit officers (the name they give a S.W.A.T. team these days) into position, one on the cables below him and one on the parapet with him.

We shared a pair of binoculars, looking through them at the Jumper, who didn't look like the kind of guy who anybody had paid much attention to before. I don't know why we all agreed about this, because even with the binoculars it was impossible to tell much of anything. Maybe black, maybe

Hispanic. Somebody said he was an Arab. Maybe thirty, maybe twenty, he was wearing a baseball cap backward on his head.

Regardless, he had his audience now. There were the three cops in the first E.S.U. unit, two helicopters, two harbor patrol boats, half the tourists in downtown Manhattan, and us. Why hadn't he jumped already? We asked, handing the binoculars around. Why don't the cops just grab him? They were three big guys after all. The one closest was sitting Indian-style right next to jumper whose feet dangled over the tower. That cop was tethered to the other two guys and the bridge's super structure. He could just reach out and boom. Like that.

But Jumper just kept on talking, gesticulating angrily sometimes, sometimes morose.

"He looks a little dingy," observed someone in the office, handing off the binoculars to pick up a call ringing through on her desk. "We'll have the meeting in five minutes," suggested someone else, wandering towards the water cooler. Soon the curious crowd at the window thinned to just two of us.

The police department had inflated a giant yellow and white mattress thingy on the ground below the parapet. Jumper just talked and talked. "He's not going anywhere," said the other guy at the window, walking back to his desk.

"Five bucks says he goes," I said.

"Dude," scolded my officemate.

"You can't bet on that," said someone else looking up from her computer. I watched for a while longer trying to keep the binoculars in focus. Then I picked up the phone and called a friend in midtown. I explained the situation.

"How long's he been with the police?" asked the friend.

"Going on twenty minutes."

"He's not jumping. No way. These guys jump in the first couple a minutes if they're gonna go. No way he jumps."

"So?"

"Five says he doesn't jump."

"I'll call you." I said and hung up the phone. The afternoon sun was making it hard to see what was going on but the two cops supporting the negotiator were leaning on the railing on top of the parapet like they were on break now. Bored stiff I figured. Each had one leg up on the railing, the one with the hard hat on had his right arm slung like a wing over the top bar. The cop on point, squatting, stood up now and shook out his legs and Jumper just talked and talked.

I took a call and made two.

"Is he still up there?" a voice called from the conference room.

"Yep. The cops look pretty bored. I bet this was going to be the highlight of the shift for most of those guys. Now, I don't know."

"Yell if something happens."

"I imagine I will."

Jumper must have looked down and seen the mattress inflated below him. The eastern parapet, the one in Brooklyn, isn't in the East River. There's a cobblestone park below it that's quite nice to visit just after sunset when the skyline lights start to shine. Anyway, Jumper got pretty agitated and tried to scoot around the other side of the tower, away from the mattress-thingy. He did this on his belly and hung his legs out over the tower to show he meant business.

"He's moving!" I yelled.

The meeting in the conference room broke up and our windows were full as the three cops dropped to their knees and crawled towards him. He waved his arms wildly.

We all made the same sound when he started to drop. A loud strangled gasp with a curse mixed in there. Jumper spun spread eagle, maybe three revolutions, before he hit an outcropping in the tower halfway down. He only made it halfway, though. As he fell he hung pretty close to the granite (quarried in Vineyard Haven, Maine) that the tower's made of.

The ambulance guys were trying to figure a way to get him back onto the roadway right now. They didn't seem to be in much of a hurry, though. The three E.S.U. cops were still on the top of the tower. One guy, I'm guessing the lead negotiator, seems pretty broken up.

Traffic out of Manhattan was starting to pick up again, now. It was just about rush hour. I must say, it tightened me up a bit watching him spin like he did. I sure wish I hadn't made that bet.

The Parakeet Book

Kenmare and Mulberry St.
by Josh Kramer

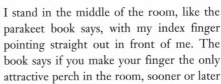

I stand in the middle of the room, like the parakeet book says, with my index finger pointing straight out in front of me. The book says if you make your finger the only attractive perch in the room, sooner or later the bird will naturally come to light upon it. So I move all the furniture out of the room, close up all the windows tightly, and I put the cage on the floor next to me. I unlatch the little clips that hold the top of the cage to the bottom. And then I lift the top off.

This very quiet bird, with whom I am hoping to build a relationship, is called Number Two. I received Number Two and his ex-companion, Number One, as a Valentine's Day present from a woman I used to go with. Her name was Johanna. Johanna used to work in my office—in fact she used to work for me.

I felt a little guilty about that, but I swear I didn't do anything to encourage her, except I did, finally, sleep with her. I always knew that Johanna was interested in me, even at her first interview, but I was able to sidestep the whole business until the Christmas party, when she asked me to dance and held herself so close I could feel the clip of her brassiere digging into my sternum. As I danced with her I thought to myself that I had been alone for a long time and here was a woman who really wanted me, though I had no idea what exactly what it was she liked about me. She didn't really like my jokes, particularly, and our conversation was only mildly stimulating. Nevertheless, I thought it might be good for me to be involved with someone again, even if she might, one day, sue me.

Johanna gave me the birds because she thought they would be therapeutic for me. She thought I was too introspective and self-involved and having a pet would "bring me out of myself." First she suggested a cat, which I rejected because Johanna had two cats, both of which I found hugely irritating. If you ever wore anything fuzzy, like a sweater for example, one of cats would rhythmically pump its front paws against you, apparently in search of a nipple. The other liked to sleep as close to your face as it could get, and it would slither up in the bed until you could hear it breathing, which I found revolting. Once I awoke from a nightmare in which I dreamt I was being smothered by Johanna, her cashmere shawl tight over my nose and mouth, but it was only the cat. From then on I wouldn't sleep over unless she locked the cats out of the bedroom.

I suggested a couple of fish. But Johanna thought that fish wouldn't have the desired therapeutic effect (they wouldn't "bring me out of myself"), because fish didn't acknowledge your existence even when you fed them, and you couldn't pet them. I pointed out that you could pet a fish, if you really wanted to.

Finally we settled on these two parakeets, a green one, and a yellow one, which I named Number One and Number Two for convenience' sake. We had a big fight about that, but I insisted they were my pets, and if she wanted to name them, she could keep them at her house.

Number One was my favorite because it seemed very cheerful and sang a lot, and it always tried to bite my finger when I stuck it in the cage, but I didn't have it for very long. About two weeks after I got the birds, I went out of town for a few days on business. While I was gone, Johanna decided to clean out the cage to wash it. She deposited the birds in a cardboard box during this operation, but somehow Number One managed to get free and started flying around the room until it finally came to rest on a window sill.

As Johanna approached with a grey army blanket held out in front of her, the bird got scared and squeezed itself into a tiny space between the upper and lower halves of the living room window, where the air conditioner was, and then it wiggled its way down the window pane until it flew out into the New York winter.

I used to think about what happened to Number One after it escaped that night. It must have been quite a sight, a little green bullet flying through the streets of lower Manhattan in the middle of a long gray winter. I imagined bundled up New Yorkers scurrying through the streets where they would come upon Number One, a little bird, bright green and yellow striped, singing its little lungs out, sitting on a stone window ledge outside the bank building next to the dirty pigeons and the muddy sparrows. This little singing native of tropical climates, who had seen nothing in its four month life but the inside of its cage, one pet store, and my small New York apartment could not help but think, "How did this happen?" as it sat on the stone window ledge of the bank building, freezing to death.

Some few weeks after Number One left, I ended my relationship with Johanna. It was an unhappy scene, with Johanna lying on the floor holding on to my leg on the fourth floor landing of her loft building, insisting that I mustn't go, that I couldn't leave her. I tried to step down but she gripped me tighter, her whole body wrapped around my left calf. It was as desperate a moment as I ever hope to see, and I knelt down and unwrapped her arms as gently as I could, which wasn't easy because she was very strong.

There wasn't much to say, really, but I tried to explain that something better would come her way soon and walked down the six long flights of stairs to the street. I could feel her eyes on my back all the way down. I can't explain how Johanna came to feel this way about me or what she thought she was clinging to as she held my leg in her death grip. Some part of me really wanted to believe that it was me that she wanted so badly. But now I think it was only that I put up so very little distraction from whatever fantasy she had going about her lover, whose space I just happened to occupy for a time.

Nevertheless, I did find myself wishing I had a camera with me on top of those stairs, so I could take a picture and send it to a woman who felt about me the way I felt about Johanna, just to show her. "See how lovable I am?" the caption would say.

So here I am, back in my apartment. Just me and Number Two. I remove the top of the bird cage slowly and carefully, so as not startle him. I am successful, I think, because he just sits there, not making a peep, waiting for whatever fate will befall him next. I stand very quietly, my index finger still pointing straight out in front of me. Without moving my head, I glance down, just my eyes, toward the cage on the floor. Number Two is still there, waiting. I nudge the cage with my foot. The bird falls over, then rights himself. I kick the cage again, a little harder this time, and the bird takes flight, suddenly, erratically. It whips around the room wildly, three times and then crashes, with a sickening "thop," into the hard, white wall. It lies on the ground, motionless, yet I stand for a moment, very still, in the middle of the room with my index finger pointing straight out in front of me, like the parakeet book says.

Everybody Poops

The Upper West Side
by Sabin Streeter

I found *Timmy's Potty* laying on the carpet beneath our bed this morning. It's a toilet training video that my wife purchased for our son about a month ago. It was odd to see it again. I remember the day my wife brought it home from the hippie bookstore. More specifically, I remember how she and I watched it together after our son had gone to bed to see if it was appropriate for him.

We've been doing this before we let him watch any video ever since we sat down as a family to enjoy the harmless-seeming *World of Butterflies*, unaware that it would end in an extremely graphic five-minute montage of birds devouring butterflies that would send our son into a mild state of catatonia.

Fortunately, *Timmy's Potty* was no *World of Butterflies*. It was just a bland little story about a boy learning how to use his potty. It had a horrible, horrible theme song, but my wife and I are used to horrible children's music. The only thing that troubled us about the video was the fact that Timmy, the boy in the story who was learning how to use his potty, looked very young. In fact, Timmy looked more like our ten-month-old daughter than our three-and-a-half-year-old son.

My wife and I spent quite a while discussing how our son would feel about this. Would watching this little Timmy kid learning how to use a toilet upset him in some way? Would it make him feel immature or unduly pressured to get on with his own toilet training? We decided that it wasn't a big deal and it didn't prove to be one. Our son watched *Timmy's Potty* a few times and didn't seem to even register that a child who was much younger than he was learning a skill that he didn't possess. Mostly, our son just liked the horrible song and the scene, early in the story, in which Timmy uses his potty as a house for his stuffed animals.

Our son tried this himself a few times, then moved on to other games. Soon after that, he lost interest in *Timmy's Potty* and probably not too long after that, *Timmy's Potty* got stuffed under our bed, another relic of our failed efforts to toilet train him.

Our son is not the only three-and-a-half-year-old who's still wearing diapers, but he seems to be one of a very small group. Most of his friends were toilet-trained sometime during their second year. According to the experience of many of our fellow parents and most of the books on this subject, there's usually a "window" in that year, during which toddlers get interested in the toilet, start wanting to watch their parents go to the bathroom, want to talk about how it all works, and find it enjoyable to sit on those little plastic potties. Supposedly, if you act during this window of child interest, you won't find much resistance to getting rid of diapers. The child will want to toilet train and will therefore do it willingly and feel good about it. And then, I guess, the child will go on to have a happy and healthy life.

Unfortunately, our son went through his "window of interest" just as his younger sister was about to be born and we'd been advised that this was a bad time to toilet train, window or not. New siblings often inspire "regression," we were told, so if we trained our son right before his sister's birth it would not last—he'd want his diapers back as soon as she showed up. And, indeed, when his baby sister arrived, our son regressed like crazy: he wanted to get in her stroller, in her crib, wear her clothes, resume breast feeding and generally, just act like a baby. It was fine with us. We were very worried that he'd resent his new sister and we were more than willing to let him sit slack-jawed and drooling like a newborn if that made him feel comfortable with her. And we were very glad that we'd ignored the window and not wasted our time toilet training him.

The problem is that almost a year has passed since my son's window of interest closed, and he's shown no further inclination towards giving up his diapers. Whenever we ask him, he always says he's "not ready." So we've waited and waited, hoping that some bright day he'll announce his readiness, meanwhile watching all of his friends toilet train and wondering if we were doing something wrong. Then, this past November, our son started having very regular bowel movements once a day, almost always at the end of his nap; never at school, never outside our apartment.

My wife and I knew this was considered to be a sign of readiness to toilet train, and when we realized it was happening, we talked to his teacher about it. She said that he'd probably ask to be trained if we gave him a little more encouragement. So we took him out to buy his own underpants and started talking to him about how his friends at school wear underpants and use the toilet, and how we use the toilet, how his grandparents use the toilet, and so on, and so on. We talked and talked and talked. We read a ridiculous book called *Everybody Poops* a thousand times and a lot of slightly less ridiculous books a comparable number of times. We bought a new plastic potty, even though we already had a plastic potty, thinking that a new one would instill new interest. We put it in the middle of our living room and let our son decorate it with magic markers and animal stickers. Our son bore all of this patiently and with good humor. He liked his underpants and the books and all the talking. He enjoyed decorating his new potty. He was even willing to sit on the potty with his clothes on and pretend he was going to the bathroom. But that was it. Any suggestion that he take off his diaper and actually go to the bathroom in the potty was firmly rebuked.

Months passed, other suggestions and encouragements were made, including *Timmy's Potty*, but our son remained unchanged. Finally, my wife decided that we should do something more active. She read a couple of books on the subject and formulated a plan: for two weeks, we would tell our son that we knew he was ready to toilet train. We'd say that we would be able to help him, and his teachers would be able to help, and he would definitely be able to do it. Instead of asking him if he was ready, we'd tell him—in a variety of ways, subtle and not so subtle—that we knew he was ready. And then, when the two weeks of preparation and encouragement were over, we'd take off the diapers and put on some underpants. He'd still wear a diapers during his naps and at night, but other than that, he'd use the potty. If there were accidents, fine, accidents were to be expected. We'd just change his clothes and show him his potty and say that next time, maybe he'd like to use it.

During the two week preparation period, we didn't talk about toilet training incessantly, just every so often, whenever it seemed appropriate. We tried to be sensitive to whether or not our son wanted to talk about it himself. We tried—but it really didn't seem to matter. Our son simply didn't want to talk about it at all. Whenever we'd tell him that we knew he was ready to use the toilet, he'd get this kind of frightened look on his face and respond, in a quavering but insistent voice, that no, he wasn't ready. If we asked him why, he'd say, "I love diapers."

This was almost too much to bear, but we kept going forward, trying new and unsuccessful ways of broaching the subject, motivated, I guess, by a fear of backing down too easily. However, as the two weeks wore on and our son continued to show fear, not interest, in toilet training, we decided to modify our plan a bit. Instead of beginning the training on a Saturday morning, we thought we'd start it on Friday afternoon after his nap. This would mean that the first period of his diaperlessness would only last a few hours: from around 5 P.M. when he gets up from his nap until 8 P.M., when he goes to sleep for the night. He usually stays home during these hours and plays with his toys and it's a comfortable time for him and we thought this might ease the transition into his new routine.

When the appointed Friday arrived, my wife took off his diapers and offered him a selection of underpants. He started screaming and crying. My wife called me at work and I told her to just wait it out. Our son, like almost every other kid, has learned to use tantrums to get what he wants. He'll often have a very dramatic initial reaction to things he doesn't like and then calm down if he realizes we're not affected by his outburst. The trick is to not be affected. I reminded my wife of this and she said that she felt it was fine to ignore a tantrum over something minor—like telling him he can't bring all of his stuffed animals to the dinner table—but that this was more serious. A bad toilet training experience can leave emotional scars. I told her I was pretty sure he'd calm down.

In the background I could hear him yelling "Give me a clean diaper!" between agonized sobs and choking noises. He was really having a fit and I was glad I wasn't there to witness it. But, after a few minutes, as I'd predicted, he quieted down, picked out some underpants and asked for a cup of juice. By the time I got home from work, he was playing happily and wanted to show me his underpants. He even seemed proud of them.

I felt that things were going reasonably well. Getting rid of the diapers was a first step—and to my mind the biggest step. For a few hours after he'd gone to bed, I felt optimistic. My wife, however, was concerned that he hadn't gone anywhere near his potty, and didn't seem inclined to. He'd had a bowel movement in his diaper at the end of his nap, as usual, and then spent the three hours in his underpants holding urine in his bladder, waiting for us to put his nighttime diaper on. My wife thought the fact he'd controlled himself for that long was a problem. I disagreed. I expected that the next day, when he'd have to wear his underpants for a much longer stretch of time— 7 A.M. until 3 P.M.—he'd either have an accident or use his potty, and that things would kind of proceed naturally from there.

But things didn't proceed. My son put his underpants on in the morning without protest, but he continued to try his best to control himself and wait to go to the bathroom until he got his diapers back at nap time. He quickly became remarkably good at this, going hours and hours without urinating, even squeezing his penis through what I guess were difficult periods. He had a few accidents but they did not deter him—he just asked for new clothes and then refused all suggestions that he try using his potty, still insisting that he wasn't ready. Soon, he stopped having accidents, and then, on the third day of our toilet training experiment, he stopped having his regular bowel movements. He was, my wife and I decided, probably constipated from worry. Or maybe all the effort he was making to control his bladder was having some kind of effect on his bowels. We didn't try to figure it out any more than that. We just stopped the toilet training. We gave him back his diapers and put his underpants the bottom drawer of his dresser and told him that he can get them out whenever he's ready. He seemed totally uninterested and hasn't mentioned the word "underpants" since. By the next day, his regular bowel movements had returned and he'd stopped clutching his penis.

My wife and I talked to the social worker at my son's school. She told us that we'd done the right thing. She said that our son will eventually be ready to toilet train and when he is, he'll let us know, and he'll do it happily and be proud of it. She said the reason we can't imagine this ever happening is that he's not ready yet.

I thought about pointing out the flaws in her argument, saying that just because you can't imagine something happening does not assure that it's going to happen—rather, most things you can't imagine happening are, in fact, never going to happen. But I decided against it. Instead, I sat there silently and smiled and held my wife's hand and felt good about our decision to abandon the toilet training. I have no idea when or how our son is going to get trained. I assume that he will, but at the moment, I don't really care. I just want to leave my son alone for a while. I am embarrassed about the way I have treated him in the last few months. It pains me to think of the hours we've spent together hovering over a potty, my face screwed up in a fake smile, watching him there, listening unhappily as I try to say in a dis-interested voice: "Would you like to practice going poop?"

Even now, writing it down, I feel sick.

Bubby's Departure

Brooklyn; The Catskills; Penn Station
by Josh Gilbert

I didn't know Bubby growing up. She and my dad had a fight when I was two and didn't speak for the next fifteen years. Bubby lived out in Bensonhurst, Brooklyn, in the same apartment my dad grew up in. We lived in California, three thousand miles away. Their differences were easily maintained by the distance, and Bubby was rarely discussed. She never sent cards or gifts on birthdays or holidays and was absent from family gatherings. For all intents and purposes, Bubby didn't exist.

Then came that summer before my senior year in high school when my parents took a fabulous Honolulu adventure tour. Sitting on a bench at a shopping mall in Waikiki, my father casually glanced at the squat old lady next to him and realized he was sitting next to his mother.

They went out for a coffee, and during this brief, fleeting moment of détente, decided it was time for Bubby to pay us a visit.

Several months later she arrived on our doorstep in Los Angeles, swearing about the morons at the airlines and the bastard from the shuttle service who dropped her bag. She ranted and raved, and for the first time in my life, I saw my father shut down in a conversation. She actually rendered him mute. As a rebellious teenager and my father's chief rival in a game he controlled, I was immediately enthralled by this.

"She's a random noise generator," my father whined to my mother several days later, helpless, after an afternoon of sight-seeing. "We're driving along and all of a sudden, out of no where, she starts telling me about five different people, using pronouns to describe each one of them. I don't have a clue who or what she was talking about. She wouldn't shut up. I almost drove into oncoming traffic."

It was borscht-belt mayhem and great theater. But more than that, she solved my secret, unsolved mystery. She was the half man, half monkey of me. No wonder my dad said "fuck" every other word and flew into those fits of loud, gibbering fury; I suddenly understood why my father and I were part baboon. He'd been raised by one. My grandmother Bubby, the four-foot-ten, fire-breathing, Yiddishe maniac.

Moments after she boarded the plane (in a wheelchair, complaining) headed back for Brooklyn, my dad came down from the proverbial ceiling and swore he wouldn't be seeing Bubby again any time soon. But her visit left an indelible impression on me and I was determined to stay in touch.

When I left for college I began calling her every few months for an aural transfusion of her vintage rants. I'd start her off with something provocative. "Hey, Bubby, how's life out there in New York?"

"What kind of horseshit question is that? How's New York? It's a fucking sewer. That whore Reagan and his little pimp Bush. Those bastards are fucking everything up. Haven't you heard all their promises and lies?!? Do you think they care? They don't care!"

After college, I took a road trip from Santa Cruz to New York, eager to see Bubby and finally catch a glimpse of the "shitbox" my dad grew up in. The shitbox he credited for his prodigious, meteoric ascension through the ranks of academia and into the wealthy suburb I called home. I wanted to see the view out their living room window: the famous Brick Wall of Bensonhurst.

"When I was eight years old," the old man said one night, during one of his own patented, angst-induced furies, "I looked out that shitbox window and I stared at that fuck'n wall and I thought to myself, I gotta get the hell out of here. I gotta get the hell outta here, no matter what it takes."

Ten years later, as a senior at Brooklyn Tech, he had the highest college boards in the state of New York and a full academic scholarship to MIT. I wanted to see the wall. I wanted to take a gander at the fold-out couch my dad shared with his brother for eighteen years in the living room of their one-bedroom rat-hole. But Bubby nixed the idea. She wasn't prepared to "entertain." Instead, she suggested we meet at the Museum of Modern Art in Manhattan. "Bubby, you like modern art?!" I was incredulous.

"Are you crazy? Who gives a rat's ass about modern art?! It's air-conditioned! You can sit in the nice, cool cafeteria all day and no one bothers you. I'll bring sandwiches."

She was right: no one bothered us. We sat in the cafeteria for hours while Bubby fulminated about how it was all my dad's fault they didn't get along and how it was actually my uncle (the homeless drifter, but that's another story) who was the real genius of the family. It was my first trip to New York and my first visit to MOMA, and it took some doing, but I finally convinced her we should take a look at the Pop Art exhibition. She reluctantly agreed.

"Jesus Christ would you look at this crap! You got a toothbrush?!" Her loud voice echoed through the wing.

"It's a Rauschenberg, you realize. He's a very famous artist. A seminal thinker. A creative genius. This toothbrush isn't just a toothbrush, Bubby. It's a concept."

"Oh what a bunch of horseshit. It's a mess. It looks like your aunt Ida's living room floor!"

POW! ZAP! KERPLOW! Bubby stole the show, blazing a trail through the gawking crowd like the chrome rocket bumper detail of a 1956 Chevy Bel Air.

Several years later, my great aunt Bea, Bubby's sister, suggested they move down to Florida to a retirement community in now-famous Broward County. Bubby was game but there was one huge problem. She was an epic pack rat. Her apartment was piled high from floor to ceiling with things she "might need one day, you never know." The thought of moving compelled her to finally consider what to do with my father's baby carriage or fifty years of newspapers or the 250,000 Sweet 'N Low packets she'd stolen from diners over the years while no one was watching.

Meanwhile, the super had "the shitbox" promised to a comrade. After two years of procrastinating and excruciating indecision, the comrade showed up on Bubby's doorstep and offered to pack her things for her, for free. The idea repulsed her, but it was an offer she couldn't refuse. So she grudgingly relented and looked on, disgusted, as "the rat bastard" packed up 350 large boxes of her essential belongings.

"How could I be so stupid to let this stupid Russian bastard bamboozle me into coming in here and packing my things?!? You wouldn't believe how stupid he is, putting china together with heavy books. Could he be any sloppier."

"Bubby, he's been working for free for three weeks."

"Nu? He's getting a wonderful apartment out of the bargain."

"You mean the shitbox?"

"I've been BAMBOOZLED!"

And with the last box through the doorway, I imagine Bubby standing in the empty apartment. Overwhelmed by a surreal, stark vision of sudden total emptiness. Since 1921 she hadn't seen the floor.

A fleeting thought of relief. All her stuff would be waiting for her in Florida. She was finally free from the sewer of New York. All those dark gray buildings, rats and morons.

As she boarded the bus to the station, a spasm of angst ricocheted through her gray matter. Sparks flying. Random images. Poor, scared peasants run screaming through the dirt streets of a burning shtetl. The statue of Liberty monolithic through the railing of a steamship on a freezing cold winter day in 1917. The oppressive smell of wet wool in a crowded room on Ellis Island.

She arrived at Penn Station and elbowed her way through the crowd and checked the time on the board against the time on her watch...panic. She was late. Of course she was late. Those morons never get you there on time. Scurrying past all the blurry faces, remembering . . .

Her husband languishing on his deathbed with two small children to feed and clothe. And no help from the community either. Those orthodox bastards at the synagogue! She wasn't good enough for them. She didn't have enough money for them to care about her welfare! The bastards wouldn't help a dying man's family. One of their own. The trash can. The sewer. Down the escalator to the train. To the tunnel. To warm weather 365

days a year and an all-you-can-eat salad bar in an elegantly appointed community center.

A strange warmth inside big dizziness.

"Excuse me, m'am, are you OK?"

There's her train. Ready to board. Ready to take her away from all this.
To that long-awaited tropical paradise.

Someone call an ambulance.

With all the strength she could muster, she muttered her last, dying
words to the unsuspecting paramedic: "Take your fuck'n hands off of me! I
have a train to catch."

Mr. Beller's Neighborhood

BEFORE & AFTER
STORIES FROM
NEW YORK

Edited by Thomas Beller

Volume I

CONTENTS

Thomas Beller 7 Introduction: After

Debra Fontaine 10 Witnessing

Charles Waters 12 The View from the WTC Plaza

Kevin McLeod 15 Don't Look Back

Thomas Beller 19 The Ashen Guy

Greg Purcell 22 Forever Falling

Bryan Charles 25 The Numbers

Carolyn Murnick 37 On Giving Blood

Tom Cushman 41 Something About Jack

Lauren Grodstein 45 The Tourist

Sam Lipsyte 49 Scenes from Astoria

Elizabeth Grove 51 This Is Bad

Adam Baer 55 The View from Long Island

Amy Brill 57 Maybe a Girl Who Loves the Ocean

Debbie Nathan 60 Profiteers and Souvenirs: An eBay Story

Alex Abramovich 64 The Scene at Union Square Park

Vince Passaro 68 Don Delillo and the Twin Towers

Betsy Andrews 71 Cosmetics Plus (and Minus)

CONTENTS

Dorothy Spears   73   God Must Be an Octopus

Elizabeth Seay   78   A Grand Candelabra

Sean Ramsay   80   Urban Renewal

Bram Gunther   82   Pet Detectives

Joseph Lieber   85   Bones

Phillip Lopate   89   Ashes

Saïd Sayrafiezadeh   96   Reflections of a Savage

Paul W. Morris   101   Zen and the Syntax of Disaster

Anne Kovach   107   Winged

Josh Gilbert   110   Terror at the Local Deli

Elizabeth Grove   114   I'm So Glad You're Alive

Phillip Lopate   118   The Good Soldiers

Introduction: After

New York City
by Thomas Beller

The skyline of New York can scare you, and I always liked that. There is one particular approach, coming across Route Eighty from the west, where you come over a rise and see the city in the distance, maybe thirty miles away, and it looks small, almost huddled. Then it disappears and you don't see it anymore and after a while you wonder if you imagined it.

Then, like a monster rising from the deep, it suddenly appears, and now it is in your face, gigantic, menacing, oblivious to you and your little hopes and aspirations. To make matters worse, you can't just drive in—you have to cross a bridge or disappear into a tunnel, and when you get to the other side you won't be able to see this skyline anymore, you'll be consumed within it.

I was driving once with a friend, a woman who had moved to New York in her early twenties and, ten years later, professionally accomplished, was about to move away.

"I remember when I first saw that," she said of the enormous mass of

building before us, lit by the late afternoon sun. "I thought, 'I'm going to make an impression on this place.'"

"You did," I said, proud of her. "You took a bite out of the Big Apple."

"Yeah," she said, "and it took a bite out of me."

I write at a time when someone, something, a force both infuriatingly specific and maddeningly abstract, has taken a bite out of the Manhattan skyline, out of New York, and the whole country. Now the city feels unbalanced, and one's eyes keep searching southward down the avenues, looking for what is not there. As Phillip Lopate points out in "The Good Soldiers," the Twin Towers had been, for all their enormity, oddly quiet structures. Now their absence is deafening and is practically all we can think of.

This book is composed of a series of views from inside the city. When you are inside the skyline, the city isn't a monolith, it's a million tiny details. In the "After" section, it's more like a broad variety of perspectives of one event. The "Before" sections are a series of essays, the "After" a series of views. Some are up close, such as Charles Waters's account of pausing on the World Trade Center plaza to finish a phone conversation with his father. Others are from a considerable distance. News of the event rippled outward and people took to their roofs and hurried to their grocers where, as Sam Lipsyte describes it from his neighborhood in Queens, they were confronted with the moral conundrum of how much soup to stockpile. Some of these essays were written in the immediate aftermath of September 11 and you can feel it in their urgency. They are testimonials, a kind of verbal photo-journalism. Other pieces were written several weeks later, and are more reflective. So even as Bryan Charles describes the harrowing details of his escape from the seventieth floor, we get a sense, also, of what the culture of the World Trade Center was like before the attack, and what it was like to work there.

No one can own the whole city, but you can own your own experience of it; writing with the backdrop of such a big city, almost all the essays in this book—all writing, really—can be seen as a kind of declaration of existence. This is especially true of the essays in the "After" section. "I'm So Glad You're Alive," is the title of one of Elizabeth Grove's thoughtful essays on life in the immediate aftermath of the attack. "It feels so weird to be alive," is the unstated subtext of all the pieces here.

I want to acknowledge the hole in the middle of these testimonials that mirrors the hole in the city: we don't hear from the dead, obviously, and we

don't hear from those who were most directly touched by their deaths. For those of us outside of that circle, one thing we can do is to hold on to the memory of how those people died.

What the pieces all share is a human scale. New York here is not one solid mass of indifferent, haughty, buildings (or people), it is not a scroll of impossibly expensive items on a menu, it is not a symbol or even a skyline. It is a place where people live. The people compose the place, and the place shapes the people. Sometimes it dents them.

This book, a kind of greatest hits from the site, was almost finished on September 10. After an initial flurry of energy—I raced down to the vicinity and tried to interview people—I sank into a state of stunned inertia. The idea of running a Web site devoted to essays and reportage in New York at such a time seemed exhausting and beside the point. But in the days after September 11, stories and accounts began to pour in. The only thing to do was to post them. These in turn lead to more stories and testimonials and the site became, in its way, another of the small and not so small groupings of stories and pictures and candles and flowers that sprang up all over the city and whose presence was such a consolation in the days and weeks that followed. The best of these pieces, especially early on, shunned any effort to interpret; they were like black and white snapshots. As we all know by now, even the color photographs of Ground Zero were reduced to a kind of ashen, monochromatic black and white. And some of these pieces have that quality.

About two weeks after the fact, still feeling rather numb, the brim of my "editor" hat pulled down low, I received Debra Fontaine's short account of the debate inside her office, which was across the street from the World Trade Center, as to whether it was right to watch people jump to their deaths. Short, vivid, ferociously real, the piece was, for me, the moment when the abstraction of it all became personal, and my feelings surfaced with raw force. OK, I thought, back to the book, this time all World Trade Center stories. We certainly had enough. But then that started to seem wrong. We need to be kept close to the very moment, the day, when time stopped. It's an important place, somehow, the smoky, ashen interstice between before and after, the during. But we are still here—time doesn't stay stopped. It rushes forward, and, inevitably, as all the stories in this book make clear, takes you with it.

Witnessing

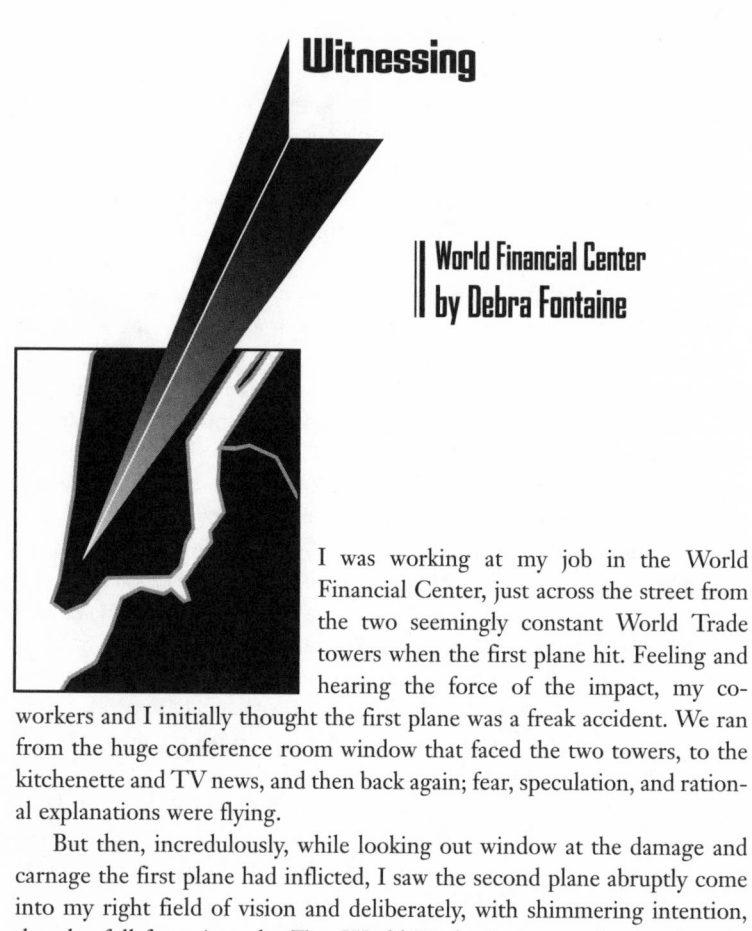

‖ World Financial Center
‖ by Debra Fontaine

I was working at my job in the World Financial Center, just across the street from the two seemingly constant World Trade towers when the first plane hit. Feeling and hearing the force of the impact, my co-workers and I initially thought the first plane was a freak accident. We ran from the huge conference room window that faced the two towers, to the kitchenette and TV news, and then back again; fear, speculation, and rational explanations were flying.

But then, incredulously, while looking out window at the damage and carnage the first plane had inflicted, I saw the second plane abruptly come into my right field of vision and deliberately, with shimmering intention, thunder full-force into the Two World Trade. It was so close, so low, so huge and fast, so intent on its target that I swear to you, I swear to you, I felt the vengeance and rage emanating from the plane.

Through that huge window and the space of the street between us, in those short seconds, its insanity seared me. It was completely overwhelm-

ing. I remember a tremendous, boiling, exploding ball of fire. I saw people jumping, falling, burning. My mouth agape, I stared at it all through wide, weeping eyes.

A co-worker said, Don't look, how can anyone watch this? But I ask, how could you not? How could you not watch these poor kinsmen, who unknowingly woke up damned that clear, beautiful yesterday morning, just hours away from a direction that no one could imagine, faced with an impossible final decision/fate: stay and burn . . . or . . . jump and fly?

Fly through a scorched sky engulfed in flames and smoke, debris and bodies . . . into a clear and cool, inviting blue sky with papers, papers languidly floating everywhere, a macabre ticker tape parade.

They deserved to be witnessed in their decision, their fate, in their final moment. They deserved to be witnessed in how they died, and to not be alone in that harsh, reeling, astonishing death.

We should all have witnessed them. We should all have stood at attention with not just one hand raised in a final, resigned salute, but with both of our hands at our throats, over our mouths, tearing our garments, making our own noises with their fall while we watched, and seen them, seen them, every last one of them.

The View from the WTC Plaza

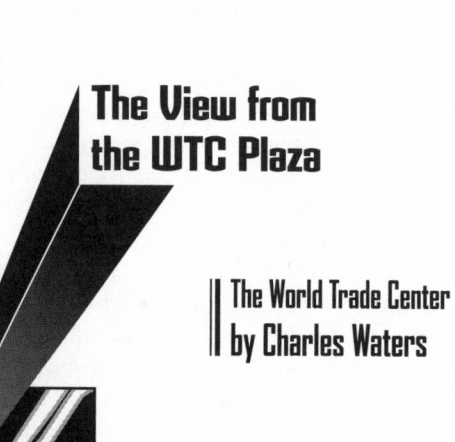

The World Trade Center
by Charles Waters

I worked on the fifty-fourth floor of Two World Trade Center. On Tuesday, September 11, I was on the plaza when the first plane hit Tower One.

Since Labor Day we had been very busy and the entire office had been arriving early for work and staying late. But Tuesday was primary day in New York and I decided to vote that morning, even though I was late leaving for work. Due to confusion at the voting center it took longer than normal.

I arrived in Lower Manhattan at about 8:38. Walking up Dey Street I decided to stop for coffee and walked across Church Street onto the plaza. I had called my father on my cell phone and I stood there talking to him, not wanting to walk inside while still on the phone. I took a seat on a bench right in front of Tower One.

"Dad," I said, "I gotta go. I'm on my way into the office."

"Okay, son," he said in his bubbly southern accent. "Call me this weekend."

As he spoke, I turned slowly, for no reason, and saw an airplane wing extended out from the building above me. An explosion. Then smoke. Then everything was frozen, very still, a perfect New York blue sky above a backdrop of explosions.

"Oh my God, Dad . . ." I was still on the phone, not realizing what I was saying. "I think . . . shit, a plane just hit the building!"

"What? Son?"

The phone went dead.

I ran when the glass and metal began to fall all around me. Only moments earlier, the plaza was full of people going to work just like me, but as I ran I saw nothing, no people, no cars. I made it across to Dey Street and into the loading dock of the Century 21 building. Then my phone rang.

"Where are you?" said my father. "Where are you going?"

"Dad, I don't know, a huge explosion, a huge plane hit the World Trade Center, I'm getting the hell out of here."

My phone went dead for the rest of the day.

On Broadway people were collapsing and crying. Much of this time is a slow motion blur. I remember a man screaming, "Fuck this, I've been to war for this country, not here."

From this position on Broadway I witnessed the first wave of people jumping from One World Trade Center. It is the most horrible thing I have ever seen. A doctor next to a group I was with fell to his knees, his stethoscope hitting the ground. Everyone seemed frozen and in shock. From there I heard but did not see the second plane hit Two World Trade Center. It sounded like a nuclear bomb.

At that point I began running north. At some point I looked back and saw Tower One's needle crumble to the ground and heard on blasting radios that both of the towers had fallen. I made my way to the Williamsburg Bridge and found my way home. Tens of thousands of people were walking across the bridge, a surreal exodus.

That Thursday afternoon I made my way back to the city. I saw coworkers and friends. The company I work for was extraordinarily courteous and compassionate with helping all of the employees. Seeing faces of others who had been on my floor was a real relief. For the rest of the day, I did very mundane activities like go to the bank, and go shopping—things that seem ed

very important in order to move past the events of Tuesday. I've met so many people who where just minutes from the building when the planes hit, everyone trying to reclaim some slice of reality by describing how they got out.

I never thought I would work in the World Trade Center. But I enjoyed my work there. Like all artists, I needed the money, but I also made many friends and learned a good deal about other parts of life, other skills that I never knew I possessed.

The views of the harbor were magnificent and inspirational. I remember ending long days by looking out the windows and feeling so very refreshed and glad to be in a city as beautiful as New York.

I always used to sign off my e-mails with, "Your Man in the Tower." But the towers are gone, and so many people have vanished with them. I have felt such anger and frustration recalling that day, more that ever in my life, but I know I will survive.

Don't Look Back

22 Cortland St.
by Kevin McLeod

September 11, 9:30 A.M. I was still nursing a baseball hangover from the night before. I had sat through a game that never started. Just as warm-ups were finishing, a forty-three minute downpour erased all hopes of watching Roger Clemens try to achieve the winningest percentage among twenty game winners. Everyone had huddled near the concessions, splitting peanuts and sipping Budweiser. Cops warned people staring at the bars across 161st Street that all exits were final. Then the skies cleared. We wiped our seats with newspapers, but an hour later the umps decided the field was still too slippery and the announcement began, "Ladies and gentlemen . . ." The crowd groaned, dispersed in silence. We climbed onto the Four train home.

Less than twelve hours later, I was on the same subway line, on a pre-work style run, on my way Century Twenty-one where a pair of wool pants by an unknown Japanese designer waited for me. The woman at the hold desk reminded me twice they opened at 7:45 and she'd keep them until 10

A.M. The Four train hit the usuals: Fourteenth, Brooklyn Bridge, and Fulton, where I oddly forgot to exit. Instead I jumped out at Wall Street, where instantly there was a change in tone.

Sirens were moving around above ground. Cops were running up the stairs. Running doesn't do it justice: they were *booking*, and the token clerk had turned his back to us, and on the phone. Upstairs was controlled pandemonium. Jayrunning was the rule. Cars were half-paused, heads pressed driver's side, cocked backwards, where up there, everywhere up there, was a wide path of dark smoke, lit at the edge with sun.

Adrenaline and urgency was overtaking Tuesday normalcy. I headed north. At sparsely treed Liberty Park, a few hundred Path train arrivals were massing, staring up in shock. Both towers were covered with shadows from their smoke. Bits of debris were slipping from behind the haze and curling earthward. Some people had cameras. They walked right by, not looking back at the towers, but pointing their cameras into the eyes of the beholders. One right at me.

I understood, they were gathering news sympathetically. What they had seen was more than enough, now they were reviewing what they had just felt, again and again in the eyes of those who had just rounded the corner and were taking it in for the first time. Gathering strength, or whatever, I decided that now was the time to join them and continue. I moved up Broadway instinctually, still not aware of the exact reason for the damage, but there was heat all over my ears: "the plane . . . fucking crazy . . . believe this, now where am I going . . . where is she, hey" and "no, no, no"repeated. A few men in dark suits were sitting on a bench. Gripping their briefcases. Cell phones were all up, straining for connections.

I stared ahead. Cars were not much of a problem. They were bouncing slowly against each other and people, who were now moving faster, were whirling forward. A woman walked by shrieking, she was trying to hold onto a coffee that was spilling. Maybe she had slammed into someone. I paused at every corner with a vista, trying to gather my thoughts, wincing, holding my jaw. Each view offered more proof, more suspense, more outcome. By Park Row, I had overheard enough: there were planes driven deep into the towers. Cops were now everywhere, confused, even arguing, "Run, Walk," one screamed, "Don't look back," yelled another, and everyone near him did.

There was plane debris in the graveyard of the church that everyone thinks is Trinity. I stood there looking at both towers, it was the final sight, just beyond the spire of St James. They were fighting gravity, furious, ablaze, ripped. Workers fell from the North Tower. A person behind me had just come from there. She was repeating a story about a man she had watched trying to slide down the ribbed exterior, but after a few floors lost his footing. She was alone and no one could look at her. Someone else whispered that she had walked by an arm.

Then a flood of conversation began. Witnessing was being shared. I looked back and the South Tower was belching more and more smoke. They came in puffs now, and other smoke species were appearing: a white mist was cascading down the floors above the pouring holes, hugging the exterior, a sign that extreme heat was baking the building. Shrieks followed every human plunge and only a few still looked. The sun disappeared behind the airborne carpet of smoke, then came back with a gust of north wind.

A minute passed. Sirens and fire trucks joined each other on Church street. Out of the corner of one of the towers came an eerie, glowing drip. First thought: welding. Firemen? Terrorists? My mind was already adapting to new century possibilities . A thick stream of molten office tower was dropping in five or six-foot long drips. Thor-like. When they hit plaza level they exploded in fireworks. You could see people running around below, dodging small heaps. The dripping glow increased and then there was a vast, heavy crack.

I blinked automatically. Its noise echoed, reverbed, built from a rumble into something louder, horrible, and the South Tower raced itself down. Vacuuming the air, the thick smoke came down with it, revealing naked blue sky instantly. And when the top floors fell inside the roaring cloud, we ran.

We ran screaming. We were still in a radius erasable by the tower. Face after face blurred, cops were grabbing the slower among us, their radios blaring: "It's falling."

We all timed a look back when we had a few feet in front and we saw the wall of vaporized concrete, and one by one we ran faster. Shoes! Slides, heels, slippers everywhere, and they were torn and beaten in the few seconds of escape. Those who knew how close the cloud was slammed into the

slower uneducated. Cars! Cars were left behind, various stages of parking and idling. I found myself on the entrance ramp to the Brooklyn Bridge. People had ignored pedestrian/vehicle segregation and were jogging to Brooklyn in the passing lane. I jumped a retaining wall and joined the northern group.

The Ashen Guy

Lower Broadway
by Thomas Beller

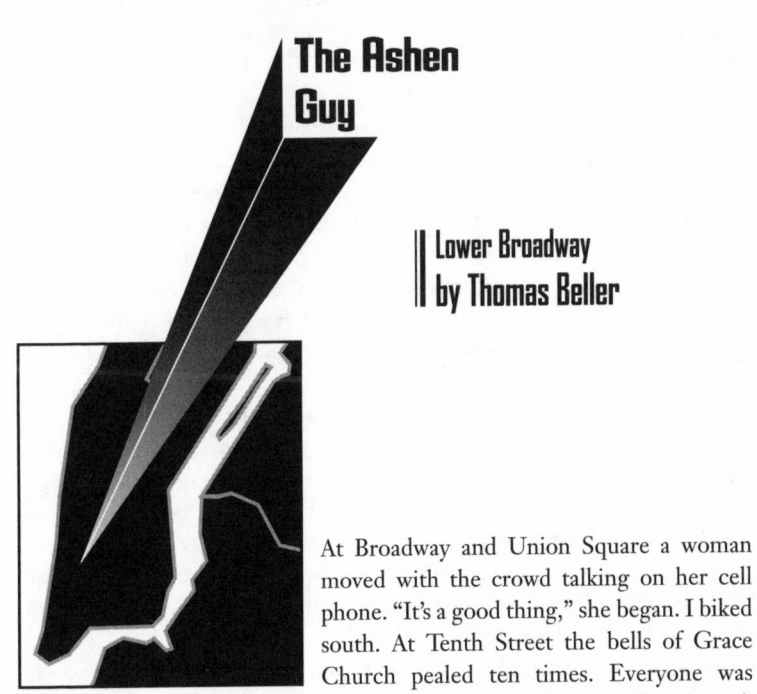

At Broadway and Union Square a woman moved with the crowd talking on her cell phone. "It's a good thing," she began. I biked south. At Tenth Street the bells of Grace Church pealed ten times. Everyone was moving in the same direction, orderly, but with an element of panic and, beneath that, a nervous energy. Their clothes were crisp and unrumpled, their hair freshly combed. Below Houston Street, a fleet of black shiny SUVs with sirens sped south, toward the smoky horrizon somewhere south of Canal Street. A messenger biked beside me. I almost asked him if he was making a delivery.

At Thomas Street, about six blocks north of the World Trade Center, the nature of the crowd on the street changed. There was more urgency and less mirth. Cop cars parked at odd angles, their red sirens spinning. The policemen were waving their arms, shouting, and amidst the crowd was a guy who had been on the eighty-first floor on Two World Trade Center when the plane hit. It was just after 10 A.M. Two World Trade had just collapsed, and

One World Trade stood smoldering behind him.

At first glance he looked like a snowman, except instead of snow he was covered in gray, asbestos-colored ash. He was moving along with the crowd, streaming north, up Broadway. His head and neck and shoulders and about halfway down his chest were covered in gray ash. You could make out a pair of bloodshot eyes, and he was running his hand over his head. A small plume of dust drifted off the top of his head as he walked, echoing the larger plume of smoke drifting off of One World Trade behind him.

"There were about 230 people on the eighty-first floor and I was one of the last ones out. We took the stairs. There was smoke, but it wasn't fire smoke, it was dry wall smoke and dust. The fire was above us."

He was shaking. His eyes were red from dust and maybe tears. He didn't seem like the sort of man who cried. He had fair skin and a sandy-colored crew cut. He was wearing chinos and Docksiders and his shirt was a checked button-down.

He was walking with the crowd, but his body language was a little different. Everyone, even those who weren't looking back, had about them a certain nervous desire to look behind them, to see, to communicate to their neighbor, but this guy had no interest in anything but in getting away from what he had just been. It radiated from every muscle in his body. To get away.

"I was almost out. I got down to the lobby, right near the Border's book store. And then there was this explosion. I don't know, I just got thrown to the ground and all this stuff fell on top of me."

By now he had dusted his head off and you could see his skin. It was pale and ashen, one of his eyes was very red. At first I thought maybe it was the dust and perhaps tears that had made his eyes bloodshot, looking closer I saw that one eye was badly inflamed.

He was joined by another man, a blue oxford shirt with a tie, mid-forties, lawyerly, who worked in the building across the street.

"I watched the whole thing. I saw the second plane hit, the explosion. No one told us to evacuate, and then the building just collapsed and I thought I better get out of here because my building could go too."

On Franklin Street the police were screaming: "There's a package! There's a package! Keep moving!"

They were herding everyone to the left, towards West Broadway. "People! Trust me! Let's go! People let's go! There's an unidentified pack-

age across the street!"

The view on West Broadway and Franklin was very good. One tower, gray sky billowing, the sky darkening.

"Do you know which way the tower fell?" a woman asked. A tall man stood behind her, scruffy beard and longish hair, his hand on her shoulder.

"It fell straight down!" someone said.

"Because we live one block away and . . . does anyone know which way the building fell?"

The man behind her, her husband, I assumed, had this very sad look on his face, as though he understood something she didn't. It was as if that consoling hand on her shoulder was there to make sure she didn't try and make a run for it.

"I don't know what happened," said the ashen guy. "I just hit the ground, don't know if something hit me or . . ."

"It was the force of the building collapsing," said the lawyer.

"I got up and just started walking," said the ashen guy.

There was a huge rumbling sound accompanied by the sound of people shrieking. Everyone who wasn't already looking turned to see the remaining building start to crumble in on itself, a huge ball of smoke rising out from beneath it, a mushroom cloud in reverse. The whole street paused, froze, screamed, some people broke into tears, many people brought their hands up to their mouths, everyone was momentarily frozen, except for the ashen guy, who just kept walking.

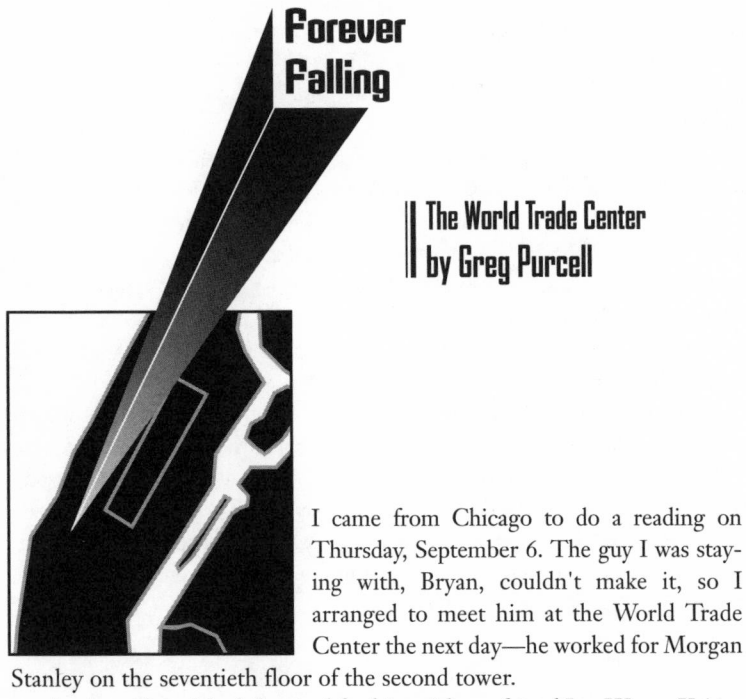

Forever Falling

The World Trade Center
by Greg Purcell

I came from Chicago to do a reading on Thursday, September 6. The guy I was staying with, Bryan, couldn't make it, so I arranged to meet him at the World Trade Center the next day—he worked for Morgan Stanley on the seventieth floor of the second tower.

At about five o'clock I waited for him with my friend Jay. We ate Krispy Kreme doughnuts and leaned on the black Noguchi sculpture. Eventually we were told by a perfectly polite security guard to get off of it, that there were plenty of nice benches around for us to sit on. The day was beautiful and we watched dancers rehearse for a performance in a large bandshell set snugly like a black catcher's mitt between the two towers.

Bryan came down late and told us that his stomach was upset. We went down into the concourse and he bought some Pepto-Bismol; we watched him drink it as if it were a beer on the plaza.

Eventually, he said, "Hey, you wanna come up and see my office?"

We followed him into the lobby of the second tower and received

passes. They snapped our pictures and then handed our faces back to us, dated and bar-coded.

He took us to his cubicle and showed us some of the brochures he had written for Morgan Stanley. "Getting your child into college can be a real challenge. Morgan Stanley can help." Stuff like that. The only decoration he had on his cubicle wall was a disciplinary action notice he had received in the fourth grade: "Bryan has trouble playing nice with the other children. He's a loudmouth. Very disruptive." He opened up his desk drawer, gave us a mildly conspiratorial look, and revealed about twenty-five half-empty jars of peanut butter, a few wadded bread bags.

"You guys hungry?" he asked.

The seventieth floor was completely deserted. We had run into a few security guards here and there, and one tiny Russian girl with ringlets in her hair, hugging an enormous textbook to her chest. She was on her way to class. Bryan took us into each of the corner boardrooms. They looked like boardrooms anywhere—grease pen boards with bits of half-erased information on them, little TVs and electronic devices that looked like video-game control pads sitting the center of the desk. But they gave us a 360-degree view of New York City and the view was beautiful. The three of us climbed up on the metal radiators and pressed our faces to the twenty-two-inch slivers of glass overlooking Battery Park, Uptown, The Brooklyn Bridge.

"Hey man, stand back," I said. "I'm going to jump over to the other building."

"I think you could make it," said Jay.

In another boardroom, I asked, "Does anyone live at Ellis Island?" I asked, Ellis Island being right under my nose, practically. From that high up, horizontal and vertical almost become the same thing.

"No, it's just a museum now. I went there last May when my Mom came to visit," replied Bryan. "It's pretty cool."

Eventually, someone asked, "What if the plane of glass just popped out while we were leaning on it?"

We all laughed but quietly stepped back a foot from the windowpane in question.

"You'd just fall and fall, forever," I think I said. Or else I just thought it.

By Tuesday, I was back in Chicago watching that very office collapse on itself on television. I was watching people leap from the merely hypotheti-

cal into daylight reality. I was thinking, maybe Bryan was in the stairwell . . . maybe Bryan was late for work . . . hell, maybe Bryan fell backwards into a locked strongbox with a parachute on it—anything—when suddenly my ability to rationalize Bryan back into life collapsed with the building itself, his tower being the first building to topple to the street.

I got an answering machine message from Bryan at about 6:30 that night: "Hey, Greg, it's Bryan. it's Tuesday, September 11. I almost died today."

I've still got that pass in my wallet. There I am, in the lobby, grinning: "9/07/01" it says. "2WTC."

Apparently, standing in the right place at the right time makes all the difference.

The Numbers

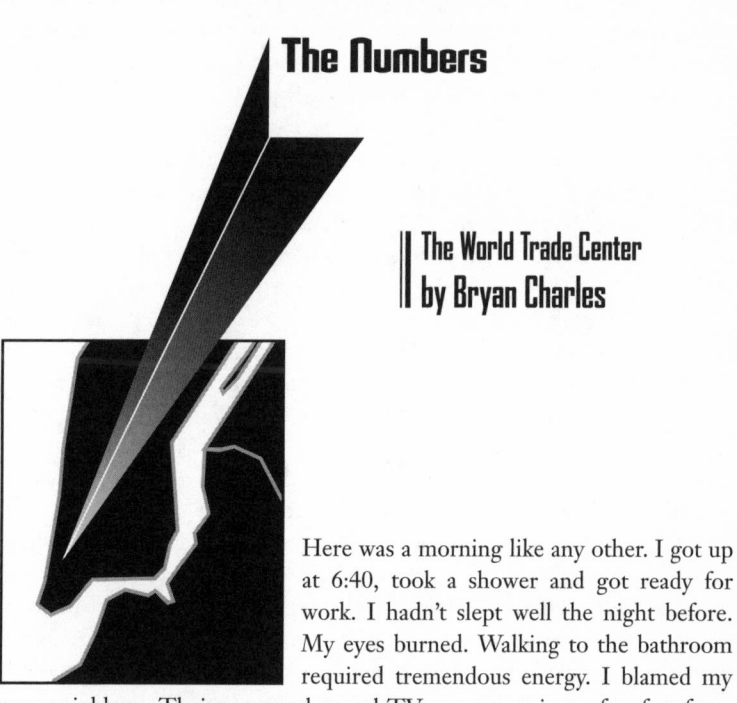

The World Trade Center
by Bryan Charles

Here was a morning like any other. I got up at 6:40, took a shower and got ready for work. I hadn't slept well the night before. My eyes burned. Walking to the bathroom required tremendous energy. I blamed my new neighbors. Their surround-sound TV was set up just a few feet from my head. The first two times I ever talked to them was to tell them to turn down their TV or stereo or whatever. Last night, I didn't have the heart to complain. I just lay in the dark and accepted it.

For several minutes after my clock radio had clicked on to Howard Stern, I contemplated calling in sick. It was a Tuesday. Nothing happens on Tuesdays. Whatever I was working on could wait. What harm could come from my sleeping in a few extra hours and enjoying the rest of the day? I could go out to breakfast, get some writing done, maybe take a walk.

But my boss was in Italy, on her honeymoon, and the more lucid I became, the more I reasoned that it would look bad, like I was trying to take advantage of her absence. I threw off the covers and got out of bed. As I

dressed, I half watched-half listened to *Good Day New York*, with Dave Price, the wacky weather guy, and Jim Ryan, the straight man. I went to the kitchen, opened the window and leaned out. My apartment was on the third and top floor. Laundry lines crisscrossed the little lawns and patios below. The tip of the Chrysler Building gleamed across the river. The sun was out, the sky was cloudless, the wind blew a little. It was a perfect day.

Outside, I took the B48 bus to Metropolitan Avenue, in Williamsburg, and caught a Manhattan-bound L train. At Union Square, I transferred to the N/R line which stopped right in the World Trade Center, where I worked as a copywriter in the Morgan Stanley marketing department. On this day, my commute was fast. The bus came right away, and both trains. I was walking along the concourse in the trade center by about 8:15.

Usually, I'd buy the *Daily News*, but not that morning. I was engrossed in a new biography of Kurt Cobain and wanted to finish it before nine. I was right at the suicide part, where the author reconstructs what Cobain might have been thinking before he pulled the trigger, what music he might have been listening to, et cetera. I did that sometimes. If I was near the end of a book, I'd sit at my desk and keep reading, reaching for random papers in an attempt to look busy whenever I heard footsteps.

I put my ID badge on the scanner, pushed through the turnstile, and got in one of the big cattle-car elevators that shuttled back and forth between the forty-fourth floor. A fact of working in Two World Trade that never quite became routine was that it took two elevators to get there. On forty-four were several other elevator banks, the second of which led to the seventieth floor, where I worked.

So much of life there was transport: the perpetual, maddening bling of elevators coming and going, escalators whose silver ridges approximated the façades of the towers themselves. Each day was a series of small surrenders to vast hidden systems of cables and electrical wiring and computer chips. Once, last winter, one of the elevators malfunctioned and either dropped a few floors or slammed into the ceiling. I think there were some broken bones. It made the news the next day.

Before heading up to seventy, as was my routine, I went down yet another flight to the cafeteria for a bagel and coffee. On my left as I descended was a new waterfall installation, two planes of thick glass pressed together as water illuminated by colored lights flowed between them. The whole

thing probably cost twice my yearly salary. Above me was a mounted TV tuned to some all-Morgan Stanley channel. The screen was cluttered with graphics, stock tickers and boxes from which the faces of analysts and other market experts telegraphed their daily predictions.

"Well, clearly this has been a rough couple of quarters for technology. But these kinds of shake-ups are all part of the game. We're in this for the long haul."

Each day I tried my best to ignore the looming presence of this TV. It reminded me of where I was, that I had gone to college to study creative writing and literature and now spent my days cranking out cheesy copy advertising about the need for careful planning in the pursuit of one's financial dreams. It reminded me that the short stories I labored over on evenings and weekends went unpublished while the brochures and newsletters I wrote enjoyed print runs in the thousands and millions. It reminded me that at an earlier time in my life I had played punk rock music and sometimes went weeks without washing my jeans, but was now outfitted in a corporate casual wardrobe purchased largely at Banana Republic, a wardrobe that rendered me indistinguishable from the thousands of other young men I saw pouring in and out of the World Trade Center every day.

That TV reminded me of a lot of things, mostly my own sense of failure. One thing it could not detract from, however, was the view.

On a clear day, walking past the cafeteria windows was like witnessing a live slide show. The Hudson River, the harbor, the Statue of Liberty, Governor's Island, Ellis Island, the tall ships on the Fourth of July. People spent their life savings and traveled from around the world to see what I saw every morning, five days a week.

Working for a multinational, multibillion-dollar financial institution may not have been my dream job, but being in that building every day sure was cool.

Out of the cafeteria, back up the escalator, into an elevator.

I had a whole car to myself, which was rare. I pushed seventy. The doors closed. The car went up.

By 8:30, I was at my desk, reading about Kurt Cobain killing himself.

When I was a senior in high school I wanted to be Kurt Cobain. A long time before that I wanted to be Jim Morrison. Both of these guys died when they were twenty-seven. Sometime during my Jim Morrison phase, I told a

teacher at my school named Ms. Schade that I wanted to die when I was twenty-seven.

"Why, because Jim Morrison did?" she said.

I said yeah. I was fifteen when I said that. Later, when Kurt Cobain killed himself, I thought, "Ah, twenty-seven, that's a good life. He must have been in pain." I was nineteen when I thought that.

On August 2, a little over a month earlier, I had turned twenty-seven.

I put peanut butter on my bagel. At work, I ate a lot of peanut butter. It was a cost-cutting measure. New York is an expensive town. Sometimes I'd have it for breakfast and lunch. In my cupboard, there were about ten empty peanut butter jars, all Skippy brand. I never threw them away. I always thought that one day I'd take them home and recycle them.

In the book before me, Kurt Cobain got ready to put a gun barrel in his mouth. I looked at the clock on my desk phone display. It said 8:45 exactly. I thought about changing into my work shoes and decided against it. (I wore sneakers to work because of all the walking I do. Kind of girlie, I admit. But New York is not the place to live if you don't like walking. Comfortable shoes are a necessity.)

A couple minutes later I heard a series of muffled booms. The floor trembled. It sounded like thunder, but closer. From where I sat, it had the odd effect of being both loud and not loud. One thing felt certain. It was very near. In fact, at that instant, I thought something was happening down the hall. I thought it was a bank of file cabinets falling over. Then a man from accounting named Leo Kirby started yelling. He didn't stop. "Oh my God! Oh my God! Oh God! Oh dear God!"

He was yelling so loudly that my next thought was, "Someone down by Leo Kirby is hurt. The file cabinets fell over on someone and crushed them." For the first time that day, I got scared. I stood up. Two guys I work with named Mark Sanford and Brian Whelan were by John Warner's office, staring out the window. I sat in a cubicle, gray walls, no window. I walked over. All I saw were thousands of papers flying through the air. Some of the papers were burning. My stomach dropped.

Mark cocked his head like when a dog hears a high pitch. "Hey," he said. He was looking out at One World Trade. "That building's on fire."

Whelan and I went to another window. There was smoke. He and I looked at each other. I could see over the cubicles, across the office, down

the hall. I sensed the chemistry of the air changing. It went from stale, recycled, artificially cold office air to something different, something I can't describe except to say it was alive. It buzzed like a high-tension power line.

Without realizing what I was doing, I went to my desk, got my backpack and walked to the hallway near the elevators, where people had already congregated. I knew a lot of them. Whelan was there, but the only other person I saw from my department was Lauren Wohl. A lot of people from the sales department were there. My friend Leslie was there. She had her arm around her boss, a woman named Zobeida. Zobeida was crying. Not very long ago, she had a baby. I saw another woman named Gail who also just had a baby. A woman from our department named Joanna just had a baby. I looked around and didn't see her. So there we were, standing around, not knowing what had happened. I thought of Leo Kirby's screams. We waited for an announcement but none came. The security guy didn't know anything. He was just standing up from his desk when I saw him.

"What?" he said when he heard the news. "Something happened to the other building?"

I looked at everyone but didn't register more than a blur of scared faces. A few minutes passed. Someone said, "Shit, the fire warden's not here. Where's the fire warden?"

But what difference did that make? The fire warden was just some cubicle worker. It's an arbitrary title they give out during fire drills. I could have been the fire warden for our floor and at that moment probably couldn't have recited my address.

More people rounded the corners and fell in with the group. I don't remember any one person suggesting that we get in the stairwell. I know I didn't say it. Probably it was a collective decision. All I know is that the door opened and we filed in. It was packed, two lanes, shoulder-to-shoulder with workers from the higher floors already making their way down. I looked at the sign by the door that said Seventy and took my first step. For a few minutes I was next to Julie Lin, from sales.

"Are you scared, Bryan?" she said, like she was asking if I were hungry.

I said yes and wondered if she was scared. She didn't seem like it. She said, "I've never seen you like this. Usually you always have something to say."

It's true. I was always joking, always goofing on having a big corporate

job. But right then I couldn't speak. My legs were crazy. My breath came in quick little gasps.

Then Julie disappeared and Whelan was on my right. Whelan was my best work buddy. He sat in the cubicle next to me and we spent whole days quoting from our favorite movies. *Fast Times at Ridgemont High*, *A Few Good Men*, *Just One of the Guys*, vintage Chevy Chase like *Fletch* and *Vacation*. We even quoted from *Kramer vs. Kramer*. He and I had a running joke about spending our days at a place that was ground zero for a terrorist attack. But that had already happened. The building had been bombed before. I was a freshman in college then. My mom picked me up one day and was driving me home to do laundry when it came on the radio.

What goes on in the World Trade Center? I wondered. *Who works there?*

I glanced up and saw Leslie walking with Zobeida. Zobeida was still crying, clinging to Leslie. I heard stories. People said that a plane had hit the side of the other tower. A plane? I pictured a tiny ten-seat propeller plane with a guy who'd just had a heart attack at the controls flying into One World Trade. A freak accident. A woman behind me was crying hard. Her red eyes radiated shock, sadness and terror. She talked to herself, and what she said was that she'd seen people jumping from the broken windows of the other building.

Around the fifty-ninth floor, there was an announcement. The whole line of people up and down stopped to listen. From behind the stairwell door we heard a voice on a loudspeaker. "There is a problem in building one," the voice said. "Building two is secure. I repeat, building two is secure. Please go back to your desks and wait for further instruction."

The voice repeated this message. Hearing that kind of comforted me, but not a lot. It comforted other people, I guess, because some of them turned around. I heard one guy say, "Well, fuck it, I'm walking all the way back up," like the whole thing was a big drag and he was annoyed.

You couldn't reenter every floor from inside the stairwell, so Whelan and I got out at fifty-five, I think it was. Lauren was there, in a big crowd. It was a weird floor, just white walls, no offices. It looked like a maintenance area, or some kind of telecommunications hub. People everywhere, roaming the halls. Tension and dread flowed through every look, every verbal exchange. A black guy came walking over, shaking his head, looking sad and tired. He said he'd just seen bodies, dozens of bodies, falling

from the other building, workers in the other tower leaping. "What?" someone said. "No."

A bunch of guys ran to look. By then I was almost as confused as I was scared. These people appeared to be telling the truth, but I couldn't believe it. I couldn't believe that anyone had jumped. It was too horrible to think about. Over the year and a half that I'd been working in the trade center, nearly everyone in my department had made at least one joke about jumping or falling out of the window on the seventieth floor. It wasn't possible to get through a work day without achieving at least a moment of consciousness about being that high up. And again, there was the view, always the view. From the corner boardroom where we had our status meetings you could see straight into midtown: the Empire State Building, the Chrysler Building, the Met Life building on one side; on the other was the Brooklyn Bridge, the East River, all of Brooklyn, on into the haze forever.

Whelan and I trudged past a cluster of people waiting to take elevators either up or down. I saw Lauren, but we got separated. Back into the stairwell.

A few floors later, maybe ten, maybe less, came another explosion. This one was loud. It was a sonic boom. The tower shook. I slipped down the stairs. People screamed and gripped the railing to keep from falling. The building, this enormous skyscraper, this national landmark, swayed back and forth like a child's toy, like a ride at the fair. A slow violent unreal rocking. This is it, I thought. Get ready to go down with the ship. My body and mind went numb. I didn't start praying, I didn't have visions of childhood, I didn't see my life flash before my eyes. I went into this white arctic zone of either acceptance or resignation or preparedness. I don't know what it was. I was blank. I was nothing. People screamed, they prayed. The screams and prayers merged into one.

"What the fuck is happening, Whelan?" I said. "Are we being bombed?"

"No," he said, "that was just the fuel tank exploding from the plane that hit the other building."

The building must not have moved like that for very long, maybe fifteen or twenty seconds, but it felt like forever.

There was a heavyset black lady about three people ahead of us, babbling an endless prayer. "Oh, please God," was all it consisted of. "Please Lord." She moved slowly, heaving her body from side to side, and I saw that she wasn't wearing shoes.

Whelan's face was tight and pale. Had he felt what I had a moment earlier, that we were experiencing our last seconds of life? I reached over with my right hand and squeezed his shoulder. The woman behind me sobbed. I turned around and touched her shoulder. I ran my hand down her back, over her sweat-soaked shirt. She didn't acknowledge me.

Sometimes the line stopped cold. Congestion on the lower floors. We'd be standing in the stairwell, not moving forward, with voices above us screaming, "No! Don't stop! Go down! Keep moving!" A moment or two of waiting, of agony, of wondering whether or not the people below were crushing each other to get out of the building, and then we'd go again.

Every few minutes I called out the words, "It's gonna be okay." I didn't believe myself, but kept saying it anyway. One time when the line was stalled, I turned to the guy behind me. We smiled weakly at each other and shook hands. The line started again. It was very hot, either from the fire above or body heat or both, and you could smell smoke.

After the explosion, life became a matter of watching the numbers on the signs in the stairwell get smaller. It was a long, slow process. Forty. Thirty-nine. Thirty-eight. Thirty-seven. Thirty-six. And so on. I couldn't tell how long we'd been in there. Time had vanished. There was no time. There was only descent. There was only counting and waiting and counting, circling around again and again. There was only concrete walls painted a grimy flesh color. Then we wound down the last ten floors. We came out on the plaza level and I looked through the big windows. Everyone did.

It was then that I realized something had happened that was far more terrifying than any of us had thought being blind and dumb in the stairwell. It was then that I realized the whole world was probably watching this on television.

The plaza with the fountain and the big gold sculpture and stage for summer concerts still set up was filled with large chunks of jagged burning metal and smoke and ash and debris. That was all you could see. It covered every inch of the ground and was still raining down. Car-sized hunks of the building, that famous sleek silver, lay burning twenty feet away. There were police and rescue workers there, guiding us. We circled around by the TKTS booth, past posters for famous Broadway shows. I saw Leo Kirby, the guy I'd heard screaming on the seventeenth floor. I said, "Did you see that?" He nodded but didn't say anything.

There was a long line for the inoperable escalator but we finally made it down into the mall area, with stores like Banana Republic, the Gap, J. Crew, Ben and Jerry's, Sbarro's and Border's. Everything was dark. There were no people except rescue workers and police and fireman. We filed past a jewelry store called the Golden Nugget. The girls who worked at the Golden Nugget wore tight clothes, a lot of make up and had bleach-blond hair. Where were they right now?

Whelan and I shook hands by the PATH train escalators. He gripped my shoulder and said, "You're pretty cool under pressure, there, Bry." I wondered what he meant. Had I been cool? Did I seem panicked? Should I have stayed behind and tried to help women, old people and the disabled? Could I have done more?

We took a right at Sbarro's. Another line at the escalator leading up to Borders, where I went every day at about three o'clock to read books and magazines for as long as I felt like it. When I looked down I saw Melissa Murphy, from sales, and Lauren Wohl and Julie Lin. I waved and smiled. Lauren waved back. The line kept moving. We went outside. The rescue workers shouted to turn off all cell phones. They shouted, "Don't look up! Whatever you do, do not look up! Just keep moving! Do not look up!" But I couldn't help it. I had to see. I turned around and looked up and there were the two towers of the World Trade Center burning. Fire and smoke poured from enormous black holes in both buildings. Real fire, giant lapping tongues of flame. The sky in the background was very clear and very blue. Crisp. Kodachrome. A postcard of someone's nightmare. It was the most terrible thing I had ever seen. Not even the movies had prepared me.

"Keep moving," the rescue people said. "Go up to Fulton to Broadway."

Dust and white ash blanketed the pavement. Fire engines, police cars, sirens coming from all around, a thousand displaced office workers. I saw bright red blood splattered in the street but not where it came from. A guy ran up with a little spiral notebook and said, "Hey, buddy, were you in there?" I nodded. He said, "Would you talk to me?" I shook my head and waved him away. The guy behind me started telling his story.

As I walked, I kept looking over my shoulder. It was all still there, still real, still happening. I never thought I'd live to see something that horrific, but there it was. I was talking to myself, saying, "Oh my fucking God, holy fuck, Jesus fucking Christ."

On Broadway, among the throngs of spectators, I found Lauren and Julie. The three of us went north. When we got to the Staples by Park Row Julie crossed the street and Lauren and I couldn't because there were fire trucks going by. I put up my finger to say to Julie wait a minute but she kept going. We lost her. Whelan was gone too. It was just Lauren and me.

Up by City Hall, I asked her what she wanted to do. She said all she wanted was to get away from the trade center. Her dad worked in the city, on West End and Sixty-fifth. She said she wanted to go there. I didn't want to be alone and I didn't want her to be alone so we kept going together. We stopped a minute later and asked this lady if Lauren could use her cell phone. She said yeah, but good luck because all the circuits were jammed. She was right. The phone didn't work. The lady was nice and smiled and said good luck as we walked away. I wanted to stop to try and calm down, and also look at the buildings because I still didn't believe what was happening, but Lauren said no. "Let's get out of here," she said.

By then we were at a weird angle and the towers were hidden. All you could see was the smoke. Soon we were on Canal Street, Chinatown, my least favorite part of town. It's always so crowded and dirty. We started east on Canal, in a futile effort to avoid the crowds. I saw the little storefronts with I Heart NY T-shirts and pirated CDs and a bunch of other junk that I don't know why anyone makes or buys. All the pay phones had long lines. We stopped and waited. There was a woman in front of me speaking Chinese into the receiver. She kept going on and on while I stood there. She didn't seem panicked or weepy. It sounded more like she was just shooting the shit. So I tapped her on the shoulder and said, "Look, I was just in the World Trade Center and I need to use the phone right now." She hung up and she and her friend gave me dirty looks and disappeared. Lauren was on the other phone, talking and crying, with her hand on her face. I think she was telling her dad or her mom that she was okay. I tried making a credit card call but the signal went dead. Lauren came over. She helped me dial and this time it worked. I punched in my credit card number.

My mom answered the phone in Galesburg, Michigan, in the house I grew up in. Her voice was very grave. "Hi, mom," I said. She started sobbing. I pictured the living room, the kitchen, our dog. I tried to imagine what my parents were seeing on their brand new big-screen TV. "Honey," she cried.

"Honey, it's Bryan." My stepdad got on the phone and he couldn't talk because he was so choked up. It was the first time I'd ever heard him like that. I'd only seen him cry once, about seven years ago. We were sitting out on the deck and he said he loved me and that he'd try his best to help me pay off my student loans. My parents were on the other line breaking down, freaking out, and I couldn't react to it. I was switched off. A part of me was still in that cold place I'd entered when I thought that Two World Trade was going to break in half and plunge into the street. I said, "Hello? Hello?" My stepdad said, "Yeah, I'm here, I love you."

Then my mom got back on and I said I had to go, there were other people waiting to use the phone. Lauren stood next to me, talking to a group of women, telling them about how she'd been in the building. I hung up.

We started walking again and I noticed for the first time that it was very sunny and hot. I had on a blue short-sleeved shirt and gray khaki pants and Nike sneakers. I had a backpack. We walked through some dirty, vacant side streets where there was nothing but workers loading restaurant supplies into greasy buildings. We went into a deli and bought water and I contemplated buying a beer.

Outside were thousands of Wall Street refugees walking north. It looked like the city was being evacuated on foot. It looked like a pilgrimage. It looked like a crusade. There were men carrying suit jackets who had sweated entirely through their shirts, ties loosened and fluttering in the breeze.

We came up through Astor Place. People were stunned and crying, wondering what had happened.

On Tenth Street we walked west and paused in the middle of Fifth Avenue, right on the center line. Two women asked Lauren for directions to West Fourth Street. They were like lost tourists who didn't know the city was burning. We looked south. There was the arc in Washington Square Park with One World Trade rising above it, burning in the distance. I thought that my building, Two World Trade, was behind the smoke.

Everyone stood in the street, numb and staring, and then it happened. One World Trade collapsed. A chorus of screams rose from the street. I reached for Lauren's hand and found it. A last glimpse of the antennae coming down and then nothing, no sound, just smoke and dust rising as it fell in on itself. It looked as perfect as if it had been wired with dynamite by a

team of demolition experts. What had taken all those years to build was gone in seconds. How many people had just been killed?

Lauren and I thought our building was still there, hidden in the smoke. I turned my head, in shock. A woman took my picture. When she lowered the camera I saw her tears. There was another woman standing next to me. I said, "But the other building's still there, right?" She shook her head and said, "No, they're both gone."

What? When the hell did that happen? And how long had I been out? Again I wanted to stop. I wanted to lay down on the sidewalk. I wanted to rest. I wanted to think. Or maybe I didn't want to think. I don't know what I wanted. But at least I wasn't alone. I was with Lauren. She was beautiful. Everyone I saw was beautiful in their grief and fear, in their just being alive.

We kept walking.

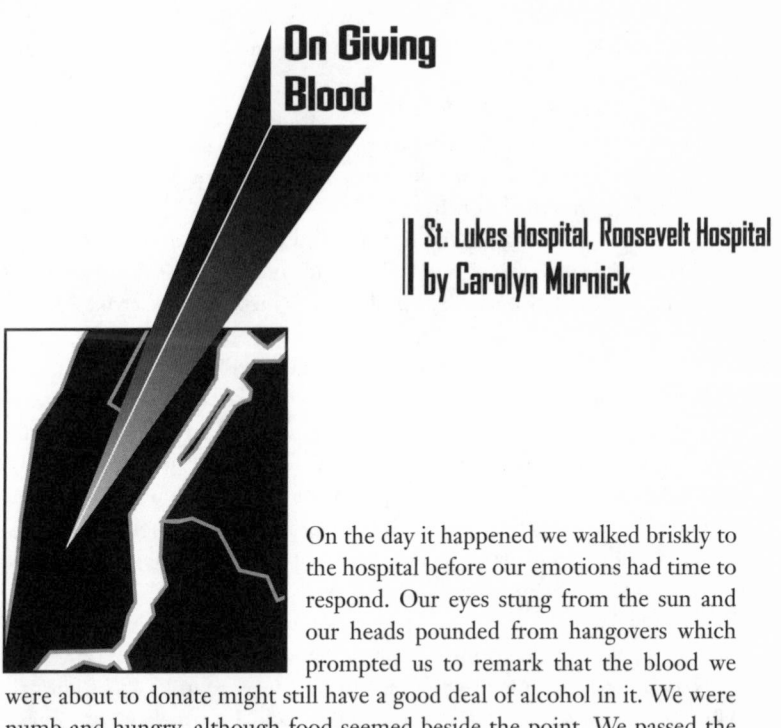

On Giving Blood

St. Lukes Hospital, Roosevelt Hospital
by Carolyn Murnick

On the day it happened we walked briskly to the hospital before our emotions had time to respond. Our eyes stung from the sun and our heads pounded from hangovers which prompted us to remark that the blood we were about to donate might still have a good deal of alcohol in it. We were numb and hungry, although food seemed beside the point. We passed the Cathedral of St. John the Divine whose bells were ringing a monotonous dirge.

It was about 10:45 A.M. There were gurneys lined up on the sidewalk in front of the hospital, and police mingling with EMTs and nurses. The scene was punctuated by the ubiquitous falafel truck that represented the only semblance of business as usual. Inside there were already about two hundred others waiting in line. They were mostly students. Some smartly dressed groups of girls, some reading textbooks. There were a few couples holding hands, and there was even an informal class meeting that had migrated over from campus. A scruffy graduate student type lectured on the Iliad to his

students in line. "And so basically when Achilles is saying, 'Fear not, but speak as it is borne in upon you.'"

The scene was disorganized and anxious but surprisingly quiet. A group of us were shuffled out into the hall to wait against one wall while another group was waiting up ahead. After about an hour we were given our first registration forms.

Have I used intravenous drugs?

Have I had sex for drugs or money?

Have I had sex with anyone who has had sex for drugs or money?

Have I had travelled in Africa?

We forged ahead, sitting and standing as the line inched along. We were headed for the "vital signs" line and I couldn't shake that acidic feeling in my throat. My pulse was racing. I couldn't tell whether it was a true sickness or simply the extenuating circumstances.

"Maybe you shouldn't do this," my friend suggested. "No," I said, "I'll wait for them to take my blood pressure and then decide."

In retrospect it amazes me that I even got that far given the disorganization and frazzled volunteers who struggled to usher an amorphous throng of about four hundred people through one of three examining room doors. At about 2 P.M. I was finally allowed to enter a vital signs room. Inside was a young medical student with curly dark hair and clear blue eyes. "Thank you for coming," he said.

I hopped up onto the crinkly paper covered table and he took my pulse on my left wrist (which turned out to be rather high—ninety-six) and then my blood pressure on my right arm, which turned out to be about normal. He then instructed me to go back outside and wait to have my finger pricked to be typed and tested for clotting.

When I emerged from the room, it was clear to me that the tone had changed. What had started as an amazingly helpful outpouring had unfortunately mutated into something overwhelming and ultimately counterproductive to the staff. A harried nurse came out and told us that there were really "just too many people here" and she urged us to leave our names and come back later and. "Only Type O's would be able to donate today."

My friend was Type O but I wasn't and I was envious of her. How much I wished I were a Type O! We all wished we were Type O's. The woman next to me said defiantly, "I'm an A but I'm staying anyway." We all wanted to be

stuck with a needle and we wanted to feel faint. We wanted to give something from our bodies and have it taken downtown. We wanted something
uncomfortable to happen to us because it felt like we deserved it.

I continued to wait, hoping for the off chance I would be able to get in
to be pricked since I had already done my vitals. As I sat in the same place for
an hour not moving, sucking on a frozen cup of hospital orange juice, I decided to give up.

I found my friend and we silently moved together across the street to
the building where they were taking the actual donations. There were fewer
people, about thirty or so had made it through the pre-screening. However,
by the end of the afternoon the number increased ten-fold because students
who were pre-screened earlier by the campus health services started to
arrive. There was an actual waiting room for us to sit where everyone was
glued to the TV. There was a table of food set up for us. It was a funny feeling—we were united in the familiar hospital waiting room purgatory, but
instead of being anxious, hoping for news about a loved one making it
through surgery, we were involved in a much different thing with little to
no promise of imminent resolution.

After about another two hours, around 4 P.M., my friend was called
down the hall. We waited in line outside the donation room and watched
three people giving blood as they focused on the mini TVs attached to their
chairs. There was again, a table full of food and another table full of hundreds of donation forms.Two nurses with glazed looks in their eyes sat
behind this table, answering questions with thirty-second clips like news-
casters waiting for answers through their ear-pieces.

It was unclear as to who would go next and the nurses seemed unable to
decide. I was sitting in the hall in a wheelchair and watching people beginning to shift in the line. "It's just so disorganized," one woman said to her
friend. "They were completely unprepared for this," said another.

Just then a young man of about thirty dressed in shorts and a T-shirt
came bounding down the hall and began shouting angrily at whoever was
listening, "I need to give blood today! Will someone get me in to give blood
now."

"I need to give blood now!" he said, raising his voice, "no one here
knows what they're talking about and everyone is telling me different
things. I am saying that I need to give blood now and no one can give me a

straight answer." There was accusation in his tone.

"Hey," said the volunteer, defensively, "we're all doing the best we can, you can just relax and I will take your name."

The argument escalated. I continued to watch from about ten feet away People around began to whisper; the feeling was not unlike the feeling just before a fight breaks out in a bar. I began to imagine what it would be like if something like that did happen—it suddenly seemed not so unlikely. What if all this futility—what if all this collective grief and guilt—what if all this inaction resulted in some kind of "mutiny-at-the blood bank"? I imagined hordes of snarling men tying up the nurses with gauze as the rest of us jammed syringes into our own arms as we amassed vials and vials of our own blood until finally we felt we had made a difference.

Finally my friend reached the front of the line. When she was about to be prepped with iodine, a nurse told her that she was ineligible due to the six months she had spent in England in 1999. "But I'm a vegetarian," she cried.

"I'm sorry," said the nurse.

We walked out slowly and silently. It was about 5 P.M. and still light outside. I had a feeling I could vomit tears—a feeling that had occurred intermittently throughout the day. Again I swallowed the emotions back just in time. "I'm sorry," I told her.

Something About Jack

Murder Ink, Broadway and 92ⁿᵈ St.
by Tom Cushman

8:30 A.M.

It's a slow morning like so many, in that I am running slow. I get into the bathtub, and turn on WCBS Newsradio. Downstairs I can hear my wife assuring our fifteenth month old that breakfast is fast approaching. And then I hear the unfamiliar sound of a plane about to fly into my house on Sullivan Street and Houston. Instinctively, I put my head down. When I realize that said plane appears to be heading for someone else's house I jump out of the tub and yell downstairs to my wife, "Did you hear that?"

"Hear what?" she answers between my son Jack's cries.

"There was a fucking plane about to crash into our house!" Incredulously, I ask again. "You didn't hear that?"

She explains patiently and politely that, between Jack's screaming and our two dachshunds barking she could scarcely hear the end of the world. Anyway, she adds, I am an idiot. I decide I am insane, get back into the tub, and turn the radio back on, thinking "Boy, it must suck to live by JFK." The guy on the radio says something about a fire at the World Trade Center. I

jump back out of the bath, and run downstairs yelling, "A plane hit the World Trade Center!" We turn on the television, and there it is; it is now on TV, so it must be true. "I told you!" I announce triumphantly.

My son, correctly, throws his bottle at me.

9:00 A.M.

I am now as clean as I'm going to get, and my wife, Melanie, has brought our son, completely covered in food, upstairs to try and attempt the same feat with him. I see a crowd of our neighbors has gathered outside watching the fire and I am struck by the fact that while I had to see it on TV to know it was real, it never occurred to me just look out the window. So . . . I look out the window. Jack is having an important conversation with his Elmo phone. Melanie joins me at the window in time to see a huge ball of flame envelope the second tower. "Jesus fucking Christ!" she screams.

"Fugginchrist" Jack tells Elmo.

Melanie asks me what we are going to do. Maybe she means in the grand scheme of things, but at that moment as head of the household I can think of only one way to meet this horror head on.

"Well, I don't know about you," I say, "but I'm going to work".

The world may be crumbling around us, but commerce marches on. My wife shakes her head in disgust. Jack is equally appalled, and throws his phone to the floor with such force it makes us all jump.

10:00 A.M.

We pick our way through our stunned neighbors downstairs, and, with Churchill-like calm, Jack waves to the people. Before leaving he addresses the faithful: "Bub-bye, bub-bye." From the corner we see that the towers are both pouring smoke. Everyone is looking up, yet strangely everyone is either standing still, or walking downtown, toward the World Trade Center. It's like we are swimming across a current. We get to the Houston Street train station and are told there are no local trains, go to Fourteenth Street. Back upstairs my wife asks me again why we are going all the way uptown to our bookstore to work. I press on with stupid determination. Melanie looks behind her, smiled weakly, and says, "Well, at least it's a hundred blocks away from here."

As we go up Seventh Avenue, people huddle around vans that have parked on the street blasting their radios. Two Italian girls walking downtown ask us where the Empire State Building is. I ask why. They say they wanted to go the World Trade Center, but . . . They shrug their shoulders.

Apparantly, any big building will suffice. Melanie suggests they try a muse-um instead. Sirens drown out the conversation, and the girls drift away. No one knows what is going on or what will happen next. Someone says they've bombed the White House and the Pentagon. As we pass Two Boots Pizzeria I expect it to just explode at any moment. The first ambulances are arriving at St. Vincent's Hospital as we try to make our way through the throng. As we go back down into the subway someone says a plane has hit Camp David. Jack is screaming "Peep Peep," in anticipation of seeing Thomas the Tank engine, or a subway train very much like him. I hope he is right.

10:45 A.M.

We are on the express train. Jack is demanding I read him his Thomas the Tank engine wordbook, but I am too interested in the conversation between two guys in suits and matching "get-me-the-hell-back-to-Long-Island" faces. They say eight planes have been hijacked. "Hey, little guy, whattya say?" they ask, suddenly aware of my son. Jack shakes his head emphatically, "No, no, no! Stow-ree!" Which is toddler speak for' you are messing with my thing here, now let's get back to the story.' And boy is he right.

11:30 A.M.

We get to the store. Our friend Jay, the owner, is there, standing in the middle of the room with all but one of the lights out. He says the first tower has collapsed . . . and everything stops. Something that has seemed so unre-al, something my brain has tried so hard to keep out comes crashing in. So many people are dead. I feel tears well up in my eyes. And just then I get hit in the back of the head with a ball. "Ball!" Jack says proudly. "Ssssh," I say, straining to hear the news broadcast. "BALL!" demands Jack, which I take to mean, "national disaster, yeah, whatever, but could you please throw me the damn ball, Dad." And I do, bouncing it to him, and he laughs, and I look at Melanie and for a second I smile.

12:00 P.M.

The second tower is down now. We try to open the store. The first per-son comes into the bookstore, and wants to discuss current events. I do not want to discuss current events with this guy.

"We're closed," I tell him.

The next guy comes in asking me to recommend some good mystery books. I do not want to do that either. "We're closed," I say.

"I came all the way from South Africa," he protests.

"We're closed."

"Why?" he wants to know. "National Security," I tell him, locking the door. I don't know where to go, but we can't stay here. Melanie's relatives somehow get through on the phones. They tell us to leave New York and come south. Well, I may not know where to go, but I ain't going there.

Jack is racing around the store, chasing Jay's dog, brandishing a roll of wrapping paper like a light saber, and yelling "Go. Dog Go!"

While we are packing up, an old woman starts banging on the window. "I need help!" she says. I run to the door and fling it open. "Where's your dollar cart?", she says accusingly, referring to the cart we usually keep outside the store with sale books. Jack falls and hits his head. "We're closed," I say.

12:30 P.M.

We start the long journey home, this time on foot. Again we are moving against the current; everyone is walking uptown as Melanie tries to negotiate the stroller down Broadway. The only cars are emergency vehicles. Everyone speaks in hushed tones. These are the only things we hear, sirens and whispers, punctuated by the odd roar of an Air Force jet that's gone by the time you look up. Melanie and I don't talk much, but Jack stands forward in his stroller and waves to the people. Occasionally, someone waves back.

2:00 P.M.

When we get to Fourteenth Street and Fifth Avenue you can really smell the fires, and I look up. And there it is. The smoke, heading off towards Brooklyn, and behind it, nothing. I am old enough to remember when those two hulking eyesores did not fill up the downtown skyline, but now they are gone. I went to the observation deck the first year they were open when I was ten, but Jack will not.

As we walk past the arch of Washington Square Park, just a few blocks from home, Jack throws his now empty bottle on the ground.

"Bub-bye! Bub-bye!" he says.

The Tourist

|| New York City
|| by Lauren Grodstein

Israel, Jordan, and the Sinai Peninsula suffered through a heat wave during the summer of 2000. In countries where July temperatures normally venture into the one hundreds, the phrase "heat wave" may seem like a redundancy, but nevertheless even the hardiest residents were miserable that summer. By the end of July, Eilat, the southernmost city in Israel, was regularly recording temperatures upwards of 110 degrees. Touching the pavement with bare skin resulted in second degree burns.

In Petra, the famed Jordanian archaeological site which was used as the hiding place for the Holy Grail in *Indiana Jones and the Last Crusade*, a group of American and Canadian tourists wandered around the old rocks and marveled at the Bedouins standing in the shadows, dressed in wool. "They are used to it," the Arab tour guide said. "The heat." The tour guide urged his visitors to buy bottled water from the Bedouins as selling water was the Bedouins' livelihood. The tourists hid from the sun in the ruins of temples and homes, and wished that they could see the site more clearly, but the

glare was leeching out color from Petra's famously crimson stones, and anyway, it was hard to stand outside without squinting.

Most of the tourists, after finishing their day in Jordan, were all too happy to board the bus back to Israel. Israel is, after all, a supernova of luxury compared to most of its Arab neighbors; even "modern" Arab states such as Jordan seem like little more than backwaters when compared to their relatively lush and wealthy neighbor. Israel has, in abundance, powerful air conditioners, public swimming pools, Italian restaurants, cold beers, and flush toilets. It has electricity and the Internet. Its women wear bikinis, carry guns, go to war. Ideologically (and unsurprisingly), it is as close as the Middle East gets to America.

However, one tourist was eager to see more of Jordan. A twenty-four-year-old Jewish-American graduate student, the tourist had never been to the Arab world before and was eager to explore as much of it as possible before returning to the relative safety and familiarity of Israel. She asked the tour guide to let her off the bus. "You are not dressed for this," he said to her, gently. She was wearing a t-shirt and shorts and had a bandana in her hair. She insisted. She gave the tour guide some money.

He sighed, and asked the driver to pull the bus over.

The town of Aqaba, in Jordan, is located on the Red Sea; Eilat shimmers Vegas-like across the water, and, if one looks far into the distance on a clear day, one can almost see the shores of the Sinai, in Egypt. The Jordanian government, which boasts friendly ties with the U.S. and a sincere desire to join the first world hopes to turn Aqaba into a genuine tourist destination. One can already find a few western-style hotels there, and even a couple shops selling alcohol. In an Arab Islamic country, these are no small things.

The tourist got off the bus in Aqaba and found herself standing alone in the shimmery afternoon heat. There was a pension across the road that the tour guide had pointed out to her; he would be staying there that evening and would be glad to show her around town, if she wanted. The pension seemed run-down, though, and the tourist thought it might be nice to check out one of the fancy hotels by the water. She began walking in that direction, but soon found herself scared to keep going. Men had stepped out of the surrounding buildings. They were staring. Some were hissing.

The woman tied her bandana over her long brown hair. "You are not dressed for this," she said to herself. The men continued to stare, some in

amazement, some in glee, but most with disgust. She turned and hurried to the pension that her tour guide had pointed out. Once she locked herself into a small, neat room, it occurred to her how little she knew. Around midnight, the tour guide arrived as promised and took the tourist out through the windy streets of Aqaba. With him, she felt more like a curiosity than an affront—men still stared but the tour guide brushed them off with a few words of Arabic. "What are you saying?" she asked him.

"That you are American," he said. "That it's not your fault."

He brought her to a rug merchant's and a magazine store, he bought her pita bread with lamb and showed her where to buy a long scarf she could wrap around her legs. The stores stayed open deep into the night, because the temperatures fell into the eighties and nineties and both shoppers and merchants could breathe. The tourist saw a few women, too, dressed in long black robes, heads fully covered. Some of them wore lipstick. A few of them were dressed in more modern fashion, and did not seem afraid.

At three in the morning, the tour-guide brought the tourist to the beach, where they sat at a table and ordered a hookah pipe and, as a special treat, bottles of Sprite. They sat quietly together at a plastic table and smoked from the hookah; they were surrounded by screaming babies, playing children, and even some men and women sitting together. There was a carnival feel in the air, as the hookahs burned sporadically, like fireflies. Soon the tourist heard splashing in the water, and then more, and then laughter heading in with the wind. Dark shapes like dolphins rose into the night and pitched themselves back into the sea.

"What is that?" the tourist asked.

"The women," the tour guide said. "They are swimming."

Dressed entirely in their chadors, heads still wrapped in scarves, the women laughed and swam together in the warm Red Sea. The tourist thought back to a few days previous, when she had suffered in a bikini in Eilat, surrounded by other women in bikinis, everyone being watched, free in some respects and shackled in others. The tourist knew that Jordan was a modern country, and she suspected that many of these women's peers in Saudi Arabia, say, or Iran, would be physically brutalized for swimming in public. But she also knew that there were possibilities for joy even in the strictest traditions, and that some women, at least in Jordan, could find freedom in the very rules that seemed to harness them.

As dawn neared, a strange man sat down with the tour guide and the tourist. In English, he said to the tourist, "I heard that you were here, and I am glad that you've come to see Jordan, but next time I must ask you to dress modestly and respect our traditions."

The tourist, sweaty and tired, wondered how the man knew she was there. She promised him that she had already learned her mistake, and that she would make a respectful return.

The tourist was no longer a tourist on September 11, 2001, when the World Trade Center was attacked. She was standing on the Brooklyn Promenade, a boardwalk which juts out over the East River, providing perhaps the best of all possible views of lower Manhattan. The tourist lived a few miles from the Promenade and had gone there that morning to drink coffee and watch the boats in the harbor. By the time she arrived, the second plane was pirouetting around the second tower. She heard the sound, saw the smoke, dropped her coffee. As both of the towers collapsed over the next hour, friends of the tourist died.

At no time have Westerners with even the best of intentions known how to respectfully engage with the Middle East. Westerners with the worst of intentions have never even tried. We have visited in our shorts, and sat tanks in their holy places. We have introduced products and values that they consider corrupt. We have supported tyrannical regimes, and we have funded guerrillas. We have done of some of these things because we think they are morally right, and some of these things because they suit our strategic needs. In the past, perhaps, we have been willing to engage in some debate about our course. But, as George W. Bush recently reminded us, there will be no more debate. Whatever hope there might have been for some brokered understanding between East and West crumbled with the towers. The foolish and fiery terrorists killed six thousand people and any hope for American compassion. After September 11, there will be no respectful returns.

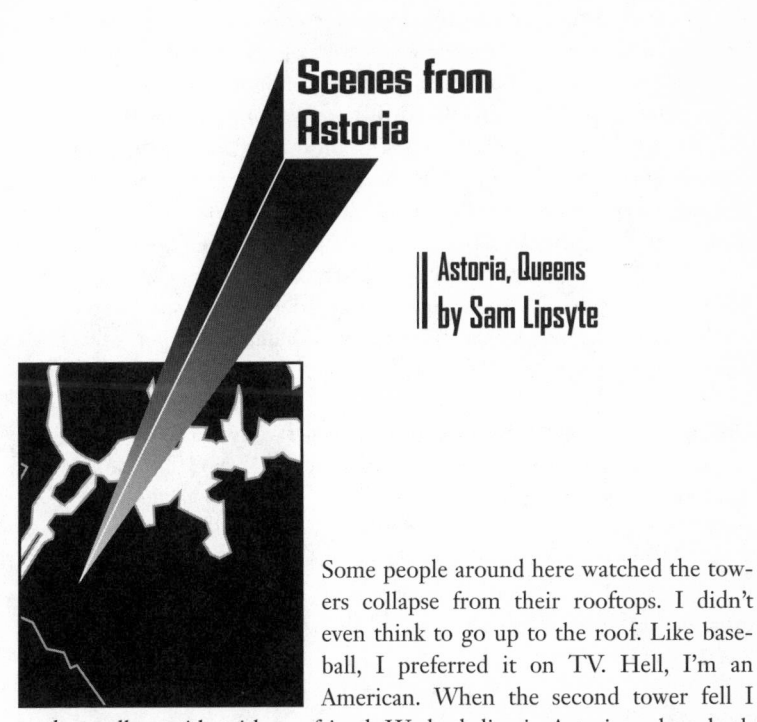

Scenes from Astoria

Astoria, Queens
by Sam Lipsyte

Some people around here watched the towers collapse from their rooftops. I didn't even think to go up to the roof. Like baseball, I preferred it on TV. Hell, I'm an American. When the second tower fell I took a walk outside with my friend. We both live in Astoria and we both work at home (well, he's a comedian, so it's more like he works at night). We walked around and babbled about the end of the world. I felt like I'd better buy a can of soup. My girlfriend was being sent home from work and who knew what mayhem was to come so I figured I'd better get a can of soup for us. Part of me wanted to buy a lot of soup but that felt disloyal so I bought one can.

Like a lot of people, I watched a lot of TV. Enough that I believe the shrinks on TV who say I have trauma from all the TV. I heard a car backfire and nearly dove into a bush. I feel myself on the verge of tears for ample parts of the day. My comedian friend said, "What happens when you bomb a nation of narcissists?" What happens is we tend to talk about our "personal experiences," like buying soup or being scared by bad mufflers.

Here in Astoria, Queens, you could smell it more than you could see it, that burning stench blowing up the river. You could make out the smoke, though. The smoldering. An exhausted reporter on Fox said he was "standing here in the rumble." Well, he was standing in the rumble, I guess.

People here have put flowers and candles out, but the mood is strange. No big vigils, no hippie sing-alongs. Just quiet sadness, a few laser-copied pictures of the missing. There's a big hand-drawn condolence sign under Ditmars subway stop from "The People of Cyprus."

The livery drivers have festooned their cars with flags. I don't blame them. I think about that Sikh in Phoenix who was gunned down yesterday. I guess that falls under the rubric of collateral damage, but whose?

The lady in the liquor store told my girlfriend that it was all so awful, just like when the U.S. lobs missiles into the Middle East. I guess that took some guts to say to a stranger. I walked by an Arab community center but it was empty except for a lone cop sitting outside, talking quietly into his cell phone. The night we all put candles out a bunch of kids with American flags came marching down our street. "This block is all Greek and American!" one of them shouted. I looked across the way at the apartment where an Indian family lives, at the Stars and Stripes they'd pasted in their window. Probably they were American, and probably they were scared. I watched all the candles flicker up and down the street, listened to the fighter jets scream overhead. I thought of all the dead, and all the people who were going to die. Then I turned on the TV and heated some soup.

This Is Bad

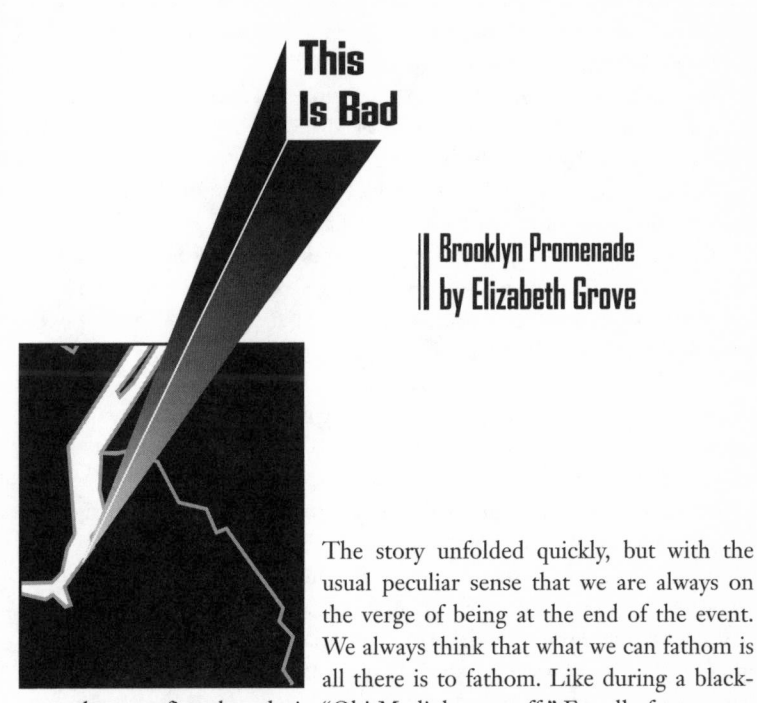

Brooklyn Promenade
by Elizabeth Grove

The story unfolded quickly, but with the usual peculiar sense that we are always on the verge of being at the end of the event. We always think that what we can fathom is all there is to fathom. Like during a black-out, when our first thought is, "Oh! My lights are off." For all of us yester-day, never has the notion that "all we know is all there is" proved so false.

There was a noise, but there's always noise in my apartment, and this sounded like a too heavy truck rumbling over hollow asphalt. The second noise shook the building, and was followed seconds later by the phone ring-ing. I couldn't hear who it was, but I could hear that call waiting was beep-ing while the message recorded. It occurred to me that I probably didn't want to be in the shower anymore. After all, if there was a "second" noise, some causal chain had been activated in my mind, and simultaneous phone calls at nine in the morning added links to that uneasy chain. But I thought maybe something had exploded in New Jersey.

The calls were from my mother and my ex-boyfriend, the former an

avid radio fan, the latter with an unobstructed view of the World Trade Center. He had heard the first noise and seen the smoke. For him there was no second noise because he saw the next plane bank directly into Tower Two.

"Paper," he said. "It looks like glitter and it's falling on my windowsill."

He said, "I'm holding a memo from 1998."

On the TV I had turned on, an anchor on Channel Two was speculating on an air traffic snafu, but she lacked my ex-boyfriend's conviction. "The plane went right for the building," he said.

A friend called then. "Hey," she said. It was the last time I would talk to anyone who hadn't heard what had happened.

But I got her up to speed. One plane would be a horrible accident, but no one was naïve enough to believe that two represented an exponential accident, so we agreed to meet on the Promenade, several blocks away, knowing already that we would be viewing the aftermath of a suicide mission. But the mind fills in the details the way it wants to and so we headed there thinking we'd see the work of two small planes flown by two suicide bombers. Not that we had a context for what that would look like, but that was the story we were going to see.

I walked down Montague Street to the Promenade. Brooklyn Heights is proud of its proximity to Manhattan and for its arguably best views of the Manhattan skyline. The star among that skyline, The World Trade Center, could catch the morning or evening light in all sorts of incredible ways. If you were on the Promenade, you were invariably feeling good about being in New York, and the view only increased that occasional feeling that you were, as mayors liked to tell you, living in the best city on Earth. On July 4th, if the fireworks are set off from the Seaport, there is no better or more crowded place to be than the Promenade.

It took a while to get there. The restaurants and stores on Montague Street were all getting their morning deliveries and small groups of people were huddled around the trucks listening to the radios. A block from the Promenade I stopped to hear the news that at least one of the planes was a hijacked 767. That meant people. People who had boarded a plane with only their usual amount of aviational apprehension. People who had known something had gone horribly wrong, but who, in the manner of all us on the ground, were probably just making up their story along comprehensible lines. Ok, they probably thought, this is bad. This is really bad. Where are

they taking us? And of course, only the ones of us left still retained the answer.

"My God," a man said, crying. "Those poor people."

I found Marian on the Promenade. She was holding her free Bloomberg radio that had seemingly been sent last year to every resident of New York City. "It finally came in handy," she said. "The Pentagon's on fire."

"Is it a coincidence?" I said, but I already knew.

"It's not usual for the Pentagon to be on fire," she said, as if I were about five. And in that split second before I asked the question I was that young. "Innocence lost" is a phrase about as overused as the Twenty-Third Psalm, and New Yorkers often seem to have little innocence to lose, but if innocence is the inability or the unwillingness to expand at the same rate as evil, then we all lost more innocence than we knew we had.

The towers were on fire. And it was bad. It was really bad. But I was surprised that the fire seemed—not contained, since it was clearly raging out of control—but limited somehow. There was still a lot of building that was clearly identifiable. Most of it was, in fact, in contrast to the smoke and flames that poured out of some upper floors like a particularly bad wound or abscess. And that is important because everyone, I'm sure, believed that as horrible as everything had become, there was an end in sight, a fire to be controlled, stories to be written, people to be grieved, repairs to be made.

When the tower went down it seemed to have the texture of sand you can hold in fragments in your hand before crumbling it like powdered sugar. Even as it happened, only a mile or so across the harbor, like some distorted mirage, like some bad video feed, there was the feeling that somehow it would stop. Somehow, our belief in structural integrity, in our lack of premonition, we could will it back to form, like some wacky trick film. In the screams and cries and oh-my-God's that filled the Promenade in that moment, in our almost kinetic pull towards the bedrock of Manhattan, there was the wish, the breath, the somatic strain to make it stop.

But it stopped at the bottom. And then it was beyond bad. It was beyond really bad. It was beyond anything we could imagine. And then we knew that there was no end to the story. We're designed for closure, perhaps a result of being born, living, and dying, perhaps a result of the twenty-two minute sitcom. It doesn't matter. When you stop being able to guess at any possible outcome, something shifts. And it shifts in particular ways.

One man, having just watched thousands of people die in front of him, strode down the Promenade, shouting, "Get out your uniforms, boys and men." A plane flew overhead.

"Why is there a plane?" someone asked. "There shouldn't be a plane."

But mostly there was a shift to silence and simply waiting for what unfathomable thing came next. The woman who had screamed loudest left the Promenade quickly. I thought about the people who must have been evacuating at that moment, probably telling themselves in the stairwells, OK, this is bad. This is really bad, but I'll keep going. I didn't know then about those who knew exactly how bad it was and jumped. Marian and I sat down on a bench together. We watched thousands of living people, moving like one entity, walking across the Brooklyn Bridge.

It was one of the only beautiful sights on a hideously ugly day. There they all came, Marian's husband among them, their backs literally to death and destruction, as they headed away. Of course, Marian's husband reported, it was no *Sound of Music* exodus, that they were sure the bridge was coming down when the tower came down, that there was a surge of panic and pushing from the back of the bridge. Still, he said, every car, every van, every bus going over the bridge, stopped at the pedestrian walkway and loaded up to capacity with passengers.

We didn't know that then. So we just watched the bridge from a distance until the smoke and ash and dust from the tower blotted out everything. And we left the Promenade then, to close windows, to try to get phone calls through, to wait for the smoke to clear so that we could see that there was nothing where there had once been something and know that even then there would be no end to the story.

The View From Long Island

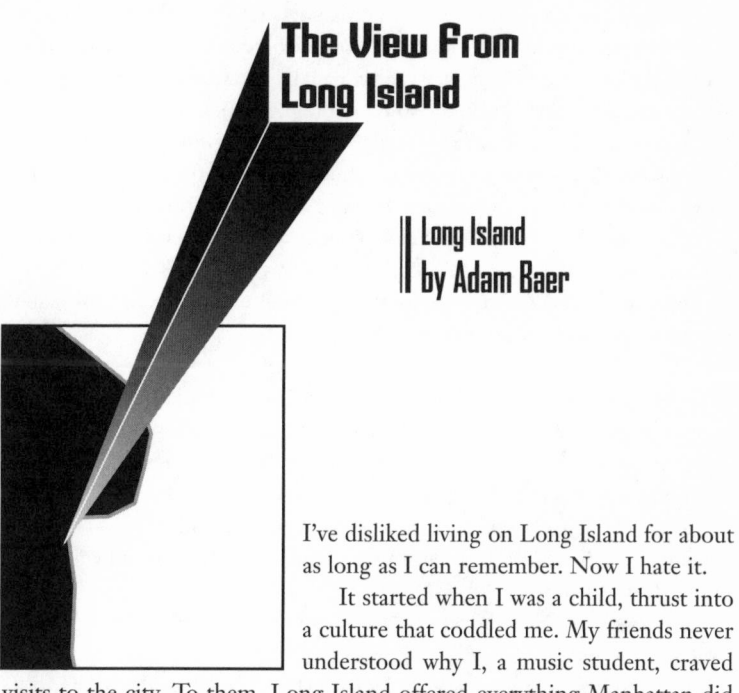

Long Island
by Adam Baer

I've disliked living on Long Island for about as long as I can remember. Now I hate it.

It started when I was a child, thrust into a culture that coddled me. My friends never understood why I, a music student, craved visits to the city. To them, Long Island offered everything Manhattan did with added bonuses: sprawling houses, trees, yacht clubs, beaches, and clay tennis courts.

But Long Island also offered something else the city couldn't, something which drove our parents to raise us here, something I'd taken for granted until now: safety.

I haven't been in Manhattan for over a week. I was supposed to travel in this past Tuesday for a job interview. Then my mother called at around 9 A.M.

"A plane crashed into the Twin Towers."

Immediately, I discounted her concern. My mother doesn't like to drive in the rain; my parents cancelled a trip to California this summer, fearful of experiencing a power outage.

Then, however, I turned on the radio, got acquainted with the truth, and, like a native Long Islander, averted danger, canceling my interview via e-mail before the second plane hit. I would not be putting myself in harm's way today, I said to myself. I'm not going anywhere near that city.

Some people—and rightfully so—consider the life of a freelance writer a boring one, an existence that doesn't make for riveting reflection. We awake, drink coffee, visit the gym, return home, check our e-mail, surf the Net, and finish whatever assignment we're currently working on.

The problem with that existence, though, the riveting nature of it, this time—living on Long Island and being a freelance writer who considers himself a New Yorker—is that I haven't been able to pull myself away from the one channel, CBS 2, my television currently receives. I haven't been able to stop viewing what I, and my locale, have sheltered me from. I watch all day and night. And I'm not planning to stop.

Like many people, I saw Tower Two leveled live from the safety of my suburb. And since, I've had a sharp pain in my left shoulder, right at its meeting-point with my neck, been short of breath, and mildly nauseated. Why? Not entirely because of the tragedy. Because I can't feel what I should about it, because I'm not there, because I can't really help.

See, I can't give blood (health reasons). I write about the arts and technology (not news). And I live on Long Island, to boot, a strip of land safely cut off from the city.

Am I still a New Yorker? Part of what's happened? Or a spoiled bystander?

I'm told not to donate food or clothes. The Red Cross doesn't need it.

So what's a guilty Long Islander to do besides donate cash?

My answer? Watch. Listen to the same information reported over and over again. Meet those who recount their escape. Force myself to experience the pain of my neighbors until my eyes give out on me.

It's a small price to pay for safety.

Maybe a Girl Who Loves the Ocean

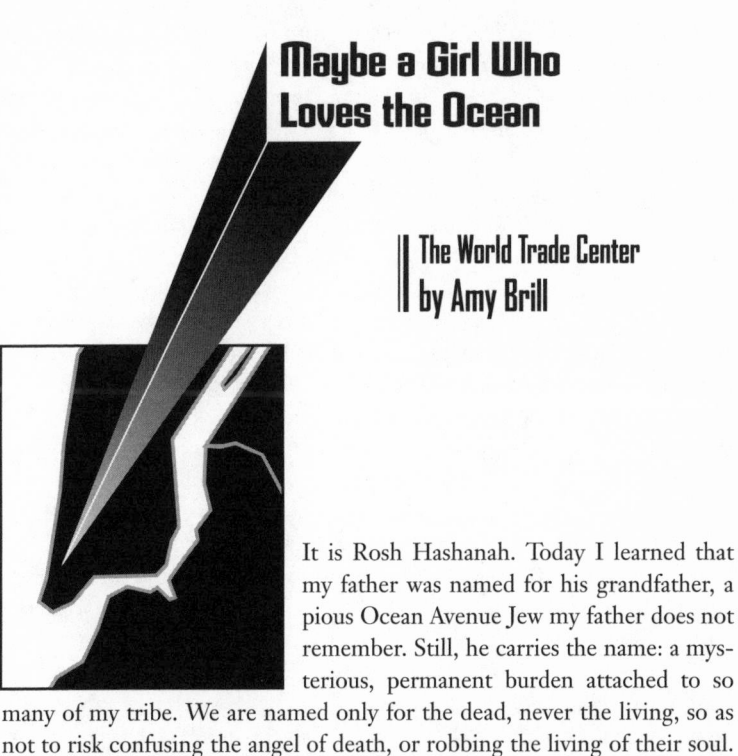

The World Trade Center
by Amy Brill

It is Rosh Hashanah. Today I learned that my father was named for his grandfather, a pious Ocean Avenue Jew my father does not remember. Still, he carries the name: a mysterious, permanent burden attached to so many of my tribe. We are named only for the dead, never the living, so as not to risk confusing the angel of death, or robbing the living of their soul. The many names of God—who is very much alive in this high, holy season in New York—are so sacred that we can't even say them out loud or print them in books. The names of the dead, on the other hand, are everywhere.

I try to talk to my brother about the devastation downtown but it is his position that bombing should be done, and if people in those countries to be bombed don't like it, they should leave and go to Tajikistan or wherever, and too bad for them and we wind up yelling at each other across the frontier of the family kitchen in Queens.

After dinner, my parents insist on driving me home to Brooklyn. We are no longer talking names, though I ache to whisper them as they come at me

from lampposts and fences and makeshift altars on corners, from television and the Internet, from newsprint and magazines: Gennie, Mario, Thomas, Marion, Lorraine, Brian, Gloria, Lisa. Michael. Touri. Klaus. Victor.

Our names are the first thing we learn to write, the last thing written about us: immortality is measured by the frequency of their distribution. Printed in bold type in the gossip columns, or in a caption beneath a glossy magazine snapshot; engraved on plaques and trophies and diplomas. But these names I'm reading are of the sudden dead, the spontaneously here-one-minute-gone-the-next dead, and with them come the dazed eyes and dull fingers of the ones who loved them, who miss them, taping and stapling and gluing them all over my decimated city, beneath the ominous and unseen roar of fighter planes overhead.

I am keeping them. The lists of names. Somewhere in my nest of drawers there is also a passenger list from Flight 103, downed over Lockerbie, Scotland. Also one from Flight 800 to Paris (I knew someone on that one). To this I will add these new lists of the dead in the Twin Towers, in the Pentagon, and on the airplanes that flew into them. It is mesmerizing work, conjuring the lives that went with them. Zoe Falkenberg: a girl with a witchy, magical name, daughter of liberals, maybe a girl who loved the ocean? Dan Shanower: cornfield patriot, loyal friend, passionate father to Dan, Jr.? Georgine Corrigan: a vivacious widow on a trip around the world? The firefighters, the officers, the EMTs, the bankers, the secretaries, the busboys. I am morbidly drawn in.

Weems, Williams, Bingham, Hansen, Olsen. I read what facts are known, study the faces on the posters and in the papers, but it is the names that stick. I think of the AIDS memorial quilt that passed through my university and how the grief that stitched the names of the dead into cotton and linen was somehow freed by the motion, the plummet and draw of the needle in and away, in and away, each gesture a tidal current, a breath. And in the end, a name, a blanket of remembrance.

I have a blanket in my head. Here are some of the names stitched in: Constance Coiner, my brilliant, fiery literature professor who died on Flight 800. Kendra Webdale who was pushed in front of a subway. Amy Watkins who was stabbed as she went home. The known and the unknown. A given, and a family. A first and a last. Letters like tiny sticks tilted this way and that, angles and crossbeams, aligned and ordered. Names are not words

like terror, murder, courage. Names are not ideas. They are markers of civilization, dominion over oblivion.

Around here, we are used to tripping over tongues, stumbling on the names of our taxicab drivers and our doctors, our shopkeepers, our neighbors and our friends. In this city, one door can lead to Bernstein, Picorelli, Singh, Angelopoulous, Martinez, Mohammad and MacDonald. The trail of knowing begins with a name. But now we who know better than anyone that a name alone is only a doorway to the vast corridors and haunted rooms of a human life—now we are left with nothing but.

When the lists are complete they will stretch the length of my arm, my body, my building, unspooling like ribbons of sorrow across the nation and the world. Already they are embedded in databases of Red Cross volunteers and printed on newsprint that will dissolve like the papers that flew from the towers and fluttered down like autumn early, crisped at the edges and bearing more, everywhere, more. A blanket of names like six thousand doors to rooms we will never enter, and it is this grief exactly, the blunt grief of an empty room, that I feel as I go down the lists and try to remember as many as I can.

Why do I study them? What am I looking for? Maybe it is an act of atonement, a way of appeasing the guilt of gratitude, for everyone that I know is, miraculously, still alive. Maybe it is a way to concretize, humanize the generic dead by affirming the human instinct to be recognized, to be known, which is to say, to matter.

Some of these names, I know, will return to my lips next week during Yom Kippur, when it is time for the mourner's kaddish and I am asked to remember the departed of the past year and to utter their names before the gathered congregation. A small token: the shape, the taste, the song of a name. It is not nearly enough, but it is all that is left to offer.

Profiteers and Souvenirs: An eBay Story

‖ Morningside Heights; eBay
‖ by Debbie Nathan

I don't tell many people about the eBay thing.

I usually just do the easy version. Like today—four weeks later already—I walked into the salon and when the Dominican beautician who does my hair asked where I'd been (you know that question: "So where were YOU when it happened?") I already knew my answer would sound significantly more noble and tragic than the stories of people who'd been drinking coffee in their apartments in Astoria, but less so than people who worked right in lower-lower Manhattan, or, God forbid, had loved ones in the towers.

I told him about my fourteen-year-old son being a student at Stuyvesant High School, five blocks from the site, about how the kids were ordered to evacuate and minutes later my son was running up the West Side Highway for his life. About how my daughter, a student at Cooper Union in the East Village, was looking out an upper-floor window and saw one of the planes go in, and she noticed little particle-like things falling, then realized what

the particle things really were. I told my beautician how I'd been en route to LaGuardia to get to Houston, where my dad had just suffered a heart attack, and how I'd seen the smoke from the M60 bus going over the East River, then ended up dragging a small suitcase on wheels all the way back to Manhattan, on foot, across the Triboro Bridge. About how my son spent the first two hours thinking I'd taken off, and he didn't know the hijacked planes were going to Los Angeles, not Houston. How I kept going into bars in places like Jackson Heights so I could see TV news, and the news kept saying the kids had left Stuyvesant just before the towers went down, and I was crying in the bars because my cell phone was dead and maybe my son, too.

My kids actually found each other after my son ran from falling Tower Two. They walked uptown, to where we live near Columbia—five or six miles at least from lower-lower Manhattan, and every few blocks they'd purchase a World Trade Center postcard. That night they addressed fifteen of these cards and stamped them. On each one they wrote: "World Trade Center destroyed 9/11/01. Tower Two fell at" and whatever time it was, to the minute. Then the same for Tower One. I'm not sure what this was all about. Were they trying to freeze history? To hunker down, like little ants in amber, in a place where, even if they couldn't move, at least they were still around? They mailed all the cards to themselves.

Which brings me to eBay.

Next day—Wednesday—my son and I went to a tourist shlock store around Forty-seventh and Broadway and bought World Trade Center butane lighters and World Trade Center key chains. Thursday I took the subway to Twenty-eighth Street, where the Koreans have those shops that sell everything by the dozen, and street vendors normally load up on Teletubbie key chains. Now there was no "normally," and the vendors wanted different goods.

"I need more *FLAGS*, man," said one disheveled man to the shop owner.

"We got no mo flag," the latter answered.

"Mother fucker, I need more fuckin' FLAGS!"

"Get out my sto, you. Out!"

"Fuck you motherfucker!"

Me, I skulked around politely and found a cache of little plexiglass "snow" cubes filled with water and groady, plastic renditions of the World Trade Center, but instead of snow they have demented-looking plastic coins

that, when you shake it up, rain down like luck on the towers. I bought three.

We had about $25 worth of this stuff and suddenly it occurred to me: "Hey, let's put it on eBay!" "Hey yeah!" said my boy. Where did we get this idea? Not from a wish to make big money, surely—our asking price for the whole lot was about $35.

I don't know quite what our motives were. But in normal life, my son is a busker. After school he goes underground at Columbus Circle with his viola, music stand and a few pages of Handel, parks himself on the downtown side of the Seventh Avenue Local stop, and plays for hours for quarters. He makes something from the city, and the city makes something of him. "Busker" has become his adolescent identity: he loves it more than anything. Now he was afraid to go into a subway station. But I think he still needed small change—New Yorker change—to feel human.

As for me, I wonder if it had something to do with Sholem Aleichem? I've been diligently studying Yiddish, and two days before the eleventh had made a pilgrimage to his grave. It's in a hoary Jewish cemetery in Queens, one so dense and chockablock with tombstones that it looks like the ghost version of a shtetl. When Sholem Aleichem died in 1916, at least 100,000 people trailed his coffin through the streets of New York, walking briskly but somberly—just as other people walked on the Triboro Bridge when I passed them with my suitcase on wheels. Right before the eleventh I was reading Sholem Aleichem's autobiography—when translated from Yiddish, its title is "From the Fair." He and his adoring, immigrant public were well acquainted with the feast-day bazaars of Eastern Europe: where Jews, peasants, Polish lords and Tsarist bureaucrats claimed their places in the world by bargaining over everything from silks to horses, to a handful of moldy potatoes. "Life is a fair," Sholem Aleichem wrote in his first chapter. "Going to the fair, a person is filled with hope." Now I was afraid to go anywhere. Yet I had the Internet. And a veritable cyber-fair: eBay.

But eBay kicked us off. We'd never done this before, so first we had to go through the registration process. Click, click. Address. Zip code. Visa number. Expiration date. Then a prim, small-font message scolded us about not respecting people personally affected by the tragedy and ordered us never to come back to eBay. Not longer after, articles in national newspapers denounced the likes of us for our perverted attempts to profiteer off other people's misery.

These days there's World Trade Center memorabilia for sale everywhere in New York. Massive reprinting from Hong Kong, assembly lines working overtime in Indonesia. Posters with the gleaming, innocent towers. T-shirts, postcards, plates, more postcards—all manufactured after the eleventh, but you wouldn't know that unless you knew that all this was very hard to find by nightfall of the first day. To know, you'd have to live here. If you did, you'd be of a mind where the big, national questions linger. But where small, local ones do too, even when they're hard to figure out.

The Scene at Union Square Park

14ᵗʰ St. and Broadway
by Alex Abramovich

Sandwiched into the fourteen blocks north of Houston Street and south of Fourteenth, Greenwich Village and the campus of New York University have formed a sort of demilitarized zone, patrolled by both civilian and military police. Below, access is restricted to officials and rescue workers. Above, New Yorkers move freely, and the city returns to some semblance of normality. Between, entry is limited to residents, and only those on foot. Businesses are half-open, papers blow, and ash covers what cars remain. A New Yorker's lizard brain can't help but notice the empty parking spaces, but the only cars moving are rescue vehicles. State Police, many of whom have traveled hundred of miles to be here, man the border's blue NYPD barricades, chatting with tourists, checking resident's bags and IDs. The shifting winds carry a strong stench of burnt plastic.

Union Square Park was distinguished first by its history as our municipal meeting ground, later by a vast subway station and stunning view of the Twin Towers. Millions have gathered here into it to celebrate (the end of

every war since 1863), demonstrate (the nation's first Labor Day parade was held here in 1882), and grieve for the dead. Tuesday morning, hundreds here watched the Towers collapse. Tens of thousands have come since, and the smell of sage and incense fills the air.

The first vigil was organized (barely) Wednesday evening by a nineteen-year-old Sarah Lawrence student whose web site listed "not getting into Wellesley" as his "greatest emotional scar." Together with other students, Jordan Schuschler taped thirty-foot long sheets of brown wrapping paper to the ground, laid out boxes of crayons and markers, and formed a huge circle of hand-holders. Those around it were invited to speak, though few could think of anything to say. The square stayed eerily quiet, the outpourings confined to paper:

Express Yourself—Be Part of The Cure

Act II: The Miracle

God give us Strength Give us Peace Grant us Freedom Shower us In Love

NYC/USA: Please don't attack Arabs. We all bled and cried on 9/11

By midnight, so many had gathered that the initial circle broke down into smaller groups of thirty or forty people, and heated arguments broke out. In one corner, a tall, redheaded Irishman stood nose to nose with a young African-American, shouting "I was born in Belfast." In another, two African-Americans engaged an Israeli in a heated debate over Palestine. "We offered them Gaza," he replied. "We offered them the West Bank." "Exactly," one of the black men said. "Who are *you* to offer?"

But most of those gathered were students—a hundred thousand live around Union Square—many of whom had left home only a week earlier. These were the same teenagers you saw at WTO rallies, and they'd brought the same arguments. "Five corporations control the entire media," one man said. "It's important that each of us make our voices heard." Perhaps for the first time, they'd run into people willing to argue with them, and if many seemed under-prepared to debate Palestinian relations with orthodox Jews (of which quite a few had gathered), or capitalism with bike messengers (who revealed themselves as strong and surprisingly well-informed supporters of the free-market economy), most rose to the occasion. The groups fractured and reformed, conversation ebbed and flowed well past two in the morning. "Please," Schuschler had said past midnight, as others shushed the

masses. "The police are watching us from across the street, and they're ready to storm us. Please, please keep it peaceful." But the police, in fact, seemed nowhere near storming. And even the screaming matches, of which there were many, never posed a threat of genuine violence. "No one inside this place hurts or touches another," a pierced, pink-haired girl said. No one was about to.

One block away, on Sixth Avenue, the flyers with missing family members had started to appear.

Twenty hours later, the crowd had grown into the thousands. Thursday evening, a group of Tibetan monks gathered in the park's main field. "The Tibetan people have a strong commitment to nonviolence," their signs read. "We pray that New Yorkers will find the strength in their hearts to come through this difficult time with a deep spirit of compromise, tolerance, love, and patience." Flanked by hundreds of New Yorkers, they chanted, sung Tibetan hymns, and led the crowd in a few choruses of "We Shall Overcome."

The original rolls of paper—now overflowing with pleas for peace, expressions of outrage and sympathy (many of them in foreign scripts), and drawings of the Twin Towers—had been covered in sheets of clear plastic, but hundreds more had appeared. People navigated not only the crowd, but the paper covering thousands of square feet of ground in the park. Men, women, and children, many of them sobbing, knelt down and read:

I know how you feel about your parents and I am sorry. Dear kids who lost there parents I feel bad because if I was to lose my parents I would be thinking who would take care of me? I am safe where my family loves me but you see I don't love my father because he said something that hearted me when I was younger. So I know how you feel to lose your parents you lost so much.

Dear Stacey, It can never be the same. I pray you are safe, happy, and smiling. We can't understand what has been done, but we can remember. You will never be forgotten. I will always love you, my future wife. I can still hear your voice. Forever, BK

A teacher at Park Slope's school for Law, Journalism, and Research put up dozens of drawings by seventh and eighth graders, some of whom had lost aunts and uncles in the explosions. At the edges, kids on skateboards and dirt bikes performed the kind of tricks you need hours of practice and

pliable bones to pull off. Cars draped in American flags cruised past. A young Brooklyn woman dressed in a *Ghostbusters* T-shirt had been standing to the side since four, playing Irish tunes and Scottish laments on the bagpipes. At 8:30 she packed up her instrument. "I can't donate blood," she said. "They don't need more volunteers. But the bagpipes have always been an instrument to boost morale and pull people together."

By 9:30, thunderstorms beckoned, and dozens began rolling up the papers. "Careful to cut only the tape," one organizer directed. Another passed out leaflets reading "WTC MEMORIAL WILL BE PRESERVED! The words and pictures of the thousands of mourning people of our city are being preserved and will be shown in schools, museums, and community centers throughout the city, the country, and we hope, the world. Please help us by treating each panel with care and respect." When I asked him who the organizers were, the man passing out flyers looked confused. "I don't know," he said. Just students." "Who are you?" I asked. "Just a student."

Most of the panels, including all the originals from Wednesday night, were taken to P.S. 1, a gallery complex in Long Island City, for safekeeping. Many were lost. The thunderstorms rolled in at one, dousing thousands of candles still lit in the park, scattering the crowd, and hampering rescue efforts taking place less than a mile away.

Don Delillo and the Twin Towers

Times Square Subway Station
by Vince Passaro

Last week ABC and Ted Koppel had on a panel of authors to comment on what has happened to our city and our world—the always-awful Maya Angelou, the cliché-laden David Halberstam, and two better sorts, NPR-favorite Bebe Moore Campbell and Jonathan Franzen. Whether it was Koppel's general density or the facts that proved too much for them no one can tell, but they added little to the available pool of wisdom.

There are a couple of authors whom we suspect *could* add to the available pool of wisdom on what is happening right now, but they won't be invited to do so, at least on ABC. Gore Vidal is one, because he is able to speak honestly about the specific sins of American foreign policy; Don DeLillo is the other, because he alone among living American writers has made a career of understanding the fragmented narrative of modern violence. His 1979 novel, *Players*, was about a bombing of the New York Stock Exchange; his next book, *The Names*, centered on violence and terror in the Middle East; *White Noise* covered "an airborne toxic event"; *Libra* did the

Kennedy assassination; *Mao II* was about the relationship of terrorism to art. Finally, *Underworld* took in all of these, in the way of the masterpiece, and moved long-legged across the landscape of violence and waste that characterized the twentieth century. They are stark, haunting, prescient works.

As for what he might say about the past week, you can look in the archives and get the idea. He once was quoted as saying, for example: "People who are in power make their arrangements in secret, largely as a way of maintaining and furthering that power. People who are powerless make an open theater of violence. True terror is a language and a vision. There is a deep narrative structure to terrorist acts, and they infiltrate and alter consciousness in ways that writers used to aspire to."

Told last week, in the aftermath of the Trade Center attack, that his name was on many people's lips, DeLillo said simply, "Well, I wish it weren't."

Last night, a friend called me. He is a newspaper reporter and was stationed somewhere down in the new military zone that has been created south of Canal Street.

"I only have one thing to tell you," he said, after we'd talked for a while about the events of the day, Giuliani, Bush, Osama, etc. "I just called to say, have you taken a look at the cover of *Underworld* recently?"

The image came back like lightning: I went out to the hall and pulled the book from the shelves, and there it was: the two towers, dark and enshrouded (by fog, much as they had been by smoke early last Tuesday morning). Before them stood the stark silhouette of the belfry of a nearby church (perhaps Trinity, or St. Paul's, down Broadway; perhaps the now-partially-destroyed St. Bernard's, I don't know the churches down there well enough to say); and off to the side, a large bird, a gull or a large pigeon, making its way toward Tower One. It's eerie and religious. At first DeLillo, after finding this picture, thought it altogether *too* religious, according to his editor, Nan Graham at Scribner. A photo researcher was hired to find an image for the cover of the book; she came back with the same image DeLillo had found on his own. In the context of the past week, the image is deeply disturbing, one more bit of testimony to his remarkable tuning.

And then this morning, on the way to work, in the mini-plaza beside the new escalators in the Times Square subway station (which are occupied in normal times by musicians and painted humans, posing as statues and the

bizarre guy who tangos with the lifesize rubber woman-doll), I came upon a memorial site. The square, tall, tiled columns (roughly similar in shape and relative dimensions to the towers) now host the many flyers of the missing, and people were gathered in threes and fours around them, reading them, or perhaps a better word would be "internalizing" them. We are, we readers, obstructing the shortcut from the One line to the R line (neither of which line now runs the One or the R trains at Times Square, but that's another story). We read them for all the desperation and grief that they reveal; we do it as a salve or a food, I can't tell which, for our own sense of desperation and grief.

Flowers and candles surrounded the bases of the columns—it would have been difficult to imagine in our past life how a flame of any kind would be a welcome sight in the Times Square subway station, but there they are, and we find them welcome. They add a religious air to the place, inescapably.

Much of New York in its reaction to this enormity of death has shown itself to be far more religious than we had ever imagined it to be, far more religious in this first week than patriotic. Later, on the BMT platform, a man is handing out small volumes, well-printed and perfect-bound, the complete Gospel According to St. John, the one that opens, "In the beginning was the Word, and the Word was with God, and the Word was God." It is the most poetical and abstract of the four Gospels; and it is surprising how many of us on the platform are taking the books from him rather than waving him off. They are shiny and of a size pleasing to the hand.

But—down the platform a bit a woman is reading a physically larger book, an older hardcover. I cruise by. I have a professional interest—or so I always tell myself, in the face of my obvious and occasionally intrusive voyeurism—in what people are reading on the subway.

It is *The Names*, by Don DeLillo.

Cosmetics Plus
(and Minus)

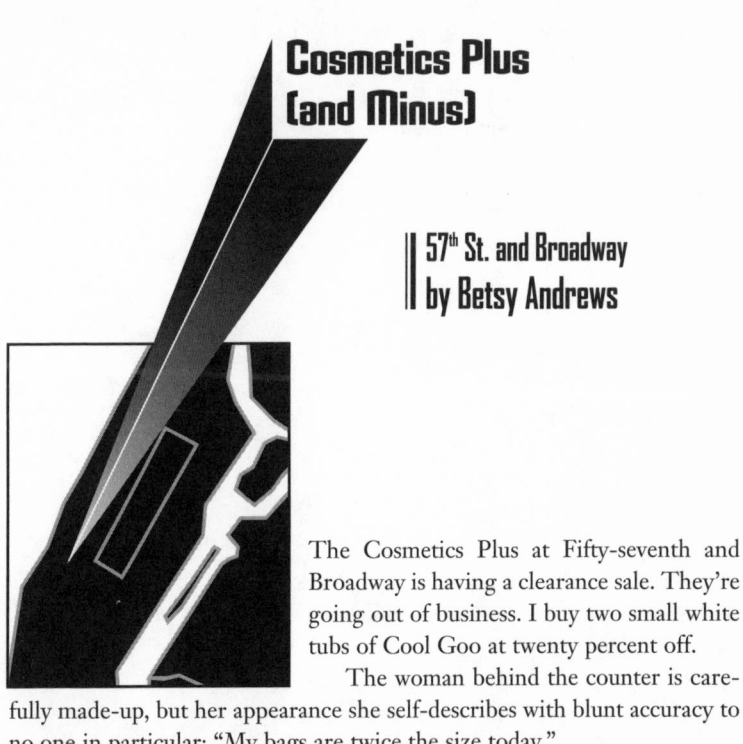

57ᵗʰ St. and Broadway
by Betsy Andrews

The Cosmetics Plus at Fifty-seventh and Broadway is having a clearance sale. They're going out of business. I buy two small white tubs of Cool Goo at twenty percent off.

The woman behind the counter is carefully made-up, but her appearance she self-describes with blunt accuracy to no one in particular: "My bags are twice the size today."

"It's been hard to sleep," I say to her. "It's just a haaaard time," she says, drawing out the word. "Ever since the Trade Center," the place itself standing in metonymically for the event, "I'm up half the night."

"That's where I worked," she tells me. "That was my job. On the mezzanine. They transferred me up here, and now it's closing."

"And your family and friends?"

"I lost like six customers I used to see regularly. They're all dead. And one of my close girlfriends."

"I'm so sorry," I say.

"First that. And all this war shit. And now this damned store . . ." She

walks away to the other register to rummage for something, to get me a bag.

"Is there anywhere else they can place you?" I ask.

"They're closing all the stores. The entire chain. Shuttered. Here you go, Sweetheart." She hands me my bag. "It's just been a haaaard month."

"Well, good luck to you," I tell her.

"Thank you," she tells me. We look each other in the eyes. We smile. Sadly. "It's just been a haaaard month."

God Must Be an Octopus

The West Village
by Dorothy Spears

We were walking to school, my two sons and I. It was their first day back since the World Trade Center attack last Tuesday. So instead of sending them with the sitter, Dona, I naturally wanted to be with them. The weather was eerily beautiful, as it has been all these days. Alex, who is eight-and-a-half, and Ferran, who is five, were holding my hands on and off, or holding my purse, or touching my elbow as we crossed the street. It was as if I was practicing being close to them, then letting go. Their conversation was light and chatty. We were smiling and I felt brave. We are going to school. We are getting back to our routines, our lives. There are more American flags than there were before, observed Alex. I looked around. It was true.

At the corner of Hudson and West Eleventh Alex said, "This is exactly where my foot was when we heard the plane. I was stepping down, like this."

He was referring to the first plane of last Tuesday's attack. I had not been with them Dona, the sitter, had told me afterward, how they'd seen the

plane flying very low overhead. Then a few seconds later, they'd heard the crash and seen the smoke. We'd both shared a moment of appreciation of Alex's typical perceptiveness. "I'm never going to fly in an airplane again," he'd announced. At the time, they—we all—had assumed the crash was just an isolated event, an accident.

In any case, I knew this had happened, that my sons had seen the first plane. And I had repeated the anecdote, along with Alex's dour pronouncement umpteen times. But repeating, it turned out, was just a way to keep the horror of it at a distance, out in the air, instead of letting it sink in to a place where I really felt it. Maybe part of our need to tell our stories is to keep the pain apart from us.

On the other side of Eleventh Street, Alex said, "This is where we heard the crash." From outside the Bleecker Street Park, where they play in nice weather, they'd seen the first signs of smoke. "Where?" I said, looking backward, squinting, trying to locate the exact view. "We can't show you," said Ferran, impatiently. "The World Trade Centers aren't there. The plane touched the cloud. Then it turned into smoke."

We crossed the street. On Eighth Avenue and Greenwich, the spire of the Empire State building began poking out as it always does.

Ferran said, "Is the Empire State Building the new highest building?"

Children are quick to remind us how little we know. Was the Empire State Building third, after the two towers? I was slow to answer. "It may be the highest building in Manhattan," I said. "But there are other higher buildings in the world."

Last Wednesday, the day after the World Trade Centers collapsed, the boys' grandmother, my mother-in-law, died of cancer. We left the city to be with family in Connecticut . At the funeral on Monday I read to a packed church of fellow mourners (for my mother-in-law was the longtime publisher and owner of the local newspaper, and also, with all due respect to her, people were in the mood to mourn.) From the Book of Revelations, I read " . . . He will wipe every tear from their eyes. Death will be no more." (At this I started crying.) "Mourning and crying and pain" (I could no longer see the words) "will be no more." Anyway, you get the picture. I came on with a strong finish, according to anyone who cared to tell me. Meanwhile it seemed to be all about the second coming. Death and crying and mourning were no more, because we were no more. In any case, I didn't believe it.

Yesterday there was no school, because of Rosh Hashanah. As I was walking up the steps of the school on Fifteenth Street, I realized the last time I'd been to the school was their first day of school. A week ago Monday. Everyone had been exchanging hugs, greetings, bits of news about their summers. Today no one looked sad. They were just passing through the doors, nodding and rushing as usual. Everyone else's first day back had been last Thursday. I thought maybe what I was feeling was something they'd already gone through.

In any case, it was upsetting to bring Alex and Ferran back to where they'd been at the time of the attack, to say goodbye to them as usual. Those hours last week when they were at school and I was wondering if they were all right, if we were all going to survive this—it was all still so fresh.

In the lobby there was a miniature model of a city, our city. I had never noticed it before. On one end were a lot of tall silver buildings, with two that stood taller than all the rest. "Look Mom," said Ferran. "The World Trade Centers are still here." His voice, like Alex's when Alex had observed the American flags, was matter-of-fact. They're fine, I thought. Meanwhile, look at me.

It was Ferran's turn to be dropped off first, as the boys informed me. He went straight into class, through a group of parents, one of whom turned to me, "Dorothy, where have you been?" he asked.

"We've had a death in the family—"

"Oh, I'm so sorry—"

"It was nothing—related," I said quickly. "Their grandmother. She had cancer."

"Well, I'm glad to see you back. We've been worried about you."

Ferran had told his teacher either about his grandmother or the World Trade Centers. "I know, I heard," the teacher was saying sympathetically, "Well, we're happy you're back."

"We saw fifty soldiers," said Ferran.

"I know," said the teacher, looking at me, as if for guidance. "The city has changed hasn't it?" I started to tell her about the day before how Ferran and Alex had stood by the West Side Highway waving American flags and thank you signs and shaking the hands of firemen. One child had asked about a certain fireman, and when his mother said, "God took him to Heaven," the child's brother put in quickly, "God must be an octupus."

Ferran made himself comfortable at the playdough table. "Bye, Mom," he said.

I couldn't say goodbye. "I'll come back and say goodbye," I said, "After I drop off Alex." On the way up to Alex's class, we ran into Alex's best friends' mother. "I'm so sorry," she said to me. "I heard." Then she glanced toward Alex. "I'm so sorry about your grandmother."

Alex was sweet, formal. "Thank you," he said, graciously.

Alex's chair was on his desk. "Well, finally," said his classmate, Xavier. "Where were you?"

"Connecticut," said Alex, quietly.

"Canada?" said Xavier, disbelieving.

"No, Connecticut," Alex repeated. Yesterday he had wanted to take a picture of his grandmother's coffin to show his class. But now he didn't want to talk about it. I asked Xavier to please show Alex anything he'd missed while he was gone. Xavier led Alex around the room. Alex returned to his desk with a work sheet and a pencil.

"Bye, Mom," he said.

"Bye, darling," I kissed him. I took two steps away. Then I stopped.

"Bye, Mom," he repeated, without looking at me.

"Bye." I was standing near the door. "Bye, Mom," he said.

"Bye," I said. "I love you." On the way downstairs I was bawling. "Hi," I said to one mother whose kids are friends of my kids. Then I passed another mother, a lingerie designer whom I hardly know. Turning my face to the wall, I kept walking. Ferran was still at the playdough table when I returned.

"Here's a piece of pizza," he said, handing me something worm-like. Then he looked up at me.

"Why's your face red?" he asked, in a voice part accusation, part humor. "Why does your face always look like that?" He sounded fed up. Another mother looked at me and smiled demurely. "Are you sad?" asked Ferran, sympathetically. "Because of the World Trade Center?" Without answering, I ran to the bathroom.

Part of me thinks kids are better at handling trauma than we are. They just accept whatever this world—what we as parents—give them. The world is what it is, we are what we are, however troubling or horrible this may be.

For parents, dropping our children off at school, saying goodbye, is an expression of unspoken faith, our ability to do this being a tacit way of say-

ing they will be safe. My difficulty in doing this reveals my struggle. Will life will go on as usual? Can it? I have been told, by World War II survivors, mostly, that it can, and it will. Still we all have our moments, and this was mine. Just as it was hard to believe that "Death will be no more; mourning and crying and pain will be no more," it was hard to believe that the world right now is any place for children.

I got over it. I had to. Anything can happen, I told myself. I just have to remember: this has always been true.

Of all the hours of TV I watched over the last week, the thing that really got me—that still gets me—was the thought of children in school receiving news of this attack. Children who had parents who worked in the World Trade Center shepherded to guidance offices or in other ways singled out. Children evacuated from the schools further downtown, finding their way through smoke and rubble. How I wished when I saw the first tower dissolve into ash that my own children were with me. How much safer I felt when I heard my husband's key turning in the door, the boys' familiar footfall signaling that we were finally together again in our home.

My crying among the kindergarteners, I knew, was not helping matters. I had to get out of the classroom. When I sat back down with Ferran, he was still making pizza. "Bye, sweetie," I said. "I love you. I'll see you later." I roughed up his hair. It was already matted.

"Will you pick us up sometime?" Us meaning him and Alex. I said yes, but not today, I had work.

"Okay," he said, agreeably. "Maybe someday. Like when the babysitter is sick." There was a pause.

"Daddy picks us up sometimes." He was talking about last Tuesay.

Out on the street, I saw the lingerie designer at a distance pulling a tissue from her pocket. Maybe she had a cold, but I don't think so. Another mother from school was speaking animatedly with a father. When she saw me, I think she noticed I'd been crying. She did a double-take. It was as if, like me, she was relieved to find another mother's face as red as hers.

A Grand Candelabra

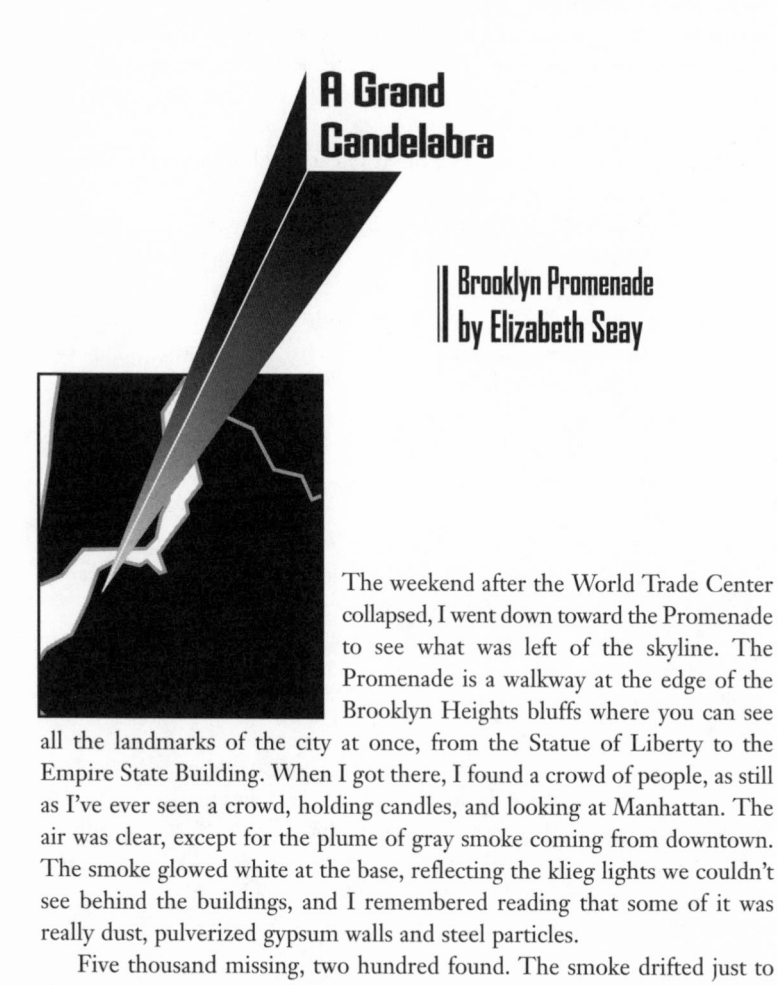

Brooklyn Promenade
by Elizabeth Seay

The weekend after the World Trade Center collapsed, I went down toward the Promenade to see what was left of the skyline. The Promenade is a walkway at the edge of the Brooklyn Heights bluffs where you can see all the landmarks of the city at once, from the Statue of Liberty to the Empire State Building. When I got there, I found a crowd of people, as still as I've ever seen a crowd, holding candles, and looking at Manhattan. The air was clear, except for the plume of gray smoke coming from downtown. The smoke glowed white at the base, reflecting the klieg lights we couldn't see behind the buildings, and I remembered reading that some of it was really dust, pulverized gypsum walls and steel particles.

Five thousand missing, two hundred found. The smoke drifted just to the south, but it had been hitting us in the face for days. Sitting near a window of my apartment on State Street, I'd watched a charred bit of paper, thumbnail-size, land in my lap. As the sun set, our eyes were drawn to lights—those of the now-empty office buildings of downtown Manhattan,

the police boats sitting on the water, the fighter jets veering overhead, and the candles everywhere. The Promenade's iron fence had become a grand candelabra, with candles stuck on the points. Some candles left long stalactites hanging from the railing. Some were down to wicks sucking up their reflecting pools. Here and there, they were grouped into shrines on the paving stones: red and white candles; a few blue candles; fat little votive candles; tall slim dinner-table candles; candles in tumblers marked for "*yarzheit*," the Jewish anniversary of the day of a death; a candle in a coffee cup that said I (heart) NY; candles in rainbow layers like the kind children make at cam; a candle in a wax-paper cup with peace sign; a candle picturing Jesus in agony and the words "*gran poder*"; a candle in a tin inscribed "*bougie verveine*"; a rose made of wax whose petals glowed a loving, human peach, the color you see at the edges of your fingers when you hold them in front of a light.

Among the candles were notes and flyers that said "God Bless America," and "We stand united," along with teddy bears, a toy fireman's helmet, and a photo of the Twin Towers. A stenciled sign commemorated the lost members of Local Fire Co. 205, Ladder 188 of Brooklyn Heights, just a few blocks away. The biggest candle-shrine stood at the flagpole at the center of the Promenade, which happens to commemorate a defeat—George Washington's retreat after he lost the Battle of Brooklyn.

There, hundreds of flames flickered furiously from a city of candles, with its own shimmering skyline. Maybe this was the city I'd been trying to see. Darkness arrived. The heat reached out. The smell was holy. People stood there for a long time, tilting their own candles to let the wax drip harmlessly, admiring a fire that was gentle, fire that, this time, they controlled, a back fire of small flames built against a great one. That night there were vigils like this all over the city. Soon after I left, the wind shifted across the Heights, bearing the smoke from Manhattan, and I went inside and shut the windows.

Urban Renewal

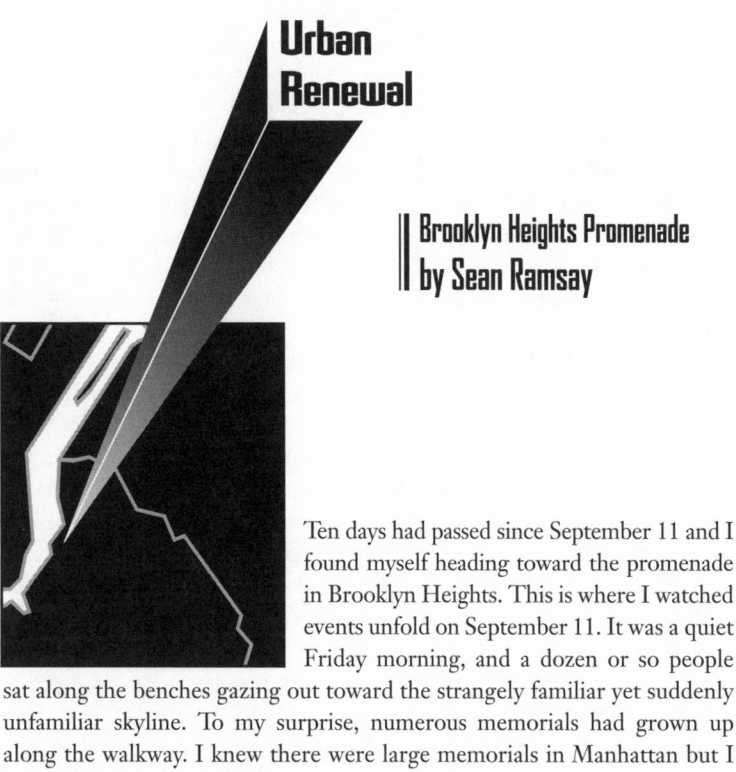

‖ Brooklyn Heights Promenade
‖ by Sean Ramsay

Ten days had passed since September 11 and I found myself heading toward the promenade in Brooklyn Heights. This is where I watched events unfold on September 11. It was a quiet Friday morning, and a dozen or so people sat along the benches gazing out toward the strangely familiar yet suddenly unfamiliar skyline. To my surprise, numerous memorials had grown up along the walkway. I knew there were large memorials in Manhattan but I didn't expect to find them here.

The railing was spotted with photos and letters and signs, the walkway interrupted by forests of half melted candles and all variety of mementos -a child's plastic fire helmet with the words "Thank you" painted on the front, a framed quote by Martin Luther King decrying violence, a vase of fresh white roses, a toy fire engine, strings of plastic flags, and innumerable pictures, postcards, and children's drawings of the twin towers themselves. The letters W.T.C. R.I.P. were scrawled on a wooden bench.

Many of the signs had appeared right after the tragedy, their hastily

copied pictures and urgent descriptions echoing the desperation of those first, panic filled days. But others, put up later, were a kind of homage, displaying three or or large photographs, showing a loved one smiling with family and friends. Someone had left a painting in which the towers, transformed from buildings into ladders of orange and blue light, reach up towards heaven.

As I made my way down the promenade, with the vacuum of the towers looming on the skyline, I read the messages of desperation, hope and remembrance. I felt connected to these faces, these families in a way I had not experienced through all the news coverage and all the discussions of justice and war and grief that consumed the airwaves.

Then I noticed a small garbage truck ahead surrounded by several sanitation workers. Beyond them, the promenade was stripped bare—candles, flowers, photos, everything—gone. Obviously they had begun to clean. And I thought, God damn, don't they know it's too soon? Don't they know we still need this, these words, these pictures, this reminder of what has happened to us—what has been taken from us? We are not finished grieving—I am not finished grieving. I decided I should say something, I should shout at them, plead with them, stop them in some way.

I knew it wasn't the workers' fault, they were just doing a job, following some heartless cleaning schedule—but it wasn't time for this yet. We New Yorkers have become accustomed to our impersonal city—its cold bureaucracy—but this once, just this once, we needed to see our city care.

Fuming, I walked over to the workers' and as I approached I could see: they were not taking the things down, but putting them back up. One at a time, the workers pulled the photos and letters and signs out of large plastic bags, repaired the torn edges with cellophane tape and attached each to the railing. Flags and ribbons were tied up, clusters of flowers hung upside down so they would keep longer, candles and toys placed into neat clusters on the ground. The memorial grew and blossomed as they worked. It had rained heavily the night before, and apparently, the sanitation department had come out, collected the objects, stored them safely, and was now carefully, gently, intently reinstalling every single piece.

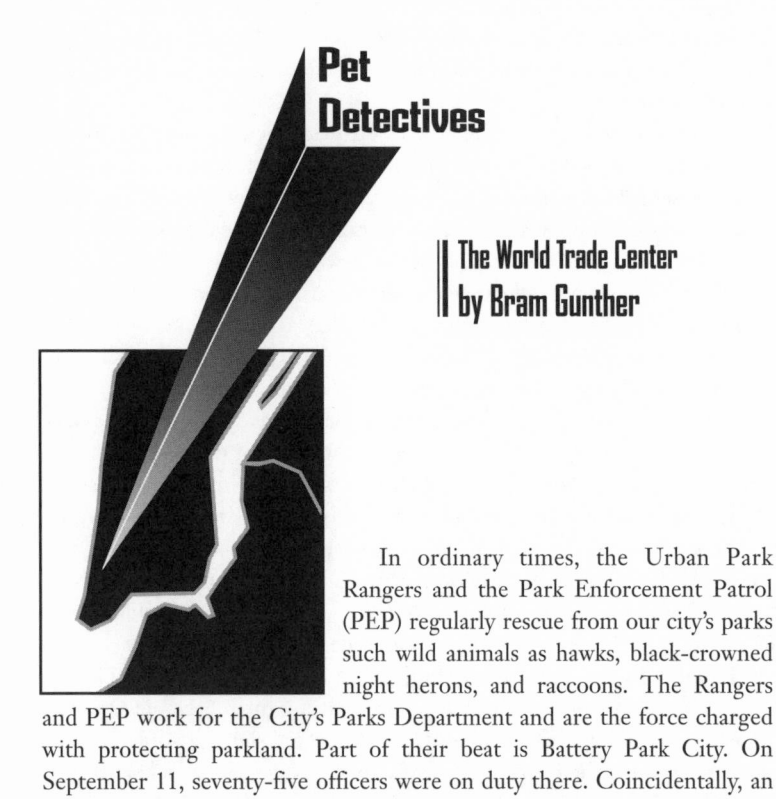

Pet Detectives

The World Trade Center
by Bram Gunther

In ordinary times, the Urban Park Rangers and the Park Enforcement Patrol (PEP) regularly rescue from our city's parks such wild animals as hawks, black-crowned night herons, and raccoons. The Rangers and PEP work for the City's Parks Department and are the force charged with protecting parkland. Part of their beat is Battery Park City. On September 11, seventy-five officers were on duty there. Coincidentally, an additional twenty-five Rangers and PEP were in a training session that was also being held in the park. When the planes hit, one hundred trained Parks Police were already at the scene.

Initially, they helped cordon off the streets around the World Trade Center. But as the Fire Department, the Police Department, EMS, and the Office of Emergency Management (OEM) hustled in, the Rangers and PEP were inevitably pushed to the periphery.

But they didn't want to just leave. Their city had experienced great harm and none of them wanted to abandon the wound. They made themselves

available to the police, to the military guard, and to OEM and set up a command center at Pier 40, at Canal Street. Their role was not central. But on Wednesday September 12, as residents from Battery Park City and Gateway Plaza drifted back to their homes looking for their pets, the Rangers and PEP happened upon their natural niche: rescuing pets separated from their human companions.

Over the next few days, the Rangers and PEP were joined by the Suffolk and Nassau county SPCAs, the Pennsylvania SPCA, the Lindhurst, New Jersey Fire Company, and the New York City Center for Animal Care and Control. Pier 40 became the center point for what Alexander Brash, Chief of the Urban Park Service, called the "largest pet rescue ever."

To organize the effort, tenants were first gathered on the pier and then organized according to their particular buildings. When a group was set, the officers drove them slowly down the promenade along the Hudson River until they reached Battery Park City.

Then, either an officer paired with a resident or a volunteer, or officers by themselves would enter the dark tombs of the skyscrapers in search of a left-alone pet.

One such team consisted of Kim Wilkins, a PEP sergeant, and Jessica Cowan, a PEP corporal. Each officer was outfitted with a hard hat that had an attached headlight, a respirator mask, and a heavy white asbestos suit. "We looked like space aliens," Wilkins said.

The officers were told that an elderly woman and her cat were stuck in their fifteenth-floor home. Not knowing the exact apartment, when Wilkins and Cowan reached the fifteenth story they began to scream and slam on doors. But there was no response. Cowan ran back down the stairs to find the janitor. However, standing there was the tenant herself. "Please get my cat," she said. She was upset.

Cowan then ran back up the fifteen flights. When she and Wilkins finally opened the apartment door, the cat ran from them in fear. The officers could only find a laundry bag to carry it in. Wilkins spotted the feline under the coffee table and "dived down."

"Nicey nicey," she said as she grabbed for it. But the cat was so alarmed it scratched her in several places. "We wrestled," Wilkins said. "I mean, I was up in this pitch-dark tower, scared deep in my heart that another plane was coming or the building was going to fall down, yet I was more afraid of

this kitty cat. It was killing me." She finally corralled it and brought it outside to her owner.

United with her cat, the woman cried, "Oh, Fluffy."

Wilkins thought to herself, "Fluffy? She's more like Satan." Then the woman said to the officers, "Where's my hat?" And Wilkins and Cowan looked at each other, wondering perhaps if they had been expected to get her hat and not the cat.

In another instance, Sara Hobel, Director of the Rangers, was approached by a small boy. He said to her, "I was put in charge of taking care of the class newt over the Jewish holiday. You have to get my newt out!" He handed her a plastic container with a note in it. The note said, "Officer, please remember to add water to this container or the newt will die."

Hobel climbed the dark, ash-strewn staircase of a Battery Park City high-rise. She opened the door to the apartment with the key she had been given by the boy's mother. She tried not to peek at things, feeling somehow as if she were trespassing. She found the terrarium that housed the newt. The plants inside were coated with dust, but, under a leaf, sitting placidly, was the newt. She put water in the container, picked the newt up and put him inside, and walked him back downstairs to the boy.

The Rangers and PEP rescued rabbits, gerbils, fish, turtles, lizards, hamsters, one white rat, parrots, snakes, ferrets, and, of course, chiefly cats and dogs. In the rescue of 1071 pets, only three animals were found dead. One cat, one bird, and one gold fish.

People's lives had been shattered by the attack and they desperately wanted their animals to be safe and at peace. In the wake of such a tragedy, all lives counted, even a newt's.

Bones

New York City
by Joseph Lieber

My grandfather, the Russian-Jewish émigré and New York painter Raphael Soyer, used to say, in his wonderful old-world accent, "New York is my country." The year 2001 finds me living in Boston in the eighteenth year of my self-imposed exile from the island of Manhattan, the village of my childhood. I am the only one in my family to have fled the nest (I do not count my brother and sister, who in their adulthood ventured across the East River to Brooklyn). Still, I have my own version of my grandfather's axiom, and, indeed, the longer my exile the tighter I cling to it: "New York," I tell anyone who will listen, "is in my bones."

Thinking about that expression now, I ponder its meaning. Bones are our foundation, of course, the deepest most innate part of us; without them we would be little more than puddles of tissue, blood and organs. But what resides in the bone? Two things come to mind: marrow, the sustainer of life, and cancer, its destroyer.

I left New York because, though it nurtured and sustained me like no

other place ever has, it also seemed bent on destroying me. It was the pace and the pressure that I fled, the heightened sense of time and movement and energy, the relentlessness of life in a world of pavement, the heavy toll it took on my body and spirit. And yet, like all expatriate New Yorkers, I am drawn back as an ant is drawn back to its hole. I left New York but the city never let me go.

Like many Americans, I wandered the shattered psychic landscape of September 11 in a confused state of shock and fear, in a condition of numbness unlike any I had known. It was such a painfully gorgeous late summer day, crystalline skies so strange against the unfolding nightmare. I spent the day frantically calling my family and my friends to make sure they were all still alive. Phone lines were down, cell phones unusable. It turned out that all of my people survived, but many were much too close.

My brother, biking on to the Brooklyn Bridge in the shadow of the World Trade Center, saw the second plane hit. He had stopped to talk with another rider about the fire in the first tower. "It was a plane," the man told him, "it was flying much too low."

"Like that one," the man said.

He and my brother watched in silence as the second plane made its now famous banking turn. They saw the explosion, the fire, the falling people. Later, my brother watched from the roof of his house in Park Slope as the towers vanished in puffs of dust and smoke, one after the other. For days, he tells me, the wind carried papers and ash to his street.

My sister, emerging from the subway at Prince Street in SoHo, noticed smoke billowing from the two towers. Strange, she thought, the World Trade Center is on fire. But the import of what she saw did not quite penetrate her consciousness. Once upstairs in the loft where her office is located, she found her colleagues at the window, a stunned group gazing south, a radio on someone's desk reporting the unimaginable.

A bit later, there was her childhood friend standing at her office door, ghost-like, covered in soot. She had walked down from the eighty-second floor of the second tower. My sister had not even known she worked there.

From the moment I learned of the attack, I felt an urgent need to be home, home in the city of my bones, home among my people. The grief hit me on the Monday afterwards, harder and more suddenly than I could have imagined, like the low back spasm that knocked me unexpectedly to

my bedroom floor two years ago.

After putting my boys to bed, I was listening to the radio, a phone-in program on WNYC hosted by Brooke Gladstone. The theme was "How do New Yorkers get on with their lives after this?"

"I don't know," I said aloud to the sinkful of dishes, "I don't know." I slumped down over a kitchen chair, feeling the enormity of our loss, the enormity of my loss. They did this to my city! They savaged my ancestral home, the island where three generations of my family have lived and struggled and fallen in love and died, the sanctuary to which my grandparents so gratefully fled the dangers and indignities of life as Jews in Russia and Poland, the center of culture and art and liberalism that spawned me and sent me out into the world. The idea of moving on amidst such overwhelming sorrow and loss seemed to me on that night in my kitchen in Boston an impossibility. This bottomless sadness has not yet passed, and it sometimes feels as if it never will.

One thing about being an expatriate New Yorker, especially one who has traveled widely and lived in as many places as I have, is that you get accustomed to having to explain yourself in a way natives of other places simply are not required to do. It is not only New York City you have to explain—yes, people actually are born there and actually have childhoods there, yes, you really did ride the subway to school—but you have to explain yourself as well. You have to overtly demonstrate that you are not a bully, not a snob, that you do not think you are smarter than everyone else (even if you secretly know that you really are what people jealously consider a snob simply by virtue of having grown up and come of age amidst such culture and diversity). You have to publicly declare the excellence of local cuisine lest you be presumed to think (as you invariably do, but never admit aloud) that it pales in comparison to New York's gastronomy. When outnumbered by non-New Yorkers—as you so often tend to be in the diaspora—you have to laugh off the constant and petty slights against your town. You carry your city with you, close to the chest and near the heart.

Perverse thoughts have crossed my mind. The one I cannot shake is this: Only in New York could anyone have pulled this off on such a scale. New York where everything is writ large—life, finance, politics, art, sports, and, yes, architecture—has now become the site of the most monstrous act of international terrorism. On the grand stage of New York's skyline, against

a pure blue sky, evil achieved its finest moment, its greatest success. Only in New York.

I talk on the phone with an old friend on West Eighty-sixth Street, two blocks from where I grew up. She tells me about the stench, how it drifts with the wind, how you never know when exactly it will find you. They say it's the smell of burning computers and desks and chairs, she says, of electrical fires and burning insulation. The odor makes her close her windows tight to the cool autumn nights. There is something else mixed in there, she says, something that makes her wake up coughing, gasping for air, edgy, ill at ease. "I don't know . . ." her voice trails off. Of course, I know what she is thinking. Silently for a moment, across the wires, we together contemplate the unspeakable. "It's burning bodies," she says; nothing, any longer, unspeakable.

Next week, finally, I am going home. I must show my five-year-old son that New York is still there, that the buildings in which his grandparents, aunts, uncles and cousins live are still standing, that airplanes are not falling from the sky. My brother, he of the Brooklyn Bridge, seems to know better. He doesn't have the dubious sense of perspective I claim to enjoy from Boston. He has not left town since the calamity. When I tell him that I want to show my son that the city is still there, he replies, "I'm not sure it is."

But like any self-respecting New Yorker—like the dozens of poor souls whom I just know stuck around to watch the terrible excitement on September 11 only to be crushed by the weight of the collapsing towers—I have to see for myself.

Ashes

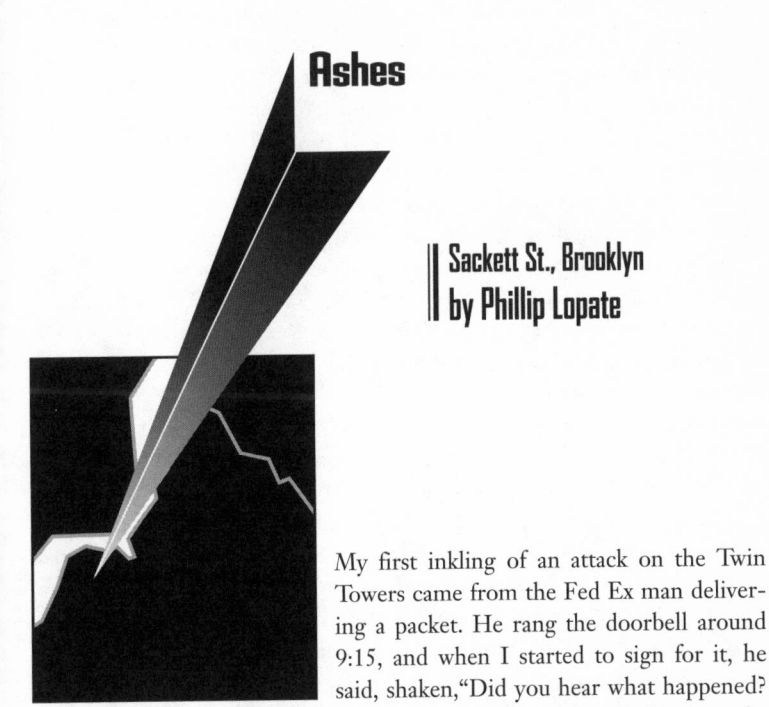

Sackett St., Brooklyn
by Phillip Lopate

My first inkling of an attack on the Twin Towers came from the Fed Ex man delivering a packet. He rang the doorbell around 9:15, and when I started to sign for it, he said, shaken,"Did you hear what happened? A plane crashed into the World Trade Center. You can see the black smoke from here." Indeed, looking down Sackett Street toward the river on that infamously sunny day, I did see a plume of grayish black cloud at the end of my block. My first response was So what? Planes do crash. I went inside, the phone rang and it was my mother-in-law, telling me to turn on the television. My mother-in-law is something of TV addict, especially if bad weather threatens; she'll keep the tube on day and night to track a rainstorm.

I had been looking forward to writing all day, now that my seven-year-old daughter Lily was back in school, and so I said rather testily that I couldn't turn the television on now, and hung up.

But something urgent in her voice disturbed me, and so, against my practice, I did put on the television, and saw the footage of the second plane

crashing into the World Trade Center. Now I was gripped, shocked, queasy, realized something unprecedented was happening. Still, I wandered by habit over to my desktop computer, and tried to punch in a few sentences for my book about the New York waterfront. Maybe because I have been so fixated on this subject, I began to think this horrifying event was directly connected to the geography of the waterfront: Manhattan's slender, lozenge shape, surrounded by rivers, made it easier for the hijacking pilots to hug the shore and spot the towers. My concentration, needless to say, was poor, but I resisted giving myself up entirely to this (so it yet seemed) public event. I am the kind of person who can write, and does, as a consoling escape from anxiety, in the midst of carpenters or other distractions. Around 10:30 I had the television turned on in my office when my wife Cheryl called me from Lily's Montessori class and said she was sticking around the school, in case they decided to close it. I replied—the resolve had suddenly formed in me, I needed to be out in the streets—that I was going for a walk down by the waterfront, to see what I could. "Why don't you stop by the school afterwards, and look in on us?" she asked. I said I doubted I would, not adding that suddenly I felt a sharp urge to be alone.

The tragedy had registered on me, exactly the same way as after my mother had died: a pain in the gut, the urge to walk and walk through the city, and a don't-touch-me reflex, *noli me tangere*. I made my way down to Columbia Street, which feeds into the Brooklyn Promenade: the closer I got to the waterfront, the harder it was to breathe. The smoke was blowing directly across the East River, into Brooklyn. There were not many people on Columbia Street, but most of those I passed had surgical masks on (I wondered if they got them from nearby Long island Community Hospital). I was choking, without a mask. Cinders and poisonous-smelling smoke thickened the air, and ash fell like snowflakes on the parked cars and on one's clothing, constantly.

It was exactly what I had imagined war to be like. An Arabic-looking delivery man had pulled over and was talking worriedly into a cell phone. It was two hours after the attack, and you could no longer make out the Manhattan skyline, all you could see was a billowing black cloud. Later, my wife told me she had actually glimpsed the top of one of the Twin Towers in flames. I found myself envying everyone who had actually witnessed the buildings on fire or collapsing. Of course I had no one to blame but myself,

having secreted myself indoors for the first few hours. I can't imagine running into Manhattan to get a closer look, but I should have gone up to my roof and looked. At the moment it didn't occur to me; I was terrified. Now I saw thousands of people on foot crossing over the bridges into downtown Brooklyn. When I reached Atlantic Avenue I turned east, away from the water, and began to encounter hordes of office workers, released early from their jobs. Not all of them seemed upset; there was a sort of holiday mood, in patches, of unexpected free time. Some younger people behind me, two men and a woman in their twenties, were even laughing as they recounted to each other the morning's events, how they had been stopped on their way out of the subway. The middle-aged and elderly, on the other hand, seemed profoundly disturbed. They had not expected anything so terrible as an attack on America to happen in the last quarter of their lives. Just as there is something unseemly when a young person dies, so the natural order of things seems wronged when the elderly, braced for their own diminishment, illness and death, must absorb the bitter, shocking knowledge of how vulnerable and perishable their society is—the world they had expected to outlast them. I myself felt, at only fifty-eight, that the attack was a personal affront to one's proper autobiographical arc, as though a messy and unnecessarily complicated subplot had been introduced too late in the narrative.

I went by the Arab shops and cafes on Atlantic Avenue, wondering foolishly if I would detect any mood of celebration. In fact, many of the Arab-owned stores had taken the precaution to close for the day; in several of the shops left open, the proprietors had retreated to the back room. To the degree that expressions among the Brooklyn-Islamic community could be made out, they looked grim, no one was wreathed in smiles, though I did not rule out the possibility that some were rejoicing inwardly. All at once, I wanted to be with my family. My cocoa-colored shirt was flecked with white ash, like residual bird shit, when I turned into the Brooklyn Heights Montessori School. The lobby was crowded with parents, many picking up their children to take them home. School seemed as safe a place for Lily to be as our house; I saw no reason to take her out prematurely. My wife, Cheryl, was standing by the door of the multipurpose room, waiting for Lily to exit with her class. They were on their way to or from dance. Lily seemed happily surprised to see me in midday; I hugged her. She trooped off to her next activity. Cheryl milled around with the mothers and some of the fathers

returning from the financial district; they were all comparing accounts, and engaging in that compulsively repetitious dialogue by which an enormity is made real.

A few days later, my wife reproached me for having shown up with ash-laden clothing, the shirttails left outside my pants; she said I could have frightened the children. I said I did not think anyone noticed me. But on some level, her reproach was justified: I was indulging the fantasy that I was invisible, not being a team player. Some sort of communal bonding was taking place, foreign to me, beautiful in many respects, scary in others.

My wife and I both felt anguished all week, but it was an anguish we could not share. The fault was mine: selfishly, I wanted to nurse my grief at what had been done to my city. I mistrusted any attempt to co-opt me into group-think, even conjugal-think.

Later that day, I went with two friends to give blood. These two gentlemen, Kent Jones and James Harvey, both fine film critics who live in my neighborhood, met me on the corner of Sackett and Henry Streets and we walked toward the hospital together. James Harvey is in his seventies, a veteran of World War II, and I expected him to have a special insight into the attack, to compare it to Pearl Harbor, say, but he just shook his head and said this was different. When we arrived at the blood donor station we were turned away; apparently so many people had volunteered that the medical technicians had run out of blood bags. (As the city learned in the days that followed, we had been optimistic in thinking that that many wounded could be pulled from the wreckage and would need transfusions.) Kent, James and I repaired to the Harvest Café, which was unusually crowded with diners. The owner and waiters seemed harried, forgetting to give us silverware. The TV was on, the volume turned so loud that it was difficult to talk. Normally, when these friends and I get together, the conversation flows, we have endless things to say; but this time we could derive no nourishment from each other's company.

Our language had dried up. Embarrassed, being writers, to say the obvious, we said little. Kent kept consulting his cell phone. James held his head and stared at the floor. I turned around and looked up at the self-same television which I resented being on in the first place, yet was hypnotized by.

When I got home, my wife was glued to the television. Uneasy about joining her in this electronic vigil, yet feeling I had no choice, nothing else

mattered, I joined her. Our daughter said, "Why do you keep watching that? They just keep saying the same things. We know that already. Two planes crashed into the building." Blasé, not at all traumatized, Lily, the customary center of our universe, was annoyed that her parents were not paying attention to her. She was right: there was something punitive about the same information, the same pictures, over and over. I realize that this has become our modern therapy in catastrophic events, the hope that by immersing ourselves in the news media, its thoughtful anchorpersons and interviews with pundits, by the numbing effect of repetition if nothing else, we will work through our grief. But for me it doesn't work: I get a kind of sugar buzz and feel nauseous afterwards.

The first day there was a bit more unexpected quality, especially shots of people running away from the explosion, stampeding, the camera flailing about. The footage's amateurism seemed to signal its authenticity. In succeeding days, I felt sickened by the slick, unending interviews with relatives of missing persons and back-stories about the victims, the same technique used for coverage of the Olympics, now applied to this Olympics of Thanatos. We must not forget the politicians' parade, their eloquence and competence inversely proportionate to their office. Most impressive was the local mayor, Rudy Giuliani, who seemed always to know what he was talking about; then came New York State's Governor Pataki, who graciously deferred to the mayor; Senator Hilary Clinton, who blustered unconvincingly, all the way up to President Bush, whose bellicosity and syntactical tentativeness embarrassed all educated liberals like myself. Most incredible were the efforts of the President to say kind things about New York, a city which he and the country at large have so often mistrusted and disliked.

That this was primarily an attack on New York I had no doubt. I feel so identified with my native city that it took a mental wrenching to understand all of America considered itself a target. I knew the Pentagon had been hit as well, but the attack on a low-rise, suburban military complex did not seem as significant, as humanly interesting. Urbanism, density, verticality, secular humanism, skepticism, popular culture, mass transit, commerce, these were the threatened values, in my view. The American flags that started appearing everywhere seemed to me entirely fitting, especially if they were taken to honor the heroic local firemen and police who died trying to rescue victims. But if they were a nationalistic statement about America as the great-

est nation, then, no, I could not join that sentiment. The only banner I wanted to fly from our brownstone window was the orange, green and white flag of New York City, with its clumsy Dutchman and beaver.

All the talk in the media that we were attacked because we were a free nation, and the terrorists who went after us hated freedom, frankly, disgusted me. Why could we not accept that an awful thing had happened to us without patting ourselves on the back and asserting it was a sign of our superior virtue? Awful things happened in the Iran-Iraq war, terrorist attacks, germ warfare, and neither county was a beacon of freedom. Awful things happened to Afghanistan.

It was quickly established that the plane hijackings had been done by Osama bin Laden's followers, and were intended in part as chastisement for the United States' support of Israel. As a Jew, I felt hot, exposed, implicated, frightened by the re-approach of anti-Semitism; I felt angry at the fundamentalist Muslim terrorists, even as I knew the majority of Muslims would condemn the slaughter; I felt angry at the Israeli government for all their past rigidities and missed opportunities, and especially at the Sharon-Netanyahu faction for having the audacity to gloat, "Now you know the pain we live under;" I felt angry at Arafat and the Palestinian people for not having accepted the concessions offered by Ehud Barat, however inadequate, and gone on to build something better from there; and I felt angry at the United States for having supported and grown bin Laden, the Taliban and Saddam Hussein as anti-Communist forces. Confused and chagrined as my thinking was, the one thing I felt sure, with thousands of innocent people blown apart, was that I did not want to hear the old argument of my radical-left friends: "When you are an oppressed people fighting a hegemonic power like the United States, you have to use the means at your disposal, and 'terrorism' is merely a label the American Empire applies to its opponents."

To be honest, we did not hear that argument, though one of my friends smugly quoted Malcolm X: "The chickens have come home to roost." People claim that New York will be changed forever by this attack. It is easy to say that, less easy to understand exactly how. A few days after September 11th, I noticed subway riders being unnaturally polite to each other, whether out of greater communal solidarity and respect for human life, or more wariness of the Other's potential rage, I am unable to say. No New Yorker expects the rest of America's warm feelings toward the city to last

very long; it is like getting licked by a large, forgetful St. Bernard dog.

Meanwhile, the towers that had anchored lower Manhattan are gone, pfft. I ask myself how I will be changed personally. On the morning of September 12 I awoke and remembered immediately what had happened, like a murderer returning to the horror of his altered moral life. I sensed I would never be the same. I have never bought the idea that suffering ennobles people. Rather, I expect that this dreadful experience will add to the scar tissue left by other atrocities of life, like the death of one's parents, the illness of one's children, or the shame of one's nation (My Lai), sorrows over which one has no control but that cause, for all that, the deepest regrets.

Reflections of a Savage

Pittsburgh, PA; Iran
by Saïd Sayrafiezadeh

As the son of an Iranian father and a Jewish mother, my sense of sorrow concerning the disaster of September 11 does not tend toward patriotism. In fact, I am repelled by it. I speak as a first-hand victim of American patriotism in 1979, the year sixty-six U.S. diplomats were taken hostage in Iran. The underbelly of American patriotism is where I resided for 444 days when I was ten-years-old and living in Pittsburgh, a city with virtually no discernible Middle Eastern community.

My father, who had abandoned me at birth, was living in Tehran in 1979 and the prospect of dropping bombs on Iran was a deeply personal reality for me. My connection to my father was tenuous at best, and I came to a very private reckoning during that time that his death was imminent and that the handful of memories that I had of him were the only ones I would ever have. The turmoil I was undergoing was in direct counterpoint to my countrymen who rejoiced noisily in the potency of American might, as American might was their might. To be sure, the underbelly of the flag is

not a pretty place to be, it is solitary and dangerous, but it reveals a great truth about the exclusivity and violence of this country, and one who has experienced it does not soon forget it.

It was not, however, American patriotism that was ultimately my great antagonizer in 1979, but rather American innocence, which fuels and drives patriotism. Of all the religions of the United States it is this religion, the religion of innocence, that most afflicts the American psyche. It obscures a clear understanding of American past and American present, and it maintains as one of its central tenets that the guilty—and there must exist innocent's opposite—resides on foreign soil and within foreign bodies. In 1979, despite having been born in the U.S. and having lived every moment of my ten years in America, I became a foreign body.

> "'Cause we could take our BB guns
> Blow your buns to the sun
> Just our Boy Scouts could wipe you out
> Some day soon, Khomeini
> You'll burn one flag too many
> Uncle Sam has got his pride
> You're about to feel his clout"
> —Song from WDLW, Boston

The yellow ribbon of 1979 was not my yellow ribbon, it was my noose; the bumper sticker of a red, white and blue Mickey Mouse, middle-finger aloft, proclaiming, "Hey Iran," was a middle-finger pointing toward me; my classmate's T-shirt of Ayatollah Khomeini's face in the center of a bull's eye, with the words "Fuck Iran," was a bull's eye containing my face and my father's face; the caricaturing of Iranians' physical features, eyes too black, beard too thick, accent too pronounced, body odor too severe, was a caricaturing of my body and the body of someone my mother had once made love to. In my pubescent years I was taught by the country I hailed from that my body was filthy and deformed.

The difficulty for me at age ten was not so much if my father was to live or die, but how I was to preserve an unpolluted sense of him within myself. Everything I came in contact with in that period conspired to corrupt him and shame me from him. A choice was proffered: my father or my American identity. I chose my father and in so doing I found myself defending Iran; I

defended Iran and in so doing I defended my father. Teachers ignored me, classmates taunted me, friends rescinded dinner invitations. I was countering what we, the population, had been taught in first-grade when we first learned about the gallant innocent American pioneers. By the time we had reached sixth-grade the doctrine was so deeply entrenched that there was virtually no way it could be effectively altered. Walter Cronkite was nightly corroborating what our history books said; my friends' parents were corroborating what Walter Cronkite said; the U.S. government was corroborating my friends' parents; and Johnny Carson was corroborating them all. To deign to suggest an alternative point of view was an heretical act, it was insulting to the complete fabric of the country. I took to carrying a piece of sharpened metal in my pocket, determined to go for the eyes if there were ever cause. I was isolated, both outside of myself and within. It was the price I paid for defending a man who, as I was forced to admit to myself years later, had not once defended me.

What I did not know then was that none of this was about myself or Iranians. It was about to what great length Americans needed to venture in order to preserve their innocence. If Iranians were guilty, after all, there would be no need to dehumanize them, they could be depicted accurately, and in the simple accuracy of such a depiction would lie their sins for all the world to see. Since this was not the case, the American media, among other entities, found itself beholdened to endless calisthenics of reproducing under-exposed, black and white photographs of Iranian men; intellectual investigations into the psychology of Iranians; footage of American flags burning in the night; rapid-fire proclamations in a foreign tongue, leaving much to the frightened American imagination. America was not attempting to reveal Iran, but to confound it, which had the reverse effect: it revealed America, its racism and its xenophobia.

> "I think we ought to round up all the Iranian students in this country, put them in one center and swap them for the Americans. I had no idea until this came up there are so many of them here."
> —Ms. Ella Belky, shop clerk, *The New York Times*, November 12, 1979

Ms. Belky is not making a mathematical error in suggesting that sixty thousand Iranians are the equivalent of fifty Americans. The American slave, after all, was valued at five to one. Dehumanization is a necessity when

a power is attempting to abscond with a nation's patrimony, which is exactly what the United States was achieving when it suddenly found itself on the other side of the gun, its shah being run out of the country and its diplomats being held hostage. An accurate rendering of American history in 1979 would have, at the very least, involved America in the hostage crisis, if not outright implicated it. If nothing more, Americans could not have gotten away with saying that the crisis began on November 4, 1979, but rather that it was another element in an ongoing crisis that had begun many years ago and included, but was certainly not limited to, the American involvement in 1953 in overthrowing Mohammad Mossadegh, the democratically-elected Prime Minister of Iran.

Americans were not privy to this history then, nor are they scarcely privy to it now. History instead has been replaced with an ingrained, all-encompassing sense of innocence which, by its nature, precludes historical investigation. It is an innocence that President Bush alluded to in his recent address of Congress. "Americans are asking, "Why do they hate us?" They hate what they see right here in this chamber: a democratically elected government. Their leaders are self-appointed. They hate our freedoms: our freedom of religion, our freedom of speech, our freedom to vote and assemble and disagree with each other." If this is a tendentious, simple-minded reading of American society and world events, it is designed to be one. Americans, despite their claims to the contrary, find solace in this depiction, and the American government, filled with dreams of world domination, is happy to oblige.

If something has changed in the twenty-two years since the hostage-crisis, I don't know what it is. The reviling of Afghanistan is that of Iran. The physical threat to Middle Easterners living in the United States is the physical threat that I lived under. And Americans, caught within their religion, that endless maze of interlocking, self-supporting elements, are still unable to extricate themselves from it because they do not know that they are trapped within it, descending further into self-congratulatory patriotism and jingoism. There is something sad and disheartening in the way the victims of the World Trade Center have been glorified. It is American life—not life itself—that is being exalted. The foreign life, as a direct consequence of such an equation, is reduced. Americans' horror and grief are being manipulated to accept impending foreign slaughter. The American

heart, in short, is being hardened to absorb a staggering death-toll that will result in untold riches for the lucky few. And somewhere in some American city there exists again a ten-year-old boy who finds himself in the middle of the tumult struggling to preserve a humane sense of who he is and where he comes from.

Zen and the Syntax of Disaster

**Broadway and Fulton St.
by Paul W. Morris**

The sound and the smoke . . . the terror of the crowds rushing past . . . a dark cloud billowing toward me in a wave of debris, determined, absolute . . .

Searching for a meaning in this memory, I look at other stories born on September 11 and see a shared vocabulary that is at once horrifying and epiphanic: "It was the apocalypse." "Like a revelation." "I thought I died and went to heaven." "There was only darkness." "I saw the light." "Then it hit me." "The world came crashing down." "My eyes were opened." "Everything looked different." "It was unreal." "It felt like I was dreaming." "I awoke into a nightmare."

Taken from first-person accounts, this is the language of enlightenment. In its syntax, we hear the words of awakening, of the struggle to see again after a blinding flash of insight. It is Saul's conversion on the road to Damascus. It is Arjuna's moksha in the *Bhagavad Gita*. For me, it was a Buddhist lesson in impermanence that I wish I could unlearn. Or at least relearn, like during a meditation retreat, or through a course lecture, or even

in one of the books on Buddhism that line my window ledge. As it happened, the lesson I learned that Tuesday morning occurred on the streets below my apartment, just blocks from Ground Zero.

The explosions arrive in swift succession during a hurried morning routine, the first as I'm getting out of the shower, and then again, inconceivably louder, as I'm preparing to leave my apartment. I crane my neck and see burning papers littering the sky seventy stories up. To the west, I glimpse a side of the south tower, on fire and smoking.

I ride down in the elevator with a neighbor who is groggy and half-dressed.

"What's going on?" he asks. "I was asleep when an explosion woke me up."

When I tell him what I know so far, what we all know by now, from the limited and confused news reports I have already heard—that two airline jets crashed, intentionally, into both towers of the World Trade Center—he says nothing. We exit the elevator in silence and walk out of our building into chaos.

On the corner of Broadway and Fulton Street, windows all along the block have been blown out by concussion force. Gazing upward, I see what I saw on the television, the towers ablaze, the same, yet different. From where I stand I observe balloons of flames twenty floors high roiling over each other, more orange than I thought possible. I smell the acrid black smoke pouring out, bleeding a deep scar east across the azure sky. It's so bright out that it's hard to determine where the heat is coming from, the sun or the fires, and if there is any difference at all. The exit wounds made by the planes look like two dark eyes gone frighteningly askew, and I stare back at them, uncomprehendingly. Later, people will say it was like a movie, like a war zone, like a natural disaster. But right now there are no metaphors. It's like nothing that has ever happened. And, as it's happening, there is nothing to understand.

Coming back to Earth, I look at the people looking up, as if a closer inspection will reveal some deeper meaning. A woman walks past, covering her mouth, gasping.

"Oh, God," she moans, "I saw bodies falling."

"They were jumping," adds another dazed woman.

"It's a nightmare," someone else says. "I have to wake up. Somebody wake me up."

Somewhere south of Chambers Street, I'm on a corner standing in a group of people, crowded around a guy with a walkman, waiting for news. Behind me, somebody is talking about a heap of twisted metal that was a jet engine a block away, and two guys holding briefcases march off for a closer look.

"They hit the Pentagon," the guy with the walkman finally says, his eyes fixed on the burning towers above us.

There is a pause as this information begins to sink in, as we weigh it against what we already know. Before we are allowed to mourn, though, a man announces, "Good! I'm glad they hit Washington, now they'll have to do something about these lunatics! It's about time they woke up!"

"It's the Palestinians, I know it," another man is saying and an argument erupts.

I'm waiting for more news to come over the radio, bracing myself for the next disaster. Anything can happen, I think. I have to be prepared. That's when the city shudders. I look up to see the top fifty stories of the south tower begin to slide off, down, and to the east. Then the rest falls in a deafening and unending crash, blanketing the corner where I had, minutes earlier, been standing, annihilating the rescue workers and vehicles that were still there. I hear the cacophony of cries: "Oh my God!" "It's coming this way!" "Run!"

And I run.

I have a recurring dream in which I'm running away from danger, but I'm not getting anywhere. The ground beneath me is like a treadmill preventing me from moving ahead, as though there were some invisible gravity holding me still. It's absurd and frustrating. No matter how hard I run, I can't go forward. When I finally wake up, I'm anxious, frightened.

Running north on Church Street, there is no clear or straight path. People are everywhere, moving in every direction. Many, like me, are racing uptown. Some dart east or west. A few don't move at all, paralyzed by their disbelief. Zigzagging through the crowds, I have the sense that I'm going nowhere, that the cloud is getting closer instead of moving farther away. I want to wake up, but there is no waking.

As I cross Canal Street, my run turns into a tired stride, a slow-motion sleepwalk through a shattered city. Suddenly, something tears through the

sky, three, two, one block away—and I instinctively duck behind a van as an F-16 flies into view overhead. I feel foolish in the eyes of commuters flowing out of the subways, unaware of the world that awaits them. We are all coming at this from different perspectives, I think, but we share a common nightmare. Maybe if I get inside, I can reverse the dream, erase what I have witnessed, delude myself into believing that the people are still alive, that the planes never hit.

I'm almost at Houston Street, heading on auto pilot to a friend's office to make a phone call, type an e-mail, get a news update, do something, anything to escape the inevitability of what has happened from dawning on me. I'm entering the building when the north tower disappears from sight. I don't look back. I'm awake now, and I've already seen too much of what is no longer there.

After a week spent displaced on the Upper West Side, I'm finally able to go home, back to the ruins of my neighborhood. For days now, I have been trying to sift through the experiences of that morning, excavating my grief from the helplessness that overwhelms me. I feel incapable of being outside for extended periods; every loud truck that passes, every siren that blares is like a sharp whack bringing me back to the present, to the harsh reality of what has happened.

I expect the worst on the way down to my apartment, imagining it carpeted with debris, glass shards blown everywhere, furniture soaked from the previous night's rainstorm. It looks like a bomb went off, I muse darkly upon entering, only because this is exactly how I left it, neglected and in disarray, but for the smell of burnt plastic. Pale sunlight streams in through windows now spotted with filth and ash. A thin layer of chalky dust covers the window ledges and the books that line them. I wonder, even more darkly, how much of that dust is comprised of the towers, how much of the people who didn't get out, of the firefighters who rushed in; how much of it is the airplanes, the passengers and crews, and how much the hijackers themselves, all of them, blown apart in a storm of whirling atoms. I wonder: how much equanimity can I bear?

I find refuge in a teaching by an eighth-century Zen master of the T'ang Dynasty named Quingyuan, who described the process of his own enlightenment in The Compendium of Five Lamps: "Thirty years ago, before I practiced [Zen], I saw that mountains are mountains and rivers are rivers.

However, after having achieved intimate knowledge and having gotten a way in, I saw that mountains are not mountains and rivers are not rivers. But now that I have found rest, as before, I see mountains as mountains and rivers as rivers."

To the pre-enlightened eyes, in other words, the physical world is just that, physical and nothing more. A mountain is just a mountain. At the moment of enlightenment, there is a new perspective, a deeper understanding of the world as it truly is: The mountain is merely an illusion, a construct of our own preconceptions. Afterward, the eyes adjust to take in everything, the physical world as well as the world of impermanence. When the enlightened mind can hold both perspectives simultaneously, there are mountains again. There, and not there. Inspired by the simplicity of Quingyuan's teaching, sixties folk-singer Donovan distilled this koan even further when he sung; "First there is a mountain. Then there is no mountain. Then there is."

Buried beneath the seeming incomprehensibility of these lyrics lies a sophisticated lesson still pertinent today.

Listening to the news report that "Everything has changed," I hear an old truth of impermanence. If the disaster on September 11 has transformed my perception at all, then I am still waiting to see how my eyes will adjust to the potential insight gained. For the enlightened mind, the vision is clear: The suffering of thousands of people is no different than the suffering of the hijackers; the destruction of the towers is proof that nothing remains unchanged. When I consider the sheer loss of life and degree of devastation, however, I know that I do not yet have Quingyuan's clarity of mind for seeing past distinctions.

This, then, is where practice begins. Here, at the place of impact, the center of gravity from which all things radiate. There is a Ground Zero inside me wherever I go. It is the home I return to and the nowhere I can never outrun. When I sit in silence, breathing deeply, I try not to think about whom and what I am inhaling, and if it even matters. I breathe in, and the city breathes out.

It's late now. My street is quiet. Only emergency vehicles are allowed this far downtown, and the urgency of their sirens have been long since negated. The smell of scorched debris is beginning to subside. It occurs to me that maybe it's only making way for something worse, the stench of decomposition. Up the block, I can hear the rumble of heavy machinery, the low, steady

thunder of a lightning flash that will sound for months to come.

Standing by my window, I remove a book from the shelf, *Dropping Ashes on the Buddha*, by Zen Master Seung Sahn, and open to Stephen Mitchell's translator's preface. "Zen teaching is like a window," he begins. "At first, we look at it, and see only the reflection of our own face. But as we learn, and as our vision becomes clear, the teaching becomes clear. Until at last it is perfectly transparent. We see through it. We see all things: our own face."

I put the book back and squint through gray-streaked glass. The flood lamps of the recovery operation illuminate the night sky. Far from enlightenment, I strain for a new perspective on an altered landscape. To the west, through a smoky haze, I can see a skyscraper I couldn't until now—the World Financial Center, blocked all these years by a mountain that first was there, and now isn't. I wonder what else I'll see tomorrow, when I wake up.

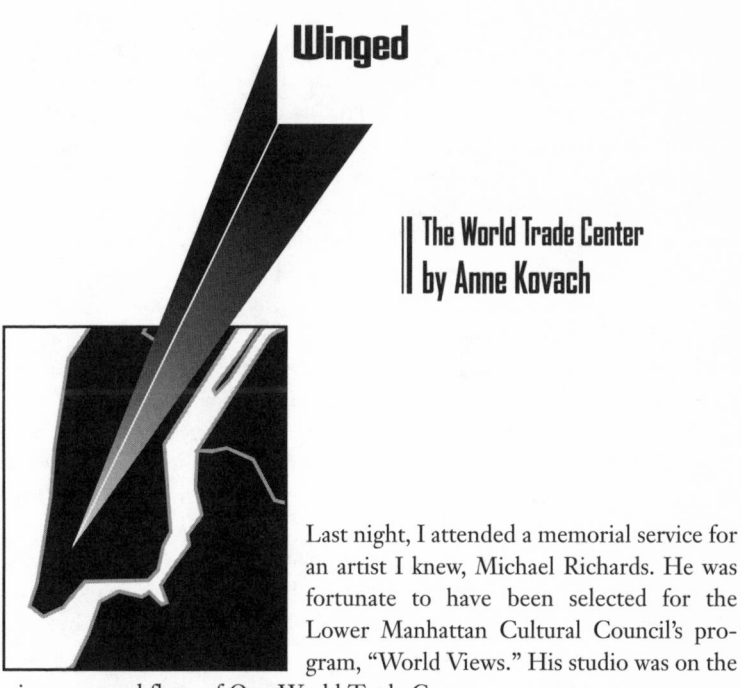

Winged

The World Trade Center
by Anne Kovach

Last night, I attended a memorial service for an artist I knew, Michael Richards. He was fortunate to have been selected for the Lower Manhattan Cultural Council's program, "World Views." His studio was on the ninety-second floor of One World Trade Center.

I met Michael two years ago when I first came to the Studio Museum. He was in the first exhibition I was ever involved with there. He was, to say the least, beautiful in every way. Not only was he awesome to look at, but his voice and nature were gentle and quiet and when he smiled, it was a mile wide. The museum offered their space for a service. It was heavy, is all I can say. Hundreds of people, family, friends, and acquaintances from various cultural institutions. It was truly moving to see how loved he was by so many people, and how for those, who didn't know him, it was meaningful for them just to lose an artist. A most uncanny thing about this is Michael's art.

One of the pieces he installed is titled "Tar baby vs. St. Sebastian." It is a full-body cast of himself in a sky diver's jump suit. In cast resin with bronze

plating, he stands monumental and tall; and instead of the arrows that pierce St. Sebastian, this figure is pierced by a dozen or more World War II airplanes. In other words this is a portrait of himself with planes crashing into him.

The second work Michael installed in this show is a piece called "Winged." It is simply a cast of his two arms extended like wings, joined at the shoulders. Both arms are pierced with several featherlike daggers that enter at the topside of his arms and come out at the underside of his arms. This piece was suspended—hung from the ceiling with monofiliment. About two weeks after this show opened; I got a call on a Saturday by a guard, telling me that the piece had fallen to the floor. The monofiliment snapped and Winged went crashing to the floor, shattering into a million pieces.

From the pile of broken parts, I kept one of his hands, and still have it in my office. Michael also worked as an art installer at various museums in the city. One woman, who worked with him at The Grey Art Gallery at NYU, spoke at the memorial service. She told us about the last conversation she had had with Michael, just three days before September 11. She said it was one of those conversations about what you want from life—what you hope for. She told us that Michael said, emphatically, "I want to live hard. I want to love hard. I want to work hard, and then I want to die."

On that Monday, before the Tuesday, I had a dream. I dreamed I was in a room of people. Some I knew, some I didn't. There was a small child there, a little boy, about three- or four-years-old. He played intently with some kind of toy in the middle of the room. I sensed that the adults harbored a secret from this boy. Then I learned what they knew. His mom had just been in an accident and had lost her life. After a while he started to ask for her. The tension in the room was so great, as no one wanted to break this tragic news to him. I felt it was wrong to leave him not knowing and wanted to end this discomfort. So, I crouched down to his height and I tried to explain to him that his mom was in an accident and that she had died.

He cried hard. He sobbed and he sobbed and he sobbed. But after a while, his sobbing changed to short breaths, then sniffles. Then it seemed his grieving stopped and he gradually engaged, once again, in play. It was then I knew that he would survive this. That this would not impact his life forever, and that he would know happiness. I then realized and considered someone would adopt him. Perhaps me. I am still processing all of this. The

connections between the events of Tuesday, Michael Richards, the dream, the power of art and our lives in this world. It seems there is so much we don't understand about how we operate in this universe, about ourselves, about each other. Perhaps this life is just a beginning. It's questionable, and that's all we know for sure.

Terror at the Local Deli

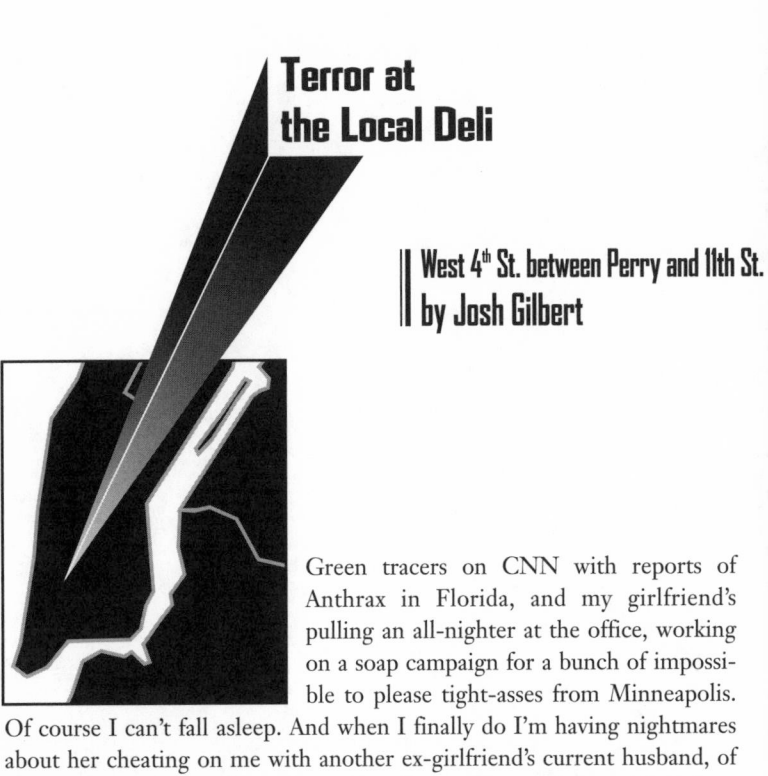

West 4ᵗʰ St. between Perry and 11th St.
by Josh Gilbert

Green tracers on CNN with reports of Anthrax in Florida, and my girlfriend's pulling an all-nighter at the office, working on a soap campaign for a bunch of impossible to please tight-asses from Minneapolis. Of course I can't fall asleep. And when I finally do I'm having nightmares about her cheating on me with another ex-girlfriend's current husband, of all people. And when I confront them in my dream after catching them making out in the sleeping car of a train headed for Italy, my ex-girlfriend's husband suddenly morphs into a gigantic heavyweight stud New York City fireman (she's been sleeping in her "I Heart FDNY" T-shirt lately) leaving me no physical or moral alternative but to focus my attention on my her, but she turns it around on me and manages to make me feel like it's all my fault, which I'm prone to feeling anyway. So there I am, up again at six in the morning, watching more green tracers and OBL talking about one hundred percent guaranteed retaliation.

Around eleven in the morning she comes home for a shower and a quick

change of clothes and then heads back to the office to present her work. I go with her like I always do to keep her company in the cab (then I walk back home because it makes me feel like I've exercised for the day).

When I get back to my West Village hood after my vigorous walk, as always, I go to the deli around the corner for a coffee and the paper before coming home and angsting about all the writing I'm behind on. Now this deli, it's a block from where we live. And like many delis in New York that aren't owned by Puerto Ricans or Koreans, it's owned and operated by Jordanians or Palestinians, depending on who you're talking to and where you stand politically on the Arab/Israeli brouhaha. They know I'm Jewish and I know they're Jordanian or Palestinian and over the years we've developed an arch-comedy fuck-you-no-fuck-you-no-fuck-you-*Do The Right Thing*- it's-all-good-in-the-hood kind of relationship.

Not today.

I walk in, intent on ignoring the memory of the green tracers and the reports of Anthrax in Florida. And I try to make small talk with my old pals from Jordan or Palestine, as usual. But there's this weird vibe in the air, and I feel it come at me when I walk in like a gust of hot air as I enter the shop. In fact, I'm so overcome with nervousness, I immediately morph into a gigantic human teddy bear. I'm here to say I love you, I decide. No ribbing or jokes or antagonistic humor today, I resolve. Like Jessie Jackson, I'm a gigantic teddy bear on a friendship mission. But it isn't working, because these Palestinian/Jordanian guys (four of them) who I know real well are giving me this very strong "we don't give a rats ass, you're a gigantic teddy bear" vibe.

But I'm still intent on rising above the tension, so I say to the owner of the deli, Abdul, I say, "Yo, Abdul, give me a hug. I need a hug from you today, Abdul." And Abdul smiles a vague, slightly plastic smile and says, "not many like you." Which is kind of cryptic, but I decide to take is as a compliment (even though it doesn't necessarily feel very genuine) because I'm a gigantic teddy bear ambassador of love, and I smile back with a broad beaming smile, and I walk toward Abdul with open arms and embrace him for an extended hug, waiting to feel the love come back my way. But his body isn't sending me any love. It's as stiff as a board. It's a no love hardwood hug like I'd never felt before in my life. I can't imagine a stiffer, I fucking hate you hug from Adolf Hitler. Which freaks me out so much, I morph out of the

gigantic teddy bear and into Gandhi, the philosophically sublime, bald Indian guru of peace and enlightenment. And I start radiating goodness and love and warmth and I start lactating and I'm standing there in the deli wearing a toga and sandals and I'm seeing light all around me and my four Jordanian/Palestinian friends at my local West Village deli.

Much to my joy and satisfaction, Abdul seems to appreciate Gandhi, and his face loosens up and he says, "come, take a walk with me to the post box down the street." And I nod, sagely, like the bald, wise man that I am. And we walk down to the corner where the mailbox is and I'm filled with light and inner peace and enlightenment and I start talking to Abdul about figuring out how to nurture love through our city's moment of hate and what does he think about all of this and where we should go from here.

Meanwhile Abdul puts his letter into the mailbox and then we walk back toward the deli and I'm walking with him because that's what we're doing—walking together toward peace and infinite bliss, and then Abdul suddenly stops and he turns toward me and says calmly but not without a significant level of edge: "Why do you think I would know what the fuck's going on? Why do you think I would know?"

Well needless to say, this question totally baffles Gandhi. Not because it doesn't make sense. But because it's so antagonistic. Which makes Gandhi mad. And he's not supposed to get mad. So he leaves me there, stranded, which makes me even angrier. So I snap back at Abdul, wounded, "Gee, I don't know, Abdul. I thought you might be able to help me figure it out. Or perhaps we might be able to figure it out together." Then I try quickly to smooth things over by telling him that I'm scared. I figure we're all scared. Which seems to hit a nerve with Abdul, but he still just stands there, pissed off, obviously waiting for me to beat it. Then Sam comes out of the deli onto the sidewalk holding the portable phone and says to Abdul, "Get rid of that guy!" And I realize "that guy" is me (!?!)

Before the "New War of 9/11," and even up until yesterday when "America Strikes Back!," I walk into that deli and Sam sees me and says to the guy working the coffee machine, "large coffee one sugar double de cup!" Just like I like it. And then he turns to me for the up-sale, smiles and says, "you wanna papeh? *Times*? You want de *Post* too? Cigarettes? Oh yeah, you quit." And sometimes, even though the Palestinian/Jordanian root of his American name "Sam" isn't Shimon, in honor of Shimon Peres, I call him

"Shimon." Today, Shimon is saying, "Get rid of THAT GUY?!?"

He knows my name. Shosh. That's what he calls me. Shosh. A word that means "piss" in about every Arabic language, according to my old friend from Iran. But what's a little piss in the name of peace, right? Shimon Peres, the "realistic dove," would trade piss for peace. But today there doesn't seem to be any room for peace.

Meanwhile, Shimon looks at Abdul. Abdul looks at me. I look back at Shimon. Shimon chuckles nervously, realizing how rude that was to say to me, his good customer, Shosh, laughs a just kidding laugh, says, "Have a nice day," turns around, and walks back into the deli. I turn back to face Abdul, but he's already walking past me, back into the deli, without saying squat.

And there I am on the sidewalk by myself, totally naked. I'm no longer Gandhi or a gigantic teddy bear and I'm most definitely not lactating. I'm just this totally confused shell-shocked individual wondering what happened to my neighborhood.

Mookie threw the trash can through my window, I realize. Fucking Mookie threw the goddamn trash can through my window. As much as I'm predisposed not to believe this would ever happen to me in my lifetime, I can't help seeing the trash can smashing through my window. Shards of glass slo-mo. I can almost see a title sequence rolling over the image.

Maybe I'm just tired and paranoid right now, I think. That would explain it. I wonder how it will feel tomorrow morning. I'll have to go back in there one more time to take the temperature before deciding I'll never go back there again.

I come home in a daze (which happens a lot lately) and I turn on the TV and wind up watching some CNN pundit fuckwit talking about the pros and cons of owning your own gas mask and finally fall asleep there on the couch Several hours later my girlfriend comes back and wakes me up. I immediately start to tell her about the weird stuff that happened to me at the deli, but she's too exhausted to hear it. Those tight-asses from the Mall of America didn't buy her work again. "But not to worry," she says like a trouper, "there's always tomorrow." Then she takes off her work clothes, puts on her I Heart FDNY T-shirt and crawls into bed.

I'm So Glad You're Alive

Brooklyn Heights
by Elizabeth Grove

For years I've been answering the questions, "You live *in* New York City? Like, right *in* New York City?" I live in Brooklyn Heights, but this is a distinction meaningful only to those with 100– zip code prefixes, so I would say yes and try to explain. It wasn't what they thought, I would say, it's not a swirling mass of faceless commuters, steel and pollution, lawless thugs, sci-fi androids, wreaking havoc while misplaced demi-Americans like me ran for cover from sub-machine gun fire, clutching dry cleaning and loaves of bread. It's not what you think, I would say. OK, there were days where it seemed like that. But, I would say, really, it's just like any other small town.

It was a partial lie, of course, the unspoken, ". . . with really good restaurants, important museums, significant theater, and the financial pulse of the world . . ." hanging heavy in the air. We liked having it both ways: little town and power capital. Let's face it, in most New Yorkers' derisive "Middle America" slurring was included everything besides Los Angeles, San Francisco, the college town where they may have spent four years, and

Seattle after Kurt Cobain.

Still, no one lives in a city of eight million. We live in villages, in many cases smaller, more provincial and more proscriptive than the little backwaters we allude to like we know what we're talking about. But in the days since September 11, we've been shell-shocked, knocked down, and made earnest. Sadly, our blood isn't needed right now and it turns out most of us don't have viable disaster skills. Volunteering at Long Island College Hospital that first day, I answered no to three questions—Did I have a car? A medical background? Know CPR?—and was given a sweet smile and a number to call on an hourly basis. Days two and three I wondered why I had never learned to weld.

Clearly, I am not alone. And that left many of us with little to do but bear witness and simply populate the city, our mere presence, our one hundred, one hundred and fifty, two hundred pounds, whatever, anchoring the city in the way the World Trade Center once did. This close to the blast site, with its mountain of rubble burning and, even in total collapse, still higher than the Washington Monument, there is little joy in being alive while it sinks in and sinks in and sinks in and we understand war is coming. But there is the accident and the necessity of being alive and somehow letting everyone know it. And we seem to be doing it by joining the rest of the country, our de facto secessionist tendencies wiped away by grief, our small town sentiments aroused by fear, and our notions of what it means to be a Rockwellian American filtered through the lens of what is still New York City.

If you somehow impossibly woke up on Day Two or Day Three and didn't know what had happened, you would have wondered where you were living. Strangers nodded as they passed on the street, beat cops stood on every corner and people came up to them to shake their hands or pat them on the backs. No car horns honked. When you went into stores, inquiries were made about your family and friends. Everyone safe? Doors were held. Lampposts were covered in notices about church services, synagogue services, mosque services, ecumenical services.

Downtown there were more signs: THE BLOOD CENTER HAS REACHED CAPACITY. THANK YOU. PLEASE TRY AGAIN NEXT WEEK. Flags flew from every stationary and moving object: homes, storefronts, cars, people. At the candlelight vigil on the Promenade on Thursday night there were more

flags, prayer, fewer renditions of, say, "My Sweet Lord" than "The Star Spangled Banner."

We fell in love with our mayor.

Had we not had been preoccupied with sorrow, rage, fear, and the sudden unfurling of history, we would've noticed sooner how weird this was. We're walking the streets and lighting candles and talking politics not so altered we don't know how altered we are. But too altered to really understand what it means to be here on September 11, 12, 13, 14, 15, 16 . . .

There is nothing wrong with this. Nothing except it's all so wrong. Not in its essence. We are Americans living in America. Even if our streets, cosmetically speaking, seldom resemble the America we think we know, you know, that America, there's nothing foolish about emulating the aspects that, once scorned, suddenly seem comforting.

But because it's a transformation informed utterly and completely by evil so profound most of us haven't yet even scratched the surface of it, it can't help but bring with it a certain shadow-self sensibility. From this, we've produced not an accurate image, but instead a retina image of a small town we think we can recall or become, that we can see when we close our eyes instead the vision of two big bullets filled with human shrapnel, instead of the World Trade Center burning hellishly and falling straight down like a KO'd brain-dead boxer.

At our core, we are already a real community, which is what this is all about, and we always have been. At the pettiest level, most of us don't even have enough square feet to make spendin a lot of time at home a comfortable option. We're out and about and rubbing elbows and rubbing each other the wrong way, and more often the right way. Confronted with lesser evils, we've come together in the face of them time and time again. There are shopkeepers, people on the subway platform, neighbors we know and who know us. The sane and loving, and there are millions of us, have always found their ways to one another.

In the late sixties there was a children's book, *Maxie*, set in New York City. Maxie was an old woman who felt useless (and if written now, clinically depressed...) so she decided not to get out of bed one morning. Before long the entire neighborhood was on her doorstep. One neighbor always woke up from the sound of Maxie's slippers on the floor and had overslept. Another knew to leave for work when Maxie's too tightly sprung window

shade shot up. Others set time by Maxie's teakettle, from her bird chirping when she fed him, when she got her newspaper and her bottle of milk, and so on. This being New York, they surrounded her bed—rather menacingly, to my child's mind—with concern and not a little irritation. So Maxie got out of bed.

My friend, Angela, had her concerns about a neighbor in the days following the blast. He'd moved in across the street, and had a bright florescent light, so she was always aware of when he was home and she could see him as he moved around the apartment with his shades up. His lights, she said, hadn't been on since at least Tuesday. Sitting on her stoop, after the candlelight vigil on the Promenade, we watched his dark windows.

Then he came home. A man entered the building and a moment later the lights on the third floor flipped on. We sat there cheering, feeling this small joy over a stranger we didn't know by name or face, by occupation or anything else, but whose absence we had noted. We imagined, only half-jokingly, going up to him and saying, we're so glad you're alive. Chances are he wasn't anywhere near the blast. But chances are he would understand.

As I write, there are plenty of lights that are not flipping on, and plenty of people feeling the pain of that, up close, or across streets, across the country and the world, people who are known or not known but who are grieved. If we are transforming ourselves, and clearly we irrevocably and inevitably are, it needn't be in parody, grotesque or otherwise, and it needn't be conjured from sheer shock and reaction. New York is not a small town, not the kind we imagine exists somewhere free from cruelty or isolation but plump with kindness and old-fashioned virtue. The flags will probably fall away or be waved for war instead of the complicated ways they're waving now, car horns will sound again, and we'll witness or perpetuate any number of little or big incivilities. But the sentiment in this new city is not a bad one these days: I'm so glad you're alive.

When you come right down to it, and New York City has, it's the only sentiment that matters. And that's not just about small town America or just about big town America or just about America at all.

The Good Soldiers

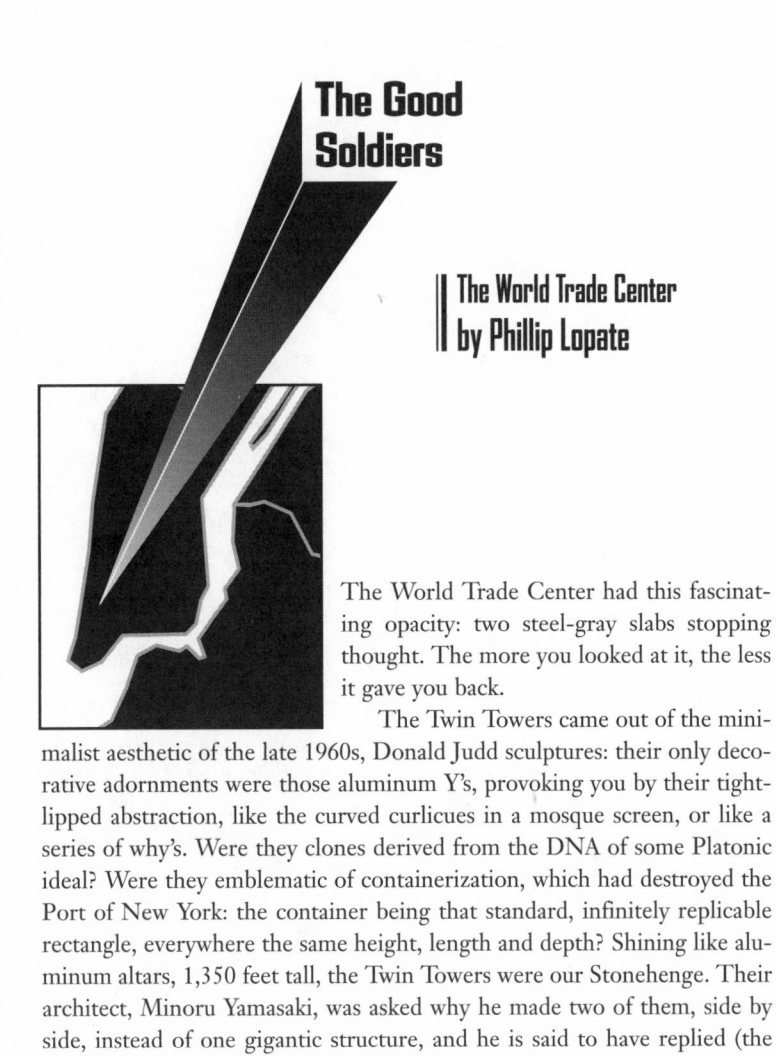

‖ The World Trade Center
‖ by Phillip Lopate

The World Trade Center had this fascinating opacity: two steel-gray slabs stopping thought. The more you looked at it, the less it gave you back.

The Twin Towers came out of the minimalist aesthetic of the late 1960s, Donald Judd sculptures: their only decorative adornments were those aluminum Y's, provoking you by their tight-lipped abstraction, like the curved curlicues in a mosque screen, or like a series of why's. Were they clones derived from the DNA of some Platonic ideal? Were they emblematic of containerization, which had destroyed the Port of New York: the container being that standard, infinitely replicable rectangle, everywhere the same height, length and depth? Shining like aluminum altars, 1,350 feet tall, the Twin Towers were our Stonehenge. Their architect, Minoru Yamasaki, was asked why he made two of them, side by side, instead of one gigantic structure, and he is said to have replied (the story may be apocryphal, but it's a good one anyhow) that double the height would have destroyed human scale.

I never found them offensive or overbearing, neither did I love them; they didn't invite dislike, they were too polite, eight-hundred pound gorillas in tuxes, having no need to beat their chests. (When they replaced the Empire State Building in the remake of *King Kong*, they offered the creature a too smooth, unvaried façade to convey precarious perching.) They were at once the most dominant and least assuming facet of the New York skyline: Don't mind me, they said.

It took seven years and a billion dollars to build them. Putting together the deal required immense muscle, supplied by David Rockefeller at the Chase Manhattan Bank, his brother Nelson, then Governor of New York (who stocked one tower with state workers when the building failed to attract tenants), and the considerable resources of the Port Authority of New York-New Jersey. Austin Tobin, then head of the Port Authority, kept up the masquerade that the spanking new towers were somehow going to be given over to trade and port functions. "How did the Port Authority—chartered to safeguard the economic health of New York's regional maritime commerce—become the agent, a half century later, of the port's displacement and decline. And what caused America's most venerable planning and development agency—once imbued with the high-minded public service doctrines of Woodrow Wilson—to transform itself into the world's biggest real estate speculator?" demanded Eric Darton, in his book about the World Trade Center, *Divided We Stand*. While I don't think the agency could have done much to keep the port in Manhattan, it does take gall to present to the public a real estate speculation as a consolidation of port services, at the very moment that these functions were being transferred to New Jersey. We were led to envision the twin towers as the vertical equivalent of all those shipping companies and counting-houses that once lined the docks, of all the shipbuilders, importers, commission merchants, marine insurance companies, brokers and lawyers whose Whitehall Street offices had overlooked the harbor.

Still, you have to hand it to them: the World Trade Center went from being a white elephant, when they began opening in 1972, to near-full occupancy of ten-million square feet of office space. Not only did it initiate the resurgence of Lower Manhattan, but its dug-out foundation stones were re-used as landfill to make Battery Park City, the true center of that revival. By 2001, the World Trade Center was valued at $1.2 billion, and the Port

Authority had managed to lease the buildings for ninety-nine years to a consortium led by Larry A. Silverstein for $3.2 billion. The city and the agency were licking their chops, contemplating how they would spend the huge profits resulting from that privatization. The electronics shopkeepers of Radio Row whose district had originally stood in the World Trade Center's path were long forgotten. But then, on September 11, 2001, the towers joined the palimpsest of multiple erasures, like a child's magic slate, which is New York.

Now that they are gone, their absence reasserts how much they climaxed the southern tip of Manhattan. Their silvered profiles ashimmer against a blue sky, like matching cigarette cases, or at night, when they became moody and noirish, were poetic postcard effects achieved only at a distance; up close, they seemed blandly off-putting, and oppressive at street level, like most sixty-five-mph architecture built in that era.

To the rest of the world—though, curiously, I would maintain, not to native New Yorkers, like myself, who would always regard the twin towers as parvenus, compared to the Empire State Building, the Chrysler or the Woolworth—the World Trade Center symbolized the Big Apple, and beyond that, the might of America, the Great Satan. Certainly the twins had the richest and most imaginative of meanings, a mystic temptation one can only speculate on, to the suicide terrorists of the Islamic jihad who attacked them not once but twice. The first time, in 1993, despite the tragic loss of life and damage to the buildings, the towers remained standing, seemingly impregnable. The structural design had called for each tower's skin to be its main strength, through light glass-and-steel facing threaded by steel columns. These columns gave the buildings their stiffness, while a cluster of central columns and steel trusses helped hold up each concrete floor. "Redundancy," the engineers call that structural backup that ensures a building's resilience, even if damaged—a word that also fit the WTC aesthetically and, now, historically. The Twin Towers were very strong, nothing compromised in the way of construction, an engineering tour de force; but no building, as we discovered, is meant to take the brunt of a jetliner, gorged with fuel, shearing through its midsection. When they collapsed, they fell straight down, not forward. Like the good soldiers they were.

SEPT. 11 SKETCHBOOK • ELISHA COOPER

view from jfk when i get off subway

singed fax that floats down to
me on my walk back through
brooklyn.

truck carrying crushed fire department
car crossing canal street

crowd at christopher street   resting firefighters on canal street